Financial Privacy

Nicola Jentzsch

Financial Privacy

An International Comparison of Credit Reporting Systems

Second Edition

With 37 Figures and 34 Tables

 Springer

Dr. Nicola Jentzsch
nicola.jentzsch@aya.yale.edu

Originally published in the series:
Contributions to Economics by Physica-Verlag Heidelberg, 2006

Library of Congress Control Number: 2007932208

ISBN 978-3-540-73377-5 2. Edition Springer Berlin Heidelberg New York
ISBN 978-3-7908-1737-9 1. Edition Physica-Verlag Heidelberg New York

Springer is a part of Springer Science+Business Media

springer.com

© Springer-Verlag Berlin Heidelberg 2006, 2007

Production: LE-TEX Jelonek, Schmidt & Vöckler GbR, Leipzig
Cover-design: WMX Design GmbH, Heidelberg

SPIN 12083411   134/3180YL - 5 4 3 2 1 0   Printed on acid-free paper

Contents

1 Introduction

Markets do not exist without the exchange of information. Information exchange is the initial phase of every economic transaction, without it market participants would not trust each other and no trade would take place. This holds for the bazaar in Kabul as well as for the electronic stock exchange in New York–in fact it holds for all transactions across all markets at any time. It is, however, of special importance for financial markets–those for capital and credit–which are known for their dependence on information. The disclosure of personal data, for instance, is a precondition for any credit contract in retail credit markets. This book is the first comprehensive analysis of the economics and regulation of financial privacy with an emphasis on credit reporting. Credit reporting agencies collect, analyze and distribute billions of information items on millions of borrowers in industrialized countries, but increasingly also in developing countries. They provide the informational structure in credit markets–and they will provide the information structure of many other markets in the future. The networks of these agencies span across financial services providers, retailers, insurers, telecom or utility providers and sometimes even transportation companies. Employers and landlords are also increasingly using such data for professional decisions. The credit report–an account of financial behaviour of an individual–is becoming the "second identity" in economic life. It will more and more determine access to and the prices of goods and services. Any book on credit reporting is only naturally also a book on the economics of privacy in general and especially of financial privacy. The impetus for this study of privacy was an article by Joe Stiglitz and Michael Rothschild published in 1997 in the Geneva Papers on Risk and Insurance Theory. In this article, the authors discuss the possibility of efficiency gains in insurance markets through the disclosure of the human genetic code. I read this article in 2000 and it immediately raised interesting questions about the economic dimension of privacy: How far will information revelation go? What is the optimal amount of information to be disclosed in markets? Where are the legal or natural barriers to information disclosure? What economic impact do they have? And maybe most important: is personal information similar to any other economic good bought and sold in markets? At first I intended to only discuss the economic impact of legal barriers–that is the impact of data protection. But as the research evolved it became increasingly clear that market forces have major (and sometimes frightening) implications for privacy. Do unimpeded market forces automatically lead to total transparency and the disclosure of everything? Markets are at the end information revelation mechanisms. Therefore, I decided to include a discussion of mechanisms at work in information markets–a topic of increasing interest for academics, because of the widespread adoption of information technologies over past decades. Credit reporting is no new invention: one of the first accounts dates back to the year 1803. In Great Britain, small communities of retailers shared negative experiences with defaulting debtors and fraudsters with their fellow traders. These local reputation systems evolved to small and then regional companies. The activity was later re-invented in other countries such as Germany or the United States. With the introduction of the computer, data collection exploded. Today, large information corporations provide data on millions of consumers and some of them even become publicly traded companies. They process information to identify and quantify credit or insurance risk of consumers, but also profitability, attrition and response probabilities or bankruptcy risk among other things. The applications are potentially unlimited.

Credit reporting agencies cover in some countries almost the entire economically active population. In the U.S., they have stored data on more than 240 million people. The trade in personal data is pervasive: information is sold for credit purposes, auto financing, mortgages, insurance, tenant and employment screening as well as marketing purposes. In developing countries it is increasingly seen as an important tool to increase access to microfinance or formal credit markets. The public in industrialized countries regards these data collections with increasing suspicion, therefore legislators stepped in to regulate the industry. Data protection legislation is the primary instrument to limit information collection and distribution, although a minority of countries apply industry-specific laws that cover credit reporting only. As of mid-2004, 80 countries around the world had acknowledged the right to privacy in their constitutions. 35 countries had implemented this right as data protection laws that cover the public and private sector or only the latter. These countries are primarily located in Western and Eastern Europe as well as in Latin America. Many more countries consider the adoption of such laws among them China, India or South Africa. Many countries in Africa are now drafting laws and regulations for credit reporting. There is no international agreement about "best practices" in credit reporting and there is no common definition of financial privacy. Different cultures pursue different approaches: in Europe there is the attitude that personal privacy is a human right. In the U.S. it is regarded as basic right that balances the trade-off of commercial interests in the data and the interest in privacy of the individual. And some countries, among them China until recently, do not even have a word for "privacy." Diverse cultural backgrounds contribute to the different styles of financial privacy regulation. For instance, the U.S. applies a narrow and industry-specific approach of regulation that targets primarily the credit reporting industry and associated information furnishers and users. The members of the European Union, on the other hand, apply comprehensive data protection laws that cover the whole private sector and not just one industry. By 2005 there were three countries in the country sample used for this analysis that applied both types of laws (Belgium, Canada and Sweden). By 2006 all EU member states had enacted data protection laws. At the global perspective, the European Union has successfully exported its regime of privacy protection, because many countries around the world have adopted laws inspired by the EU Data Protection Directive. Among these nations are the candidate countries in Eastern Europe, but also Latin American countries. At the moment it is unclear what approach will prevail in African and Asian countries, but applying two laws is no preferable way. The next challenge will be the international harmonization of data protection standards, because they might become an obstacle for the global trade in financial, insurance or other services. It remains to be seen if consumers will start to directly trade with each other based upon credit information or if–like a friend of mine imagines–it will be possible to point at anyone on a crowded street in Mumbai, India, and draw a credit report upon that person.

The term "privacy" denotes different concepts in different cultures. In the U.S., the historical meaning of privacy is non-interference by the central government. The origin of the American understanding of privacy can be traced back to the colonial times and the "writs of assistance." These writs gave the officers of the British King broad discretion to enter and search private homes in order to prosecute violations of British custom laws. After the Independence, the Fourth Amendment to the Constitution stipulated a general protection against "unreasonable searches and seizures." In 1890, Supreme Court Justices Louis D. Brandeis and Samuel D. Warren argued that this was to be interpreted as a "right to be left alone." For many decades coming, the American legislation enacted laws that primarily targeted the balance of law enforcement agencies and the privacy interests of individuals. This "government versus citizen" focus changed somewhat in the 1960s as companies introduced large mainframe computers, but the concept of privacy still remains different from the European understanding. It is a broader concept that includes physical and informational privacy. The Fair Credit Reporting Act of 1970 was the first federal law that implemented financial privacy provisions in the private sector in the U.S. With this legislation the country embarked on the path of narrow, segmented and incomplete regulation of an industry that is better understood as information network with data exchange among many participants across *different* industries. U.S. legislators nowadays typically discuss the economic trade-off and the balancing of the interests of different parties involved in the exchange.

In Europe, privacy is regarded as human right. This conviction has its origins in World War II. The war demonstrated that data collections in the public and private sector could be misused for the prosecution of politically "undesirable" people. The National Socialists seized data collections in Germany, France and the Netherlands to identify and locate Jews among other people. Today privacy is constitutionally protected in most European countries and it is enshrined in many international agreements. In the 1960s, civil rights activists on both sides of the Atlantic started to discuss how privacy could be preserved in an environment of pervasive computing power. Germany became the leader in data protection action: on October 7, 1970 legislators in the state of Hesse enacted the first data protection law. Although this act became law in just one state, it served as an example for other countries in Europe. Today the word privacy is primarily used to refer to the protection of sensitive data about individuals. I use the term "privacy" for "data protection," something that would be called "information privacy" in the U.S. Financial privacy in this respect is the protection of information about personal financial behaviour.

Although this book is a survey on the economics and regulation of financial privacy, I do not intend to propose an "optimal" data protection regime. Due to the international focus of my work, I came to the conclusion that countries have considerable variance in their tolerance of privacy intrusion and that pragmatism sometimes prevails. Policy makers have to balance consumer and industry interests, and depending on the strength of lobby groups and consumer associations, the "political economy of privacy" varies across nations. With some risk of being very general, the above explanations demonstrate that there are cultural, economic and political determinants of privacy. Countries may embark on a certain development path, but they can learn from past experience as well as experiences in other countries. One of the purposes of this book is to explain the historical development of credit reporting and its regulation. Credit reporting has implications for millions of people–but only a minority seems to know that credit reporting agencies exist. Credit reports increasingly become the "access code" to financial services, telecommunications, insurance, sometimes even employment and transportation. For the industry that uses such data, personal information implies consequences for efficiency, productivity, risk management and market contestability. This convincingly points out that the topic should not be left to lobbyists, lawyers or legislators alone. In the past, there has been little academic interest in the "economics of privacy." I hope to fill this void by approaching the subject as follows. In the theoretical sections of this book, I discuss information markets, law and economics and the microeconomics of privacy. This approach allows me to underpin some of the observations about these peculiar markets that follow later in the analysis.

In the second edition of this book I have revised and updated some of the sections and I have included a comparison of public and private credit systems. The descriptive part also discusses the history and regulation of credit reporting, these sections have been expanded and updated. Such a perspective allows insights into endogeneity of factors that might later emerge and complicate the analytical part. Additionally, I provide an overview of the international political economy of privacy as there are several international agreements and guidelines that state privacy rules. These contracts are reviewed and compared. The econometric analysis is based upon the insights from the theoretical and descriptive historical part of the survey. In this part, I construct an index of data protection to find out more about the impact of data protection acts that is the effects of data protection on credit report sales and the effects of credit reporting on defaults or overall credit risk in the market. It is not intended to have a long and complicated technical analysis here. Rather, this part provides some insights into the interaction of data protection with credit market variables. The main purpose of this book is to provide a comprehensive theoretical and analytical treatment of financial privacy with insights about regulation and economics that go beyond the existing literature. This is especially the rigorous discussion and analysis of credit reporting regulation.

Around the world, there is an increasing number of credit reporting agencies and more and more countries enact data protection laws. In the industrialized nations there is the paradox that a rising amount of information is shared while at the same time consumer protection is also on the rise. With this book, I hope to contribute to a better understanding of the benefits and problems of financial privacy and its regulation. Credit reporting will evolve worldwide and become more pervasive. By the time I had finished writing this book I was convinced that this research not only covers the information structure of financial services markets, but that such reporting might be the foundation of many other markets in the near future.

2 Theory of Information and Privacy

Despite more than thirty years of research in information economics, the knowledge about the effects of asymmetric information in markets is far from complete. There is a large body of economic literature dealing with information problems, but this literature is incoherent, because there are different approaches to information. Some authors regard it as economic endowment, others as tradable good. There are microeconomic and macroeconomic perspectives. The economic implications of information are multi-dimensional and no model can integrate them all at once. For providing an accessible overview, this chapter brings together different strands of the economic literature. In the following, I discuss information markets, institutional economics and the microeconomics of information and privacy. To fully understand the competition in information markets, some basic features of information must be understood first, such as non-excludability, non-rivalry, immateriality or the structure of the production costs. Next, it is important to appreciate other factors that do play a role: network economics as well as other demand-side and supply-side features. Further the reader is introduced to the economics of markets for personal information. Credit reports are information goods that are compiled from information items specifying the financial and consumption behavior of an individual. Some of the problems identified in the sections on information markets re-emerge here with interesting welfare implications for the individual. I apply property rights theory, discuss negative externalities in markets for personal information and show that there is imperfect appropriation of information that creates interesting problems such as identity theft. Economic theory is also helpful in explaining industrial concentration tendencies in such markets and the rise of "information power." An extra section is devoted to versioning and "purpose creep" to show how profit can be increased by using information for different purposes, some of them even unrelated to the purpose for which it was collected in the first place. Any discussion of the economics of information and privacy is incomplete without the latest models on privacy. The latter is called the "microeconomics of information and privacy." Only recently some economists (mostly in the U.S.) have started to apply game theory to model privacy problems with some remarkable insights. First, models that belong to traditional "information economics" will be discussed, but this is then narrowed down to models that stylize problems of personal privacy. This discussion sheds some light on the basic interaction of information disclosure, incentives and welfare distribution. The upcoming sections will show that many of the problems observable in today's information markets can be explained by applying economic thinking and tools. Some might consider the trade in personal information as only an input to the provision of financial services. However, credit reports themselves are products bought and sold on markets. And this market reveals some peculiar features with implications for bargaining power and welfare distribution among market participants.

2.1 Competition in Information Markets

Information is materialized in products such as books, CDs, films or newspapers while at the same time it has the characteristic of being immaterial. It can be distributed via airwaves, paper or digital media. Hence information is difficult to define and sometimes even more difficult to commodify and not easy to formalize in theoretical economics. Babe (1994: 42) argues: "Information, however, does not fulfill the definitional or conceptual requirements of a commodity, thereby placing the discipline in a crisis concerning its own internal validity." Although this is a radical statement, I show in the following sections that information markets and information goods have features that challenge conventional economic thinking (without, of course, overturning it).

2.1.1 Information Goods and Property Rights

Information goods are distinct from classical goods in several aspects. One simple and popular definition is "everything that can be digitized" (Varian and Shapiro 2001). Another explanation states that such goods are "goods consisting of data, information, and knowledge content, typically with high sunk costs that are traded online at a close-to-zero marginal cost of production." (Lopes and Galletta 2002: 1). Some digital goods are more than this, they are *network goods*: they provide an original utility, but this utility rises with the number of other users of the same good. This is the case for software, for instance. Many information goods are what in technical terms would be considered "systems." *System goods* are bundles of complementary components that are sold together such as CDs and CD players. The analogy also works for information: Marketing data bundles together the consumer's preference for beer with the information that she is a smoker, for instance. If these data items are correlated, they are *complementary*. Information has some public good features, as it is *non-excludable* and non-rival. It can be very expensive or even prohibitively costly to exclude others from the consumption of the good, for example. This is illustrated sufficiently by the enormous difficulty to cope with product piracy. Only through legally enforced property rights (trade secrets, patents, copyrights or trademarks) others can be potentially excluded from the use of the protected information. Sometimes this problem can be circumvented by bundling information together with a good that is excludable (Varian 1998: 9), but not always as information is immaterial. *Non-rivalry* means that there is almost no scarcity, because theoretically the good can be replicated without limits (*"infinite expansibility"*). This is one of the peculiar features of information goods compared to physical ones: *theoretically* unlimited production and replication possibilities exist.

It is well known that *public goods* are a reason for market failure (the other reasons are natural monopoly, externalities and asymmetric information). If the benefits from the production of such goods cannot be fully privatized, "under-provision" of the good might be a consequence. And users, on the other hand, have an incentive to free-riding that is to use the information without paying for it. Non-excludability is also a problem once the information is sold–the seller can potentially further use it, "there are natural limitations on one's ability to commit not to use information once acquired that is, 'it's hard to forget'." (Kahn, McAndrews and Roberds 2000: 2). Another problem is *experience good* character and that the value of information becomes clear only *after* its consumption. But once information is consumed why pay for it? The seller must reveal meta-information that is "information about the information" so that the consumer can find out if it is worthwhile to pay for it. The production costs for information goods are typically characterized by *economies of scale and scope*. The initial high fixed costs are followed by low and in some cases almost zero marginal costs. Of course, an increasing number of copies of an original data set could be accompanied by further costs such as technical assistance. In credit reporting, the copying and sale of credit reports is cheap, in some cases as low as 0.05 Euro per inquiry. However, the sale might be accompanied by questions and complaints from consumers implying additional costs for credit bureaus that are also not fixed. The general rule of thumb is that costs vary little with the quality of the information good. In competitive markets, prices are driven down to marginal costs–this is the reason why information providers rarely sell their products in competitive markets as marginal costs are almost zero (Varian 1998: 5). Through different competition strategies, they try to create a market niche. The model best describing this market is the monopolistic competitive market.[1] The competition strategies will be described in a section further below where I discuss the supply-side of information markets.

The explanations above show that information goods depend on a legal infrastructure defining property rights. It is well understood that markets cannot be analyzed if institutions are not considered. Legal systems are incentive systems–if a law is modified it changes the incentives of economic agents and their behavior. Legal and economic systems cannot be regarded as independent from each other, a notion that has been promoted by new institutional economics.[2] This field consists of transaction cost theory, theory of the firm, property rights theory and agency and information problems.[3] The approach was a reaction to neoclassical economics and its static and timeless world of passive utility maximizers on the demand side and reactive price-takers on the supply side. Thorstein Veblen and John Commons among others criticized this paradigm. The authors argued that institutions are not given, they evolve over time, laws, regulations, norms or contracts are constantly challenged, are overhauled or replaced. These institutions, however, restrain the behavior of economic agents, because they limit the set of social choices. Sometimes, new institutional economics also contains theories of public choice, jurisprudence and legal processes (so-called "law and economics"). Law and economics reduces legal problems to economic ones where the actors' incentives are analyzed under varying legal constraints. This approach is helpful when applied to the analysis of information markets, which I will do further below. The origin of works on property rights can be traced back to Coase (1960). The theory of property rights is concerned with the establishment of ownership rights, their economic impact or remedies for violation of such rights. Economic transactions are essentially regarded as *exchanges of bundles of rights*. Cooter and Ulen (1995: 72) state that property creates "a zone of privacy in which owners can exercise their will over things without being answerable to others (...)." Property right regimes exist in a variety of forms ranging from capitalist economies (private property, privacy) to communist economies (common property, no privacy). And property rights can have different features: (1) Specification (that is specified vs. unspecified property rights); (2) Divisibility (that is undivided vs. shared property rights); (3) Dynamics (static vs. dynamic property rights); and (4) independence

---

[1]   In such markets, competitors have some monopolistic price flexibility.
[2]   The term goes back to Williamson (1975).
[3]   These approaches are taught in industrial organization as in Carlton and Perloff (1994).

(that is independent vs. interdependent property rights that are related to one another). For instance, property rights are specified when their legal assignment to one person is clear and not controversial. In reality, information ownership is not always clear. This is important in credit reporting, where a lot of controversy revolves around the point of who the rightful owner of credit information is. Undivided property rights denote rights owned by just one person. In the United States it is typically the company that collects the information that obtains the ownership. However, one can also think of situations where property rights are split and are assigned to different parties.[4] It is important to note that the division and distribution of property rights influences the *distribution of welfare* between economic agents–this will be discussed in greater detail further below. Static property rights refer to those that do not change over the course of the property relationship, whereas dynamic ones are subject to change (leasing is an example of a dynamic property right). Although the static perspective of property rights usually prevails, I will show in the descriptive part of the study that the legislation in credit reporting has changed property rights by locating them more and more at the individual. Some rights are related to one another, whereas others are independent, examples of dependent rights in credit reporting are the rights to access information and to have it corrected. Naturally, the first is a precondition for the second. Altogether the reader should be aware that different combinations of the above features exist and that they determine the ownership structure pertaining to information goods. Is there a way of optimally assigning property rights to information? This question has sparked a lot of controversy and will be discussed in upcoming sections.

According to the Coase Theorem, the initial assignment of property rights does not matter for the *efficiency* of resource allocation, meaning from an efficiency standpoint it does not matter which party owns the rights as long as they are clearly defined. Hence, "optimal assignment of property rights" is not a question–it simply does not matter for market efficiency. Parties can negotiate with each other and agree to contracts, if there are any positive or negative effects that are not priced into the transaction externalities arise. In this case one party can compensate the other for possible damages.[5] The theorem, however, holds only in a world of zero trans-

---

[4] One party might have access, the other might use the information, and the third might have the right to sell it.

[5] Coase (1960) criticized Pigou for his understanding of externalities and his interventionist view that only government (by demanding taxes and subsidies) can internalize externalities. Coase argued that it does not matter what party holds property rights as long as the parties can negotiate they are able to internalize externalities.

action costs, full information and total flexibility in contracting. The theorem is somewhat counter-intuitive and has led to cases, where economists argued that victims of environmental pollution should *pay* the polluter to stop the harmful activity. This ignores any responsibility and source of the damage and as to whether such proposals would be politically feasible. But there are many other problems with the theorem and there are many other problems with the assignment of property rights or negotiations. Anderlini and Felli (2000) show where negotiation costs are introduced, parties run into a circle of negotiations about the negotiation costs. Ishiguro (2002) argues that if the full information assumption is dropped, the theorem only weakly holds under asymmetric information. Any attempt to prove or falsify the theorem usually results in the conclusion that it only holds under very narrow assumptions.

The most important point is that exchange of goods never takes place in a perfect Coasian world. For instance, "bargaining is costly when it requires converting a lot of private information into public information." (Cooter and Ulen 1995: 85). The ability to reveal information influences the bargaining power of economic agents. Bargaining power, in turn, influences how the surplus from the transaction is divided among the agents. Altogether, we must accept that the distribution of property rights *in fact matters*. Communication between parties in the negotiation process does not have to be clear, cultural differences and political hostility among negotiation partners can contribute to inefficient outcomes. Additionally, the more parties are involved and the more distant they are from one another, the more difficult the negotiation and enforcement becomes. I come back to this point when I discuss the markets for personal information. Allen (1999: 898) notes, that the literature usually argues that there is a monotonic relationship between property rights and wealth: "Given that trade is the transfer of property rights, there can be no trade (and hence no gains from trade) in the absence of property rights." The author further explains that if there is a continuum between the two extremes of "completely undefined property rights" and "completely defined property rights," the gains from trade might increase the better the property rights are defined. Closely related to this literature is transaction cost theory that acknowledges costs for using the price-mechanism such as costs for search, bargaining, monitoring and enforcement (Coase 1937, 1998; Williamson 1975, 1985). Only naturally, specification of property rights lowers transaction costs. Property rights determine who benefits more from trade and they have implications for welfare distribution. The better property rights to information are defined the lower the transaction costs. Whoever owns property rights to information has the power to shift surplus accruing from the transaction.

2.1.2 Network Economics

Although the study of network economics dates back to the 1970s, it has gained increasing attention during the second half of the 1990s. One of the first formal treatments of networks is provided by Rohlfs (1974): a model where the value of service depends on the number of other subscribers. Some of the insights from this literature apply to financial privacy. In fact it is not possible to fully understand competition in credit reporting industries without the economics of networks. The next sections present a brief overview of the main features of networks. Physical networks consist of compatible parts, such as nodes and links or connections, gateways and adapters. Some examples are telecommunication networks, railroads or electricity nets. Non-spatial nets, on the other hand, are not geographically fixed. They are typically *"virtual"* meaning that they are based upon a common standard such as language or software. Gottinger (2003: 2-3) provides a topology of networks that describes star, tree, crystal or web architectures. Credit reporting resembles a two-way star network, because credit report users (that are at the same time information furnishers) rarely exchange information directly with each other, instead the credit bureau acts as central circuit for data exchange.

Figure 2.1
Credit Reporting Activity

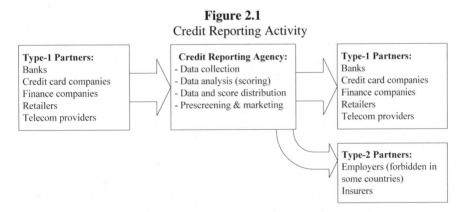

The activity is depicted in Figure 2.1. Type-1 partners deliver information and withdraw it ("reciprocity"), whereas type-2 partners only withdraw information. Network characteristics may influence market structure, firm behavior and performance and economic outcomes. Credit reporting is an industry based upon an information network with reporting standards. Therefore I apply the insights from network economics to credit reporting with some qualifications like other authors have applied them to finance (Economides 1993, 1996). A major feature of networks is *path depend-*

ency, a feature discussed at length by David (1985). Path dependency is characterized as a stochastic sequence of events that influence future outcomes (Arthur 1989: 117). It can explain why networks depend on initial conditions–a small modification in the initial conditions magnified by increasing returns may yield large variations in outcomes (Arthur 1994: 86 - 89).

Path dependency is controversial among economists and for its illustration it is mostly pointed to anecdotal evidence (Brown 2000, David 1985, Shapiro and Varian 2001). One popular example is the QWERTY problem (David 1985).[6] Liebowitz and Margolis (1995) doubt the existence of the problem. This discussion is not presented in detail, as it is sufficient to state that path dependency plays a role for adopting standards–also informational standards. For instance, once specific information types are exchanged in a country it might prove impossible to return to a regime that uses other types of information. Additionally, once the data have been shared it is "out there" and it is questionable if the development can be reversed. For instance, once a country has decided to share positive and negative information, it can be difficult to revert to a negative-only regime. Networks can also involve considerable *switching costs* that determine the degree of lock-in of users. Companies create some of these switching costs as a reaction to intensifying competition. Shy (2001) notes that switching costs affect prices in two ways: for consumers who are already locked-in, firms have monopolistic price discretion, for outsiders firms compete intensively to lock them in only later. Shapiro and Varian (2001) have provided the following examples of switching costs: (1) Costs for breaking an existing contract; (2) Costs for training and learning; (3) Complementarities (switching costs due to specific standards); (4) Search costs; and (5) Loyalty costs. Switching costs reduce the impact of competition. Closely related is *excess inertia*. Excess inertia means that a more efficient technology is not adopted, excess momentum means that firms switch although they would prefer to maintain the status quo. Farrell and Saloner (1985) explain with a dynamic standardization game played by firms, how excess inertia or excess momentum arises. The existence of one dominant network with specific standards might make is difficult for another network to penetrate the market. In credit reporting firms have to agree on technical

---

[6]   The keyboard design QWERTY was originally developed for typewriters to avoid jamming, but then it locked its users in. The mechanical problem of jamming does not exist in computers but QWERTY is still in use today. Changing to another keyboard design involves retraining. Altogether the argument is not convincing as everyone knows who uses German, English and French keyboard designs.

reporting standards and definition of terms such as "default" or "delinquency." Different reporting standards in various countries are an obstacle for cross-border credit reporting activities and market entry might be difficult if there is one dominant incumbent.

Classic economic theory assumes constant returns to scale or decreasing returns. In such settings, no firm gains market power and competition drives market prices down to marginal costs. There is one unique solution entailing no profits for firms. Variation in the initial conditions leads over and over again to the inevitable result of just one market equilibrium. Is the market in disequilibrium, it will soon move back to the equilibrium ("stability of the outcome"). The world of network-based economics, however, appears to be different. The set-up of networks usually entails high fixed costs. Moreover, in many cases the de-installation of the net is costly.[7] This holds if it cannot be used for other purposes. Returns are an increasing function of the size of the firm: total costs decrease as output increases. This has also been discussed for information goods, where the investments in knowledge and research are high and the marginal costs of reproduction are trending to zero. Gottinger (2003: 6) states that in software industries "there is no natural point of exhaustion at which marginal costs begin to exceed marginal revenues and at which it becomes uneconomical to increase production. That is to say, in this industry there is always the case that the more products produced the lower the costs per product." There is a strong incentive for firms to price discriminate in order to include new buyers to increase sales. This insight has interesting implications for personal information, as we will see. Small variations in initial conditions are magnified through increasing returns and may tip the adoption of a network towards the market result. Some of these markets might be even monopolized. For many decades, increasing returns served as a justification for tolerating one dominant firm. Today, smaller firms can survive in such markets in case of asymmetric regulation.[8] Liebowitz and Margolis (1996) are critical with regard to the above explanations. They state that research and development are not just incorporated in high fixed costs, they are also part of variable costs in form of support or sales services: "Our claim is only that knowledge is always a component of goods, that the knowledge share of total cost is not necessarily greater now than it was in the past, and that the fixed-cost attribute of knowledge need

---

[7] This is subject to change due to technical progress, where electricity providers can offer telecommunication services over the same network.

[8] In telecommunication networks the incumbent firm has to provide competitors with access to the technical network. This is an example for asymmetric regulation.

not overwhelm other cost components." (Liebowitz and Margolis 1996: 14). *Economies of scope* are typical for network markets, because many consumers shop for whole systems such as videos and video recorders. In this case, conventional competition is replaced by competition "for the market" (Farrell and Klemperer 2001: 5 - 6). Compatibility is usually achieved through standard setting, the activity and its welfare implications have been analyzed by other authors (Economides 1988, Economides and Salop 1992). More important in this context are *"informational complementaries:"* they correlate specific items of information, facts or events. For instance, there is a correlation of the demand for toys and clothes for children (Shy 2001: 2). These correlations are of greatest interest to marketing firms, in credit reporting they play a major role. Firstly, credit information is increasingly used for marketing purposes. And secondly, credit risk is the statistical correlation of variables such as payment behavior and the probability to default. The correlations that exist in the data are used for assessing insurance risk as insurance scores are based upon credit report information.

Network externalities are distinct from network effects: they only become externalities if they are not included in the price.[9] There are direct and indirect network externalities, positive and negative ones as well as those that exist on either demand or supply side. Not every network generates externalities, for instance, one-way star networks (such as broadcasting networks) do not imply positive direct demand externalities. For the individual viewer, it does not matter if another viewer is added. In credit reporting an increasing number of information furnishers produce a more complete picture of the consumer–this is a positive externality. However, if the consumer is privacy-sensitive, she might not want to have her personal data disclosed to many parties. In this case negative externalities of data sales might arise for the consumer. There is a relationship between network size and network value (Gottinger 2003: 17): According to the linear assumption the marginal value of new nodes (or participants) is constant and does not change by adding more nodes. The logarithmic assumption states that with growth of a network, marginal value diminishes. At their limit, network effects are either zero, very small or even negative. The third assumption is known as "Metcalfe's Law:" It assumes an exponential relationship by stating that a network's value is $n(n-1) = n^2 - n$

---

[9]   Through side payments between adopters or through pricing by the seller such effects can be internalized.

with n denoting the number of network participants.[10] Networks might grow in non-linear and self-reinforcing fashion or they decrease and die away quickly (so-called self-negation). Markets with network effects have been called "winner-takes-most markets." The market share of the largest company can be a multiple of the market share of the second largest, and so on (Economides 2003): "In equilibrium, there is extreme market share and profits inequality." The feature of increasing returns by adding more nodes or more participants is controversial. DeLong (1997: 3) notes that the most valuable connections of networks are created at first: "The first uses of modern telecommunications and computers (…) were the highest-value uses. Later uses are lower value uses (…)." This is also supported by historical observations about the telegraph, where Krugman (2000) notes that the telegraph connected the largest cities first. Liebowitz and Margolis (1996: 1) also find the empirical importance of network externalities and increasing returns overrated. Their example is the telephone network: most subscribers call a small number of people such as relatives and friends. After these parties have been connected, it does not matter how many more people are added to the network. Gottinger (2003: 18) states that early additions to the network add exponentially to its value, but later additions diminish in their marginal value. For credit reporting, the latter could be the case. As soon as a certain amount of data is collected, the predictive power of the data might not increase much further, but the number of mistakes and errors in the data might increase. Networks also tend to display *critical masses* that are positive and can support different sizes in equilibria (Economides and Himmelberg 1995, Rohlfs 1974). The smallest size observable in the equilibrium is the so-called critical mass. If this mass is not reached, the network will not survive. Equilibria are either instable or points of attraction to which the network moves because of bandwagon and network effects (Rohlfs 1974). This means that either nobody or everybody adopts a technology: "What happens depends on expectations (everyone will do what they expect everyone else to do), and may be unpredictable or, at least, depend on things omitted from a simple model." (Farrell and Klemperer 2001: 8-9). It is possible to observe a *"tipping effect"* in expectation-based competition: if enough consumers assume that the general public adopts a certain product, this product will eventually prevail. All in all, the following points may be summarized: Credit reporting agencies resemble star networks as they act as circuits among several interconnected participants. Path dependence and lock-in play a role in the

---

[10] The original quote is: "In a network of N users, each sees a value proportional to the N-1 others, so that the total value of the network grows as $N(N$-$1)$, or as N squared for large N." (Metcalfe 1995)

adoption of the technology, but also in the adoption of reporting standards. As soon as firms have embarked on a specific standard of reporting, they have to re-program their systems and re-train their employees if they want to switch to another system. This might be costly and lock them into a specific system. Since credit reporting can be best characterized as competition among networks rather than individual firms, switching costs will arise as well as excess inertia. The nature of this kind of market facilitates industrial concentration and market forces might bring about oligopolies. This is exactly the case in credit reporting, where two or three dominant firms seem to be the rule rather than the exemption.

2.1.3 Supply-side Characteristics of Information Markets

The intensity of competition in information markets increases the incentive of companies to employ strategies that help to reduce competition pressure. In monopolistically competitive markets, firms face a downward sloping demand curve where the demand elasticity defines the space for price changes: if price changes are too large, consumers will switch to another competitor. Considered the high fixed costs and almost zero marginal costs, how is it possible for producers to recover high fixed costs? Maybe "cost-based pricing makes little sense and value-based pricing is much more appropriate"? (Shy 2001: 182) In the following, I discuss prevailing competition strategies in information markets such as price-discrimination, bundling or flat-rate pricing. Figure 2.2 presents three forms of price setting:

> ➢ First-degree price discrimination (personalized prices, left);
> ➢ Second-degree price discrimination (quantity and quality based discrimination, middle); and
> ➢ Third-degree price discrimination (group pricing, right).

The aforementioned strategies are common in industries with large fixed costs. Price discrimination can only be applied when three preconditions exist: (1) the firm has some market power; (2) the firm acquires information about the consumer's willingness to pay; and (3) resale of the good can be prevented. The latter is important, because otherwise it is possible for one consumer group to pay a lower price and to re-sell the good to another group facing higher prices. There are several methods to prevent resale and for services resale is often not possible altogether.

Figure 2.2
Price Discrimination

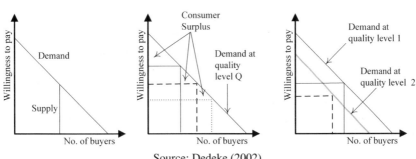

Source: Dedeke (2002)

In the left figure, a personalized price is charged and the good is sold to the consumer at the maximum price she is willing to pay. For several reasons, this idealized price discrimination will rarely occur. Practically, the firm has to know the consumer's reservation value. This, however, is private information. The consumer's surplus from a transaction is the difference between reservation value and market price that presumably lies below the reservation value. The surplus can only be maximized if the reservation value remains private information. For now, we leave the other two forms of price discrimination and briefly discuss the first-degree strategy.

Ulph and Vulkan (2000, 2001) discuss *first-degree price and product differentiation* in a competitive environment. They state that extraction of surplus for firms increases when they charge prices that approximate the reservation value. At the same time competition may intensify, because now firms compete for every single consumer. Under specific circumstances, firms might be worse off and consumers are better off with personalized prices, especially if intensified competition dominates surplus extraction. Yet, this only works under the assumption of full information. In their 2001 paper, the authors study the incentive of producers to price-discriminate and to establish mass customization.[11] An alternative method to generate price discrimination is two-tiered pricing (also called two-part tariff). Consumers are charged a lump-sum fee for access and for each unit consumed or usage of the service. Theory predicts that this pricing strategy leads to the same output level as perfect competition. The result is Pareto-

---

[11] Mass customization is defined as situation "in which firms can offer a whole range of finely differentiated products at the same constant marginal costs without having to incur additional fixed costs on every differentiated brand they offer." Ulph and Vulkan (2001: 3)

efficient by maximizing social welfare. The distributional consequences of such price discrimination, however, are striking: The consumer ends up with no surplus as the firm extracts it all by perfectly approximating the consumer's reservation value. The reader should keep in mind that the Pareto criterion does not imply an equal distribution of the surplus. In the case of perfect price discrimination, the distribution of the surplus is highly unequal to the disadvantage of consumers.[12] Theoretically, there is no single price anymore that clears the market. Instead one is faced with multiple perfectly personalized prices. Credit reporting helps to reveal information about individuals and it helps to approximate their reservation value with regards to financial services or insurance offers.

Second-degree price discrimination is pricing according to different quantities or qualities of a good. Volume-based pricing is common in many information industries, also in credit reporting. Another approach is quality-based price discrimination (*versioning*) ranging from artificial degradation of the quality of a product to time-based discrimination. Consumers have an incentive to sort themselves into these different categories of quality and time. The strategy to offer multiple levels of quality to heterogeneous consumers is also known as "vertical differentiation." The welfare consequences are the following: The price menu offered by firms provides a self-selection incentive for consumers. By introducing additional prices for lower volumes, the producer can capture a greater share of surplus *without* altering the total quantity offered. This appropriation of surplus is a "rent-shifting" to the disadvantage of consumers. The model outcomes depend on the consumer's utility function; some authors assume linear utility functions creating some counter-intuitive results such as nonprofitability of price discrimination in a monopoly. Bhargava and Choudhary (2002) or Jones and Mendelson (1998) discuss the utility functions and associated problems in greater detail.

In the case of *third-degree price discrimination*, different prices are charged for the same good. As consumers belong to groups with different price tolerances, the group with the lower demand elasticity is charged a higher price. Grouping of individuals according to characteristics such as age or profession is also called third-degree price discrimination: "If willingness to pay is correlated with observable characteristics, such as membership in certain social or demographic groups, prices can be keyed to these observable characteristics." (Varian 1997: 2) It is clear that credit

---

[12] A necessary condition for Pareto optimality is that the marginal willingness to pay equals the marginal costs.

scoring constitutes exactly this kind of correlation. It is controversial if third-degree price discrimination leads to an improvement in social welfare. Although one may identify a Pareto-efficient solution, there is rent-shifting by the producer. Different authors have discussed the welfare implications: Hausman and MacKie-Mason (1988), Layson (1994) and Schmalensee (1981) as well as Varian (1985). Unfortunately, there are no general results emerging from this literature despite probably some key points: third-degree price discrimination can expand the market to previously underserved consumers, it is beneficial where there are strong economies of scale, but it may later constitute a market entry barrier.

Altogether welfare effects are not clear set aside the extreme case of personalized prices. Such effects depend on the form of the consumer's utility function and if output expands or not. There is a strong tendency of firms in industries with large fixed costs to engage in this kind of price-setting behavior.

Another competitive strategy employed in information markets, however, is *bundling*–the sale of two goods in a bundle. As in the above cases, a firm can choose different strategies. The bundling literature acknowledges *pure product bundling* where only the whole bundle can be purchased or *mixed bundling* where the firm offers both the bundle and the individual goods. If one product has to be purchased to obtain the other, this is termed *add-on bundling*. If the latter enables the consumer to get the second good cheaper, it is called *mixed leader bundling*. There is an abundance of examples for bundling such as software packages, CDs, journals and newspapers. Credit reports are bundles of different items of personal information. Bakos and Brynjolfsson (1999, 2000) have elaborated on this firm behavior–in their 1999 paper they analyze the case where a multi-product monopolist bundles large numbers of unrelated information products. The profitability depends on the *Law of Large Numbers* that predicts that it is easier to target the consumer's average valuation for a bundle than selling goods individually. This so-called *"economics of aggregation"* leads to greater sales, profits and efficiency per bundled good compared to the unbundled one. However, this only holds in the case of information goods, where marginal costs are close to zero. Other authors have discussed valuations of consumers in detail as well as bundling in competitive environments (Chuang and Sirbu 1999, 2000; Fay and MacKie-Mason 2001). Bundling may lead to intense competition, because consumers either buy the whole bundle or nothing. At the same time, firms increase their market power, because bundling allows them to deter newcomers. This strategy bears the risk of market monopolization. The welfare implications, however, are not always clear and not robust. Lastly, strategies of versioning and bundling are complemented by *flat-rate pricing*. The information producer grants consumers or other parties' unlimited access to the service based upon a flat rate (the rate stays the same for different usages or amounts of data retrieved). This strategy is popular in Internet industries and for content providers who demand subscription fees. Sundararajan (2003: 1) shows that the introduction of fixed-fee pricing increases both consumer surplus and total surplus, but suggests: "in nascent information markets, firms may profit from low flat-rate penetration pricing, but as these markets mature, the optimal pricing mix should expand to include a wider range of usage-based pricing options." This author aside, there are few theoretical works on this subject matter, especially compared to the thriving bundling literature. Some works worth mentioning are those of Fishburn, Odlyzko and Siders (1997), Hayashi (2002) and Oi (1971).

2.1.4 Demand-side Characteristics of Information Markets

There are interesting features on the demand-side of information markets as well. In the treatment herein, I separate firms and consumers as some peculiarities associated with an individual's information demand cannot be observed for firms and vice versa. Yet other characteristics are of more general nature. Let us start of with a discussion of the individual and then organizational demand for information. Varian (1999: 13) coined a *"Malthus' law of information."* At his time, Malthus was concerned with a linear growth of food production that faced geometric population growth. Varian notes that the supply of information grows exponentially, but its consumption grows only linearly at best. The author has estimated that the world produces between 1 and 2 Exabytes of unique information per year that is approximately 250 megabytes for every man, woman, and child. This data production is popularly termed "information overload." Human information processing and information overload are typically discussed in cognitive economics and in computer science. I may only briefly mention it here the interested reader is referred to Davis and Olson (1985) or Paquet (1998). Individuals show decreasing marginal utility in their consumption of different information items. Yet, in the case of identical information the utility derived from the second information item is zero. Human brain capacity limits the processing of information. This capacity varies from person to person, of course. Experiments show that adding information up to a critical point increases human performance, but further addition will decrease performance, because overload occurs (Davis and Olson 1985, Handzic 2001 and Paredes 2003). Information overload reduces the quality of human decisions. Computational capacity limitations are typically accompanied by *bounded rationality*: individuals tend to choose any aspiration level, which is not necessarily the optimal one just to not further process additional quantities of information. In a now famous quote, Simon (1971: 40-41) states:

> *"What information consumes is rather obvious: it consumes the attention of its recipients. Hence a wealth of information creates a poverty of attention and a need to allocate that attention efficiently among the overabundance of information sources that might consume it."*

He notes that recipients incur a large part of the costs of information. This insight has sparked a discussion about "economics of attention" (Aigrain 1997, Goldhaber 1997 and Lanham 1994). I do not further explore this literature here. Behavioral economics that incorporates psychology seems more promising as it provides more realistic assumptions about individual decision behavior. Neoclassical theory assumes that consumers are Bayesian updaters who maximize expected utilities and who calculate probabilities of outcomes of their actions and employ different strategies based upon this decision rule. However, as various experiments have shown, this is not an adequate description of human behavior: "There are numerous experiments to describe how individuals process information incorrectly, that is, in ways inconsistent with Bayes' rule." (Pesendorfer 2006: 718).

In complex situations humans tend to employ other methods of reasoning: they recognize patterns, use heuristics and build hypotheses that are replaced by new ones if needed (Arthur 1994). Behavioral economics dates back to Nobel Prize winners Kahneman and Tversky (1979), who demonstrated that decision-making under uncertainty exhibits peculiar anomalies, which are not reflected in the rationality theorem of economics. These anomalies are in fact frequent deviations from this theorem. For instance, individuals tend to ignore available (technical) information such as probabilities and instead base their actions on heuristics. *Heuristics* are simple rule of thumb, that is an easily accessible and simplified representation of a situation and of how to react to it. This, of course, must not be congruent with reality.

Information costs and search costs are crucial in this context. Stigler (1961) has proposed a search model for information that can be applied to the demand side of the market. Individuals will demand information up to the point where the marginal cost of additional information equals or exceeds its expected value. Assume there are two goods x_1 and x_2, where for one good the price information is freely available while for the other it is costly to obtain. Utility is defined as $U = u(x_1, x_2)$ for the two goods x_1 and

x_2 and the budget constraint is defined as $w = p_1x_1 + p_2x_2 + p_iI$ with p_i denoting the price per good and unit of information and I denoting the amount of information acquired. Further it is specified that $p_2 = p_2^e = f(I)$, the expected price p_2^e decreases as more information is acquired. The utility maximizing investment in information is reached at $\frac{x_2dp_2}{dI} = p_i$.

At this point, the expected reduction in costs for the searched good equals the marginal cost of information. Once this point is reached, no further searches are conducted. From now on, the consumer ignores better prices–a sign of bounded rationality. The subjective value of information is increasingly an object of intensive study. Raban and Rafaeli (2003), for instance, explore the *endowment effect*. In their experiments, participants had to buy and sell information, but apparently they valued information they owned much higher than information they did not own. They also had a strong inclination to purchase information, not to sell it, even though the information had no real objective value for them. The authors attributed this behavior to risk aversion (not loss aversion).

What about the behavior of individuals in situations where they have to disclose personal information about themselves? Acquisti and Grossklags (2004) explain that individuals often claim they are concerned with privacy but then trade off information in return for only small rewards. The authors explain that individuals act with limited knowledge about the consequences of information revelation. There is often no full assessment of the associated privacy risks. In this sense one can state that *immediate gratification* from information disclosure in the short-run weights heavier than the "cumulative risks" that build up over the long-run when the economics of aggregation and correlation kick in. Although the disclosure of bits of information in one transaction might not be considered intrusive, the aggregation of this information across transactions and economic spheres is considered to be very intrusive. Acquisti and Grossklags (2004) also explain that there are self-control problems, hyperbolic discounting and underinsurance. *Hyperbolic discounting* explains that there are high discount rates over short horizons and low ones over long horizons. This impacts decisions and can lead to underinsurance as long-term risks are not appreciated adequately. It is somewhat paradoxical that there is an abundance of information accompanied by limits in processing power, but that at the same time demand for information seems to increase. For example, decision makers usually derive positive confidence from increasing information collections. Davis and Olson (1985: 256) have two explanations for this phenomenon: (1) the psychological value of unused opportunities and (2) information as a symbol of commitment. The *"theory of unused oppor-*

tunities" explains why people pay a premium to live in large cities without ever using the cultural opportunities offered. The premium is paid for the unused opportunity. The same holds for information collections: Large data collections in firms or bureaucracies around the world are almost always justified, even if the information is hardly ever used. Only storage and back-up costs seem to limit the demand for information as well as in many cases data protection laws. Feldman and March (1981) have suggested another explanation for the excessive information demand by organizations: They propose that much of the information gathered in institutions is for surveillance and not for decision-making purposes and that use of information is a "symbol of commitment" to rationality and competence. It therefore creates confidence in decision-making abilities. Companies have far larger capabilities to store and process information, but there are still limitations despite the extreme price reduction in computing power. In 1965, Gordon Moore (the Co-Founder of Intel) observed exponential growth in the number of transistors per integrated circuit. He predicted that a doubling per year would continue. In subsequent years, data density has doubled approximately every 18 months. This is the co-called "Moore's Law." In addition, there are now many technologies available for data compression. Scoring models and credit scores (the quantification of credit risk) are an excellent example of such data compression, where large amounts of data are reduced to a single three digit statistic, the credit risk of a consumer.

In the above sections, the supply and demand sides of information markets were characterized. It was argued that information goods induce price or quality discrimination, bundling or flat rate pricing. In credit reporting, one frequently encounters volume-based pricing, bundling of data items and versioning, where credit bureaus sell the credit information for different purposes. The sale of credit information for employment purposes is increasingly forbidden in countries around the world to protect consumers from its severe consequences. While mainstream economics assumes that there is a rational trade-off in information searches, experiments show that this must not be the case. Endowment effects can explain some irrational phenomena in information markets. For the information demands by firms, however, especially the theory of unused opportunities and symbolic commitment seems to play a role.

2.2 Markets for Personal Information

Is personal information just like any other economic good? The following sections are intended to approach this question from a theoretical point of view. For quite some time, there have been virtually no studies on a specific type of economic good: personal information. Sensitive personal information is bought and sold by a wide variety of institutions: government agencies, marketing firms or insurance and financial services providers. Through the adoption of information technologies, institutions have greatly expanded their information-processing capacities. At the same time information underwent an unparalleled commodification process–it is now bought and sold just like any other product. In the introduction to this book, I have mentioned that my original research interest was the economic dimension of privacy. In the following I turn this question around to ask: what is the impact of market forces on privacy and hence welfare distribution? It has been argued above that an individual's characteristics are correlated with credit or insurance risk and that this allows a more precise approximation of the willingness to pay. The input into scoring models is financial data, employment and CV information and sometimes life-style or health information. Again, is personal information similar to any other good bought and sold in the market? For obvious reasons: no. Personal data might entail severe welfare implications for the data subject in case of disclosure.[13] In the economic sphere, it is valuable because of its effect of redistributing welfare among transaction partners. Control over personal information determines negotiation power, allows conclusions about the willingness to pay and influences the terms of trade. Individuals have to balance the willingness of disclosing information with the expected returns from trade. Personal information receives special protection in many countries, data protection laws govern what may be collected and commodified and limit production and distribution of information products. Often these laws constitute the only barrier against the incentive to collect and centralize many different types of information items about individuals. Societies around the world are in ongoing struggles to find regimes that balance economic interests in information and the right to privacy. As we will see, the public goods features of information goods can create considerable problems if sensitive information is involved and these problems constantly challenge the balance.

---

[13] In some cases the expression "welfare implications" is euphemistic. Apparently there was a case in the U.S., where a stalker went after actress Rebecca Schaeffer and murdered her. He had found her residential address through the California Department of Motor Vehicles.

2.2.1 Intellectual Property Rights in Personal Data

When it comes to personal information, the main question is who is considered to be the rightful owner of that information? The person who collects the information? The data subject to whom the information refers? The answers to these questions vary across nations. In this section, I present an overview of the discussion of granting an intellectual property right to personal data. Maybe personal information could be better safeguarded by property rights protection or by contractual approaches? Samuelson (2000: 1127) discusses the advantages and disadvantages of property rights in personal information and contrasts that with an alternative market-oriented regime. The advantages of the property rights approach are the following: Individuals would have the right to sell their information, thus forcing companies to internalize some of the costs they currently externalize.[14] Data subjects would take part in the trade in information and could set their individual price for privacy. Samuelson (2000) states that the U.S. law limits the disclosure of personal data: "(T)he rationale for these legal protections has not historically been grounded on a perception that people have property rights in personal data as such. (...) Indeed, the traditional view in American law has been that information as such cannot be owned by any person."

In the U.S., however, credit bureaus do own the data and therefore can use it more freely. There are many cases, where U.S. law assigns more rights to firms in terms of how to handle data than to individuals, although this seems to change now. So far, only weak rights were granted to individuals to stop firms from using the data for marketing purposes. Americans also have minor possibilities to stop governmental agencies from selling their personal data such as driver's license information. In many cases further uses of information (the primary purpose and use aside) are usually unknown to consumers. They typically reveal information only for the obvious use in the primary transaction, for instance, for getting credit (see Figure 2.3). Secondary transactions such as the sharing of information with a credit reporting agency must not be obvious to the consumer. It depends on the data protection regime as to whether this transaction occurs with or without knowledge of the data subject. Further tertiary transactions such as the sale to telecom or marketing companies, however, often happen without any knowledge or consent of the consumer. The general attitude in the U.S.–not in other countries such as Germany–is that information is merely some by-product of an economic transaction.

---

[14] Such an externalization would be the case if a company that collected personal data sends marketing material to persons that are not interested in the products.

Figure 2.3
Credit Reporting Transactions

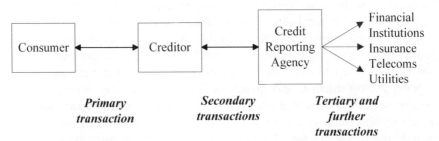

Primary	*Secondary*	*Tertiary and*
transaction	*transactions*	*further*
		transactions

Note: The sale of credit information for employment purposes is forbidden in some Euro-pean countries and does not conform to the principle of selling personal data only for re-lated and not unrelated purposes.

With little specification of the rights to the data in the primary transaction, the consumer has no power for determining the terms of trade in the sec-ondary let alone any further transactions. Usually firms claim that they are the owner of the data. In this setting, externalities may arise, because the consumer is typically not involved in the price-setting process in the sec-ondary transaction. One advantage of specifying intellectual property rights in information is, that the market would solve many problems through the price mechanism. But this solution also has drawbacks. For in-stance, there might be substantial transaction costs associated with negotia-tions concerning information privacy. Laudon (1996a) has argued that there has to be an infrastructure that backs the trade in information. The move from a regime of free information use to one of property rights might not be without friction. A major problem in privacy transactions is *"alienability."* In common economic situations, the owner who sells a good looses any control over it with regard to further transactions with that good. This is not the case for personal information: if the data subject looses all control over the data after the first transaction, there is a regime of no data protection at all. This is not a purely theoretical argument, in many developing countries there is no legislation protecting personal data. Samuelson notes that privacy is a fundamental human right that would be traded away if personal information became personal property. It is well known that property rights regimes are inherently regressive. Samuelson finds that "standard models of property rights seem unsuitable to achieving information privacy." (Samuelson 2000: 1146). Therefore, she prefers a default rule that forbids certain activities with the data, until the parties override it with an agreement. With some qualifications this is the case in European legislation. Also, certain uses of the data could be licensed and the license rights would not be transferable unless the licensor grants the right to sublicense. No new intellectual property rights would have to be established in this case. Defenders of the market solution claim that conflicting privacy interests can be reconciled through the price mechanism by finding the optimal price for personal data. However, the optimal price depends on the ability of market participants to reach mutually acceptable contracts.

Kang (1998) shows that if there would be two rules (opt-out and opt-in) the costs associated with opt-out might be higher than with opt-in and that this inequality will grow over time: "Unless the parties agree otherwise, the information collector should process data only in functionally necessary ways." (Kang 1998: 1259). Litman (2000) states that the proposal to treat personal information as a property right is more than thirty years old, it has been originally suggested by Westin (1967: 324-325). The author claims that the major appeal for the property rights approach stems from its feasibility and the idea that low transaction costs will allow individuals to negotiate privacy terms. Property law gives the owner the right to sell or license a good: "If privacy is a property right, and individuals have an ownership interest in facts that describe them, (...), and people who cared about their own data privacy would have the means to secure it." (Litman 2000: 1297). She states that ownership of facts such as personal information might be inconsistent with the First Amendment of the U.S. Constitution. In her opinion, the bargaining of privacy terms will neither be easy nor cheap and the gain from it remains unknown: "The market in personal data (is) the problem. Market solutions based on a property rights model won't cure it; they'll only legitimize it." (Litman 2000: 1301). In her opinion, such a solution provides only "illusionary protection." Instead of the "privacy as property" notion, she writes that the complete opposite is thinkable: the so-called anti-property proposal. Under this proposal personal data cannot be property and it is illegal to buy or to sell it, just as it is illegal to buy and sell humans. One could still share information, but nobody would own it. The above explanations show how difficult it is to find a solution to the privacy problem. It is also clear that in the past, countries have established regimes that treat this question quite differently. Whereas in Germany there is the rule of thumb that "everything is forbidden until explicitly allowed," the U.S. pursues the opposite "everything is allowed until it is forbidden" rule for uses of personal data. None of the countries reviewed in this survey, however, has established a true market for person information where individuals also participate and set prices.

2.2.2 Negative Externalities in Information Markets

For physical networks path-dependence, lock-in and excess inertia play an important role. Complementarities, compatibility, coordination and standards are also important. There are remarkable economies of scale and scope as well as different kinds of externalities. The result is that perfect competition must not necessarily lead to a unique market solution, but that it is likely that multiple equilibria arise. But are these insights transferable to information networks? In the following, it is assumed that an information network consists of all users that share personal information under the same standards and protocols. The question is whether these networks do have special characteristics. Although data are immaterial the distribution of information goods depends on physical networks, it was explained above that credit reports are similar to system goods–meaning that they bundle together complementary information items (*"economics of correlation"*). For that matter companies transfer their information to the central repository. The data are then distributed to the parties that delivered them. Shy (2001: 164-195) defines three kinds of information reproduction: vertical, horizontal and mixed reproduction networks. In the first case, each agent makes one copy for the benefit of another user. If this copy is not worsening the quality as for digital information it may well be reproduced infinitely. In horizontal reproduction, each consumer makes a copy from the original provider. In mixed reproduction, data are first copied in horizontal and then in vertical fashion or vice versa. Apart from the quality of copies, the interesting feature is certainly the pricing of information, which depends on reproduction networks. For instance, in mixed reproduction networks the risk of illegal copying or other illegal uses may rise with an increasing number of furnisher/users. Therefore, systems should be designed in a way that this risk is reduced. Complementarities and standards also play a role in non-physical networks. Information collection has to be standardized–hence common reporting standards (technical specifications) and language are important. Some creditworthiness data may be useful originally, but many credit record items are useless until they are bundled together with other items to provide the bigger picture (so-called "*economics of aggregation*"). However, in turn, the whole credit report might be not of much value if it lacks the most important item such as bankruptcy information. If credit reports depend on network structures are network effects observable? It was explained above that there are demand-side and supply-side externalities. If a new firm enters the data pool of a credit bureau and contributes to it, there are positive effects for all other participants. Usually this is priced in by rewarding the entering company for the contribution in terms of lower prices. Externalities in the original sense would only exist, if the agency does not take the network effects into account. Credit reporting agencies either set volume-based prices or differentiate according to access technology used or according to information delivered (positive or negative data). But some also charge fixed transaction fees or only a lump-sum for access.

What about negative externalities? Negative externalities arise when personal data are sold without the consensus or knowledge of the consumer and these secondary transactions do not take the consumer's cost-benefit calculations into account. However, for the consumer's strategic considerations it is important to know what the exact welfare implications of information disclosure or non-disclosure are. Varian (1996: 2-3) provides a simple example. A buyer usually wants a seller to know that she would like to buy a certain good. At the same time, however, the buyer does not want the seller to know the maximum price she is willing to pay. Vice versa the seller does not want the buyer to know the minimum price he would be willing to charge. Both sides could exploit such information to their own benefit. Market participants are very well aware of this and often strategically disclose misinformation.

Theoretically, an unlimited number of transactions with the information are possible after the first one happened (so-called "*unlimited expansibility*"). Of special interest in credit reporting is the third transaction, when the credit bureau sells the information to other market participants in some cases even thousands of other market participants. Should data subjects have the right to block the disclosure of information or to be at least compensated for it? This touches upon the very question of the definition of property rights and the possibility for enforcing them. If the property rights would be fully specified and located at the data subject, many of the secondary and tertiary transactions in the market place would not take place due to restrictions imposed by the data subject. Moreover, the data owner could specify the "terms of privacy," that is purposes as well as terms of storage and processing of data. Varian (1996: 5) stresses that many privacy problems are a consequence of *to little information* that has been shared for defining the "terms of privacy." This kind of property right specification will probably reduce the amount of information in the market compared to a situation of unspecified property rights. The owner will try to conceal adverse personal facts, because he or she now has the incentive *and the power* to prohibit usage. It is not clear if a reduced amount of data in the market decreases efficiency. Traditional economic approaches regard more information as better, their benchmark are full-information scenarios or total transparency. However, the literature I discuss in the section of the microeconomics of information shows that other information scenarios might be optimal. If property rights are specified and located at the firm involved in the primary transaction, it can sell the data freely in the market place. This may generate negative externalities for the individual. The optimal location of property rights depends on the information shared such as positive or negative information (see Box 2.1).

Box 2.1 Positive and Negative Information

Negative information: Negative information consists of statements about defaults or arrears as well as charge-offs and bankruptcies. It may also include statements about lawsuits, liens and judgments that are obtained from courts. This kind of information may be collected about individuals or companies. It is also called black information. Negative information is information about contractual breaches.

Positive information: Positive information consists of assets and liabilities as well as guarantees. It sometimes includes detailed statements about outstanding types of credit, amount of loans and repayment patterns as well as further information like employment and family history. The extent to which positive information is collected depends on the data protection regime prevailing. Such facts may be collected about individuals or companies. It is also called white information. Positive information are facts about contractual compliant behavior.

Some information is better located at the data subject to control disclosure and uses of information. However, property rights to other facts such as negative information about an individual (bankruptcy information), might be better not located at the individual as there is a strong tendency to conceal such information, despite the fact that it could be beneficial for society in general. This information, however, should still be subject to quality-improving measures (such as access and correction rights). What are the costs associated with negative externalities? Many authors assume costs of time and attention that are posed upon the individual (Varian 1996, Laudon 1996a, 1996b). Laudon (1996b: 42) describes this as direct and indirect costs that are either large amounts of unsolicited mailings or time and attention that are lost. In addition, marketing might lead to a shift in rents. The costs of loss of attention cannot be estimated, but the waste in human capital and money due to misdirected marketing efforts. Over the course of the 1990s, response rates to credit card solicitations in the U.S. were constantly decreasing as the American Financial Services Association (2001) reports (see Figure 2.4). In 2005, card issuers mailed out the record number of over 6 billion solicitations. This, however, came with a record low response rate of 0.5%. The main reason for this low rate is the saturation of the market, 75% of the U.S. households have one or more credit cards with the average being 2.4 cards in 2000. Despite this saturation "a typical household receives more than three credit card offers *per month throughout the year.*" (American Financial Services Association 2001, emphasis added).

Figure 2.4
Credit Card Mailings in the U.S.

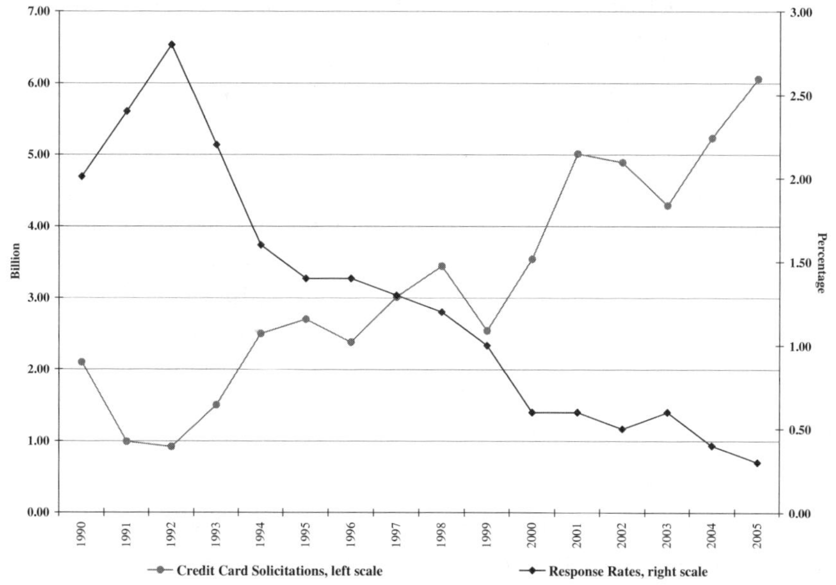

Source: Consumers Union

In the process of acquiring new customers, the quality of cardholders has constantly decreased–a phenomenon analyzed by Black and Morgan (1998). The authors show that increased access to credit worsened the mix of credit card holders and affected the risk of delinquency. New card holders tend to earn less, work in cyclical blue-collar jobs and are more willing to borrow. The appeal of direct mailing is that it is still contributing a major share to the generation of new credit card accounts. In 2000 approximately 68% of the new accounts were opened after a mailing (American Financial Services Association 2001). However, the vast majority of offers are simply tossed away. Junk mail costs millions. In a survey conducted by the European Commission (2001), the authors state that junk e-mails cost users worldwide approximately 10 billion Euro per year. Internet marketing firms collect information about individuals stemming from their interaction with websites. With such information personalized advertisements may be sent to the consumer, even if he or she did not give consent. The point to be made is that such negative externalities do have a price and are based upon sub-optimally specified property rights. Laudon (1996b) writes that firms typically argue that they mix data such as address with other information such as lifestyle. By doing so they would add value to the data in a way that justifies their ownership to such data. He argues:

> "*If a thief steals your car, fixes and paints it, and mixes it with a fleet of stolen cars, then indeed the thief has added value to the car and the collection. But these actions by the thief do not therefore transfer the ownership to the thief. To argue that information gathering institutions add value to my personal information by compiling, collating and mixing in a database, does not solve the question of ownership.*" Laudon (1996b: 43)

In information markets where property rights are located at the company, there is an excessive use of information for purposes other than those originally specified. Arising negative externalities cannot be internalized without a change of law and information property rights. A further aspect is: the more parties are connected to the information network, the more have access to the information shared. This only increases the probability of privacy breaches, usually conducted by either employees or family members of the victim. The network architecture is important when privacy policies are designed. If information is copied from a single source (horizontal reproduction) it is efficient to locate the primary responsibility for data quality at the central source. Credit reporting networks, however, are mixed regimes, where copies are made from a central source, but at the same time data are distributed to affiliates. This means several parties are interconnected, share and co-own the information.

2.2.3 Imperfect Appropriation of Personal Data

The section on information goods described characteristics such as non-excludability, non-rivalry, experience good, economies of scale (and scope), immateriality, and indivisibility. It was explained that there is imperfect appropriation of data: it is in many cases prohibitively expensive to exclude others from its use–even more so if the information has already been shared.[15] In the following the main problem arising from this feature (identity theft) is discussed. Credit reporting can be a tool against identity theft, but it can also be a source contributing to it. Identity theft denotes a situation where individuals mask themselves as somebody else to benefit

---

[15] This is the case for Social Security Numbers in the U.S.

from access to credit and other services. It is the illegal appropriation of another individual's identifiers such as Social Security Number, driver's license, financial cards and account information. In 2003, the U.S. Federal Trade Commission (2003a) conducted a survey on the subject matter. It showed that an alarming 27.3 million Americans had already been victims of identity theft in the past five years up to publication of the study. In 2002 the number stood at 9.91 million Americans or 4.6% of the population. The welfare implications from identity theft can be enormous for the individual. Approximately half of the victims discovered the crime after noticing suspicious movements on their accounts. Some statistics on the crime are summarized in the Table 2.1.

Table 2.1
Identity Theft in the United States

Indicator	Total ID Theft (2003)	Total ID Theft (2006)
Percent of population affected	4.7	4.0
Number of people (million)	10.1	8.9
Average fraud amount per victim (US-$)	5.249	6.383
Average consumer costs (US-$)	555	422
Average resolution time (hours)	33	40

Source: U.S. Federal Trade Commission

There is currently a discussion in the U.S. to what extent the credit reporting system facilitates identity theft. Lopucki (2003) states: "As a legal matter, consumer credit reports were available to anyone with a 'legitimate business need,' (...) and as a practical matter they were available to 'virtually everyone.'" There are some inherent problems in the U.S. system of identification, where thousands of people may have access to personal data. There is no national identification system, usually name, address and Social Security Number serve as unique identifiers. Both are easily appropriated. The more difficult it is to prevent others from the use of personal information, the higher negative externalities will be. Lopucki (2003: 1280) notes that credit files are notoriously incorrect containing typos in Social Security Numbers and misspelled names. A further problem is the system for documentary identification issued by the U.S. government such as the driver's license. For issuing this license, the Department in charge accepts either the social security card or the birth certificate; neither document includes a picture of the person holding them. Furthermore governmental institutions also engage in selling driver's license information. It is amazing that the absence of a national identity system increasingly generates privacy problems, but the majority of Americans are opposed to such a system because of *privacy concerns*. The path dependency debate has shown that as soon as a country embarks on a specific development path, standards in the market place may be difficult to change, something that is observable in the U.S. Additionally, the right to access personal information is cumbersome for U.S. consumers. I have explained that the ownership to information is based upon the notion that the data collector has added some extra value and therefore is the rightful owner. The consumer, on the other hand, only receives access after identification and payment of formerly US-\$ 25 (!). This had to be regulated by law and stood at approximately US-\$ 8 in 2004 adjusted for inflation. Commercial users of credit reports pay far less than US-\$ 1 and only a couple of cents in Europe. The industry justifies this asymmetric pricing by arguing that dealing with follow-up questions by consumers is expensive. To remedy some of these problems, a variety of policy proposals have been put forth, but these cannot be discussed here. The part of this study on regulation will allow some conclusions in this respect. For now it is sufficient to say that legislators in the U.S. have introduced a free credit report once a year for monitoring of possible identity theft. More radical propositions put forth that the system should be turned upside down and that consumers should be able to choose to become the client of a credit reporting agency through an opt-in regime (Solove 2003: 1269). It is argued that the consumer should be the owner of information and advise the bank to what credit reporting agency the data should be send. In this case credit bureaus would directly compete for consumers. But why is identity theft in general not such a big problem in European countries? "One reason why it has been such a problem in the U.S. is the traditional use of social security numbers as an identifier–a piece of information that, when linked to the name and address of the individual, makes it relatively easy for a thief to assume an individual's identity." (The Register 2004) For a long time, credit reporting agencies sold credit report header information and Social Security Numbers.[16] The reason for these developments is an inadequate specification of property rights and the feature of non-excludability inherent in information. There are authors that have linked the smaller extent of the problem in Europe to its privacy legislation (see Clements et al. 2003). In the report, the authors argue that "strong existing European legislation, which defines clear privacy and data protection rights" contributes to a lower number of identity theft cases.

---

[16] Credit headers are identifying information at the "top" of a credit report. This information typically includes personal identifiers and Social Security Number.

2.2.4 Concentration of Information Power

Scale economies lead to strong concentration tendencies in markets for personal information. This by itself is nothing negative as there may be still fierce competition among oligopolists. From a regulatory point of few, coping with few companies instead of many certainly increases effectiveness of oversight. Economies of scale are based upon the law of mass production. They lead to an increasing diversification of the use of personal information. The specific competition strategies in information markets induce price discrimination, bundling and versioning. Most of these strategies can be observed in the market for personal information with some interesting side effects for the individual to whom the information relates. Again, the competition strategies and the structure of production costs will very likely lead to concentration of the industry. Most of the companies that are active in credit reporting are not exceptionally large (when compared to marketing companies) although this might change. As of 2006, two of them–Equifax and Experian–were publicly traded companies. In 2001, Experian had revenues of US-$ 1.2 billion, Equifax US-$ 1.1 billion and TransUnion US-$ 1 billion. Within the period of 2000-2005, profits were between US-$ 370-500 million. Acxiom, which is one of the largest marketing information providers in the U.S., had *profits* of US-$ 1.1 billion in 1998 alone. Credit reporting agencies reduce asymmetric information and bundle information processing in markets. Additionally, they realize scale and scope economies and lower the costs that would arise if banks would have to search the information individually. This is welfare improving and increases the productivity of the banking industry. However, the public increasingly monitors credit reporting with suspicion. One of the reasons is the pervasiveness it reached in the 1990s. Table 2.2 presents the estimated coverage rates of credit bureaus and one credit register in the United States, Germany, United Kingdom and France. With such information collections it is possible to follow consumers through their life cycle and through different lifestyles. The coverage rates of the economically active population range from 30% for smaller agencies to 90% for the larger ones. The numbers are estimates by the author based upon different sources such as company websites, industry officials and newspaper articles. Many companies guard the exact number of individuals stored in their databases as trade secret. However, in general it holds that the expansion in terms of information collection is–set aside regulatory measures–only constrained by technological capacity limits and economic usefulness of the information.

Table 2.2
Information Indices in Credit Reporting

Country	Company or credit register	Year	Individuals stored (Million)	Economically active population	Info index (coverage)
U.S.	Experian	2006	215	236.266.000	90.99
	TransUnion	2005	200	236.266.000	84.65
	Equifax	2005	n/a	236.266.000	n/a
UK	Experian	2006	45	58.652.592	76.72
	Equifax	2005	25	58.652.592	42.62
	Callcredit	2005	33	58.652.592	52.26
GER	Schufa	2005	60	70.986.000	84.52
	KQIS	2004	21	70.986.000	29.58
FR	Banque	2005	2.3	47.094.372	4.88

Note: "Individuals stored" are estimates by the author based upon information from different sources. Economically active population are all inhabitants +15 years (ILO data, national data for Germany and France, all data for 2005), Banque denotes Banque de France.

Theoretically, the coverage of the population could soon be universal, meaning that economically active population is covered by 100% in countries with positive-negative information sharing. Table 2.2 shows some countries with high coverage rates (U.S. and Germany), whereas France (a country with a negative information regime and a public credit register) has a low coverage rate. In countries with negative information regimes, the number of people stored in databases is far lower as only a small fraction of consumers will get into arrears, delinquencies or defaults. Many data protection activists regard positive-negative information sharing with suspicion, as millions of consumer profiles are stored. This has been one of the arguments in France to not turn the system into a positive one.

2.2.5 Versioning and Purpose Creep

This section is an overview of the problem of versioning and "purpose creep" related to the use of personal information. These two problems stem from the various competition strategies discussed above. Again, the reader is reminded that versioning and bundling strategies entail specific problems when personal information is traded. In markets for personal information, data collections are increasingly centralized. This leads to a correlation of different variables with one another—and hence of different fields of economic life of a consumer. I have described this as "economics of correlation." The picture of the risk associated with consumers is more comprehensive the more firms enter the reporting network. However, there is a trade-off: "Consumer access to credit, housing, insurance, basic utility services, and even employment is increasingly determined by centralized records of credit history and automated interpretations of those records." (Consumer Federation of America 2002: 2). With the centralization of databases the score might become the "entry code" to economic life. "Purpose creep" describes the tendency to use information for more and more purposes–also those that are unrelated to purposes for which the information was originally collected. Assume the case where the company collects data for the assessment of creditworthiness, but then sells the information for marketing purposes or employment purposes. This has been discussed above as "non-transparency" of further transactions to which the consumer has not given consent. The practice of selling information for purposes other than the original one can have negative effects for individuals. Over the course of the research, an increasing number of countries counted cases where consumers had been locked out of the job market. This is an alarming tendency, but also an excellent example of purpose creep. For instance, students in the U.S. found themselves declined for posts after having defaulted on their University loan and in South Korea debtors could not get jobs after the credit boom had come to a sudden halt. In March 2004, the finance ministry of South Korea stated "personal credit information providers will be asked to temporarily withhold some people's credit records from employers so as to facilitate the hiring of credit delinquents." (Asian Pulse 2004) They even considered a one-year suspension, "to facilitate hiring of those who have been shut out of the job market because of small debts that they have incurred." Ministry officials are quoted with the words that if these people cannot find work, they cannot pay off their debt and get out of arrears, which leads to a vicious cycle.[17] Even in the U.S., the subject has been regulated. Credit reports were not only used for hiring but also for determination if the person should keep the job. The Consumer Reporting Employment Clarification Act of 1998 now unambiguously states that the consumer has to give written authorization, without it no consumer report can be obtained for employment purposes (read: opt-in). This is an example, where negative externalities led to the regulatory shifting of property rights away from the data collector and towards the individual. Consumers also complained that insurance firms use their credit records for determination of their risk premium and for adjusting insurance rates. The latter outraged consumers in the U.S., who never had a car accident while holding the insurance police, but saw their rates re-adjusted. By 2003, 19 states had

---

[17] This measure is implemented for those that incurred smaller debts and arrears only.

issued regulations of "insurance scoring." Insurance companies use credit reports for their underwriting policies and to set premiums. They typically use their own risk-prediction models, but also derive the risk of somebody filing a claim from the credit data (so-called insurance claim risk). The rule of thumb is that somebody who has a low insurance score has a higher propensity to file a claim. In addition, this score is based upon the credit score, because there is a correlation: the lower the credit score, the higher the risk for filing a claim. This illustrates how the economics of correlation increasingly leads to purpose creep.

There are limits of information sharing and purpose creep. Many regulators in Europe have established that information should only be used for the purpose for which it was primarily collected and not for any other unrelated purposes. In addition, there are retention periods for the use of such information. Bankruptcy and default data usually have to be erased after a couple of years. This is supposed to offer the possibility for a "fresh start" for borrowers after they have defaulted. If information could be collected and stored for an infinite amount of time, information asymmetries would theoretically vanish (Vercammen 1995). This would undermine the cause of the existence of information sharing mechanisms. The Vercammen model will be discussed in the section of microeconomics of privacy. Further, regulators typically also restrict the set of variables that can be collected. Usually restrictions encompass sensitive information, which might be substituted by other data that is less predictive. It is a political question as to whether sensitive information should be shared. The two authors who provided a theoretical argument for negative information sharing are Padilla and Pagano (2000): Information sharing creates a disciplinary effect and increases the borrowers' incentive to perform–the borrower knows that deviant behavior will become public knowledge and that it will be shared in the community of credit granters. Information sharing, however, might also have unwarranted effects. In their model, the fuller information sharing weakens the borrower's incentive to perform and interest and default rates are the lowest if only data on defaults are disclosed. If banks share all the information that is available to them, theory predicts that adverse selection is eliminated but so is the disciplinary effect (Padilla and Pagano 2000: 1953). Therefore, complete information sharing is not the answer–a certain degree of asymmetric information must be sustained in the market otherwise the incentive to share information will be eliminated and with it the justification to engage in this beneficial activity. Credit reports will always provide an incomplete picture and there might be circumstances leading to bankruptcy that are rather difficult to predict. This holds for divorce, health problems, unemployment or other sudden shocks to the income stream or expenditure side of a household balance sheet.

Some industry officials even joke that default rates before and after the introduction of credit scoring are exactly the same, because of the unpredictable life events. Concerning the countries for which preliminary data are available, it can be stated that repayment difficulties, default and bankruptcy are often due to the occurrence of unexpected life events that disrupt the household's budgetary equilibrium. These shocks can come from two sides–either the expenditure side with a sudden increase or from the income side with a sudden drop in income.

Table 2.3
Reasons for Default, Bankruptcy or Overindebtedness

Country	Reasons for Overindebtedness	Percentage
Austria	Poor household management	26
	Unemployment	21
	Divorce	20
	Housing debts	16
	Other reasons	17
Belgium	Unemployment	19
	Excessive charges	16
	Non-financial causes	15
	Divorce	18
	Illness	7
	Deceased	5
	Unexpected charges	3
	Other reasons	17
France	Unemployment	42
	Divorce or deceased	20
	Illness	11
	Reduction of social benefits	4
	Other reasons	23
Spain	Income reduction (unexpected life events)	58
	Bad financial management	12
	Lack of information	26
	Other reasons	4

Note: Some of the numbers do not add up to 100, because multiple reasons could be cited. Source: Jentzsch and San Jose Riestra (2006)

Table 2.3 indicates that credit card bills, unemployment, divorce or medical bills and often several of these factors clumped together can cause inability to finance debt. The number of people who intentionally misuse credit and default strategically is rather low and typically overrated in the theoretical literature. The vast majority of borrowers try to pay off their debts in a timely manner. And unfortunate borrowers might have negative life events clumped together (for instance, divorce and unemployment), but their credit risk is still lower than the risk of strategic defaulters. Other information input, however, could potentially increase the prediction power of scoring models: GDP growth rates or regional economic conditions have not been included in scoring models in the U.S. due to public disapproval. As will be discussed in the section on credit scoring the failure to not make such adjustments can lead to inefficiencies. In summary, it is obvious that markets for information goods are not strictly comparable to markets for traditional goods. Information has some peculiar features that may create problems if it is traded like an economic good. This especially holds for personal information. The legal infrastructure for information sharing changes the property rights and therefore the features of the good. Thus the trade of personal information is sensitive to the legal environment. To understand information markets, features on the demand and the supply side must be analyzed. In such markets, individuals have a privacy preference that is inversely related to the expected welfare implications of information disclosure, meaning the higher the potential benefit from information disclosure the lower will be the preference for privacy (or the incentive to conceal). Some information items will have negative welfare consequences such as bankruptcy information, leading to higher credit risk and higher prices for credit. The individual will have an incentive to conceal that fact. Demand for personal information is driven by the efficiency of the "economics of correlation" where it is possible to predict risk or approximate profitability in areas unrelated to credit (insurance, employment). The next sections discuss microeconomic theory, incentives of data disclosure and their effects on market outcome.

2.3 Microeconomics of Information

In the upcoming sections, the reader is introduced to the microeconomics of information and insights derived from models that stylize asymmetric information problems. Such problems are, of course, nothing new to economists. Stiglitz (2000: 1441) argues that early economists such Smith, Marshall and Mill were aware of information problems, but they did not consider their far-reaching implications. The common model known for featuring complete information is the Walras general equilibrium model. Many academics argued that costs associated with information such as search costs could easily be incorporated into models without invalidating the fundamental welfare theorems (Stigler 1967). Today we know that this is not quite right. The implications that spring from asymmetric information are so rich that a new subfield of economics developed. In the following, I introduce to information economics and discuss credit market models with an emphasis on adverse selection, credit rationing and information sharing. The primary focus will be on consumer credit market models, although I also included some of the commercial lending models.

2.3.1 Information Economics

In information economics, two kinds of situations are distinguished: uncertainty and asymmetric information. Uncertainty describes situations where all market participants are incompletely informed to the same extent. Hirshleifer (1973: 31) states that "(U)ncertainty is summarized by the dispersion of the individuals' subjective probability (or belief) distributions over possible states of the world." Information is an input that changes the probability distribution. The upcoming sections primarily concentrate on asymmetric information, because the strategic implications arising from it are richer than those from uncertainty. Asymmetric information generates insights concerning wealth distribution, market efficiency and market structure. The literature acknowledges two problems of asymmetric information: adverse selection (hidden information) and moral hazard (hidden action). Moral hazard is "hidden information" and generally acknowledged as problem of asymmetric information (Macho-Stadler and Pérez-Castrillo 2001: 9). *Asymmetric information* describes the problem of private information held by market participants *before* the relationship is initiated. In markets where this problem is severe, information must lead to discrimination otherwise markets break down. Externalities in markets with asymmetric information might also lead to a role for government in terms of targeting at Pareto improvement of market outcomes. *Moral hazard*, on the other hand, describes situations, where agents hold private information *after* the transaction has begun. The actions during the relationship are important, such as careless negligence that might lead to negative outcomes for the transaction partner. If it is not possible to observe the actions of the contract partner, effort levels cannot be contracted. A common phenomenon in moral hazard markets is rationing. The provider would like to offer a greater amount of her good or service, but this alters the incentive structure for the transaction partner. Market participants have found ways to circumvent such problems: Banks and insurance companies screen and monitor applicants and there is a possibility to signal certain characteristics. Guarantees allow the buyer to draw conclusions about the quality of a used good, for example. The implications of information problems cannot be overrated. Severe information problems will lead to the absence of markets–still a problem in many developing countries today.[18] In theoretical models, asymmetric information might lead to multiple results (separating or pooling equilibria). In separating equilibria economic agents signal their types by choosing a specific action. In pooling equilibria, all agents make the same choice. Which role might government play here? Orthodox theory sees only a very limited role, because of the risk of regulatory failure. It is, however, not admissible to compare incomplete information situations to those of complete information. The first are always likely to be Pareto-inefficient (Stiglitz 1987). Rather the question must be if governments can improve market outcomes in an imperfect world: the comparison is not perfect versus imperfect world but "imperfect world" versus "imperfect world with regulation." The first and second model generations are not formalizing information sharing. The origin of the first generation of models is Akerlof (1970). The Nobel Price winner showed with his "market for lemons," that the market price affects the quality of the good offered.[19] He modeled the market for used cars as symmetric and asymmetric information situation. In the latter, it is impossible for buyers to tell the qualitative differences of cars offered. Bad cars (that are traded at the same price as good cars) tend to drive good cars out of the market. Akerlof called this "modified reappearance" of Gresham's law. Yet, he was the first to formalize adverse selection processes based upon information asymmetries (and not the intrinsic value of the traded good). Additionally, he could show that in certain price and quality ranges, no trade takes place (Akerlof 1970: 490-491). This astonishing result describes a break down of markets if there are severe information asymmetries. Remedies against this quality uncertainty are guarantees and reputation, both facilitate trust and are further scrutinized below.

What are the effects of asymmetric information in credit markets? One outcome is credit rationing, where demand exceeds a completely inelastic supply at any given interest rate. Supply-demand adjustments might then take place through non-price related instruments such as collateral or a borrower's equity. Over the past decades, a huge body of literature attempted to show that credit rationing is consistent or inconsistent with the rational profit-maximizing behavior of lenders or that it either exists or not in the equilibrium (Azzi and Cox 1976, Hodgman 1960, Jaffee and Modigliani 1969, Jaffee and Russell 1976, Stiglitz and Weiss 1981, 1983). I will

---

[18] For instance, until recently, consumer credit markets have been nearly non-existent in developing countries and only slowly formal lending to household evolves.

[19] "Lemons" is a nickname for used cars that are defective. The model assumes good used cars and defective ones (lemons).

not discuss this literature in detail as it leads to far away from the topic of interest. The second generation of models includes interesting extensions that will only briefly be noted here. One part of the literature revolved around the question if rationing existed at all, as mentioned, because lenders have other instruments to adjust their supply to the demand such as loan size or they use collateral and interest to screen investors (Bester 1985a, 1985b). This allows the design of the self-selection mechanisms in contracts that lead to a separating equilibrium.

How do markets resolve information asymmetry problems? The most important mechanisms are screening before the relationship begins, monitoring during its existence and the termination of contracts in case of contractual breaches. Screening, as mentioned, is the ability to identify and distinguish different qualities of customers or clients (Akerlof 1973 and Stiglitz 1975). In the latter article, Stiglitz discusses the economic benefits and costs of screening and determines the equilibrium amount of screening under various institutional arrangements as well as its effects on welfare distribution. He notes: "Thus, by its very nature, screening information has important effects on the distribution of income." (Stiglitz 1975: 283) It tends to increase inequality. In the full screening equilibrium, the productive group of workers and the more unproductive group have lower net incomes (compared to a no-screening equilibrium). This is due to the fact of a subtraction of screening costs from the productive group's income. In addition, the less productive group is now singled out as such and does not receive the average wage anymore. The conclusions from the above are that multiple equilibria exist in imperfect information models with some being Pareto-inferior to others. Stiglitz shows that Pareto-inferior equilibria can entail either too much or too little screening.[20] Screening allows credit institutions to discriminate between different risk categories ex ante, typically through creditworthiness tests and credit scoring. This enables risk-based pricing. Monitoring, on the other hand, describes situations in which the bank observes ex post the borrower's behavior. Credit reports that contain payment behavior map the borrower's behavior during the relationship. Many models of this generation are concerned with the costs and benefits of screening as well as its optimal amount in the equilibrium (see, for an example, Such 1985). There are very few papers on screening in consumer credit markets. Some newer exemptions are Gehrig (1998), Mester (1994) and Khalil and Parigi (2001). Mester (1994) is interested in credit card rate "stickiness" which she investigates by using a screening model of consumer credit markets. The initial observation is that while the

---

[20] And sometimes no equilibrium exists at all.

costs of funds have fallen in the past, credit card rates have remained high. The author shows that banks only sometimes use collateral as a screening device. Depending on the parameter region of the model, the equilibrium may be a separating one, where lower risk borrowers choose secured loans and higher risks choose unsecured credit card loans. Other parameter values suggest a pooling equilibrium, where everybody chooses just credit card loans. The author shows that a change in the banks' costs of funds can have an ambiguous effect on the credit card rate: it does not need to decline with the decrease of the costs of funds.

Khalil and Parigi (2001) are interested in how the bank balances ex ante screening and ex post monitoring activities. Here, income of borrowers is prone to random shocks and for banks it is virtually impossible to perfectly anticipate default risks. The authors find mixed strategy equilibrium. The borrower leaves lenders in uncertainty about future income realization and lenders in turn keep borrowers uncertain about their auditing efforts. One result is that the more the lender screens, the higher the probability that the consumer does not default strategically. Intuitively, the optimal amount of screening is set at the point where marginal costs equal marginal benefits. Above a certain level of accuracy, further screening is not worthwhile. Further, Gehrig (1998) shows that banks can use creditworthiness tests that generate imperfect information about borrowers. When they adjust the test characteristics strategically by investing resources in the screening technology, credit markets become less contestable, because this investment can turn out to be an entry barrier. The higher the ability to separate risks, the more selected is the pool of pre-screened borrowers left to the firms that want to enter. If the incentives of screening are reduced, the quality of the overall loan portfolio declines and the economy incurs higher aggregate risk. This leads to the recent literature that is models that incorporate proprietary information. Dell'Ariccia, Friedman and Marquez (1999) consider adverse selection as market barrier. Banks are faced with uncertainty about the borrowers' creditworthiness and only after already lending to borrowers, they are able to reject riskier ones when refinancing. For firms that enter the market, adversely selected pools of borrowers are a severe problem. Dell'Ariccia (2001) analyzes the effects of informational asymmetries on the market structure in the banking industry with a model of spatial competition. In his model, the lending relationship enables banks to gather creditworthiness data about their borrowers (so-called "learning by lending"), which results in an informational monopoly and, thus, market power: "However, in the process of lending, banks gather some proprietary information about borrowers' creditworthiness, so that over time, they may partially resolve the problems associated with information asymmetries."

(Dell'Ariccia 2001: 1958). The author assumes that the type distribution of new potential borrowers is public information, while the type of the individual borrower remains unknown until the end of the first period. The credit history of a borrower is publicly available, the bank, however, may learn additional information. Informational barriers to entry arise due to the knowledge advantage of the incumbent bank concerning its borrowers. The conclusions from this model are interesting. The author is able to show that different degrees of adverse selection correspond to different degrees of market concentration and that information structure, market structure and bank conduct are interrelated. It also shows that economies have specific shares of known and unknown borrowers: For instance, in developing countries where no credit reporting systems exist, the share of unknown borrowers is higher than in industrialized nations and even there it differs from country to country due to different coverage rates of the credit-active population. Informational barriers are lower where the share of unknown borrowers is higher. Thus, it is the composition and not the absolute size of the credit market that matters. The author states that informational asymmetries are not the only obstacle that limits the degree of competition in credit markets other factors are capital requirements or regulatory systems. In a similar model, Marquez (2002) shows that proprietary information has an impact on the structure of the banking market. Proprietary information is not transferable to other creditors, thus borrowers remain unknown to market newcomers. Still, banks probably know more about their clients as can be extracted from a publicly available credit report. The more banks compete, the more they become informed about a smaller and smaller pool of unknown borrowers. The author shows that the emerging entry strategy in banking markets is merger and acquisition (Marquez 2002: 917). Banks acquire the customer base and with it the customer data. There are a number of analytical problems that are not addressed by the first and second generation of models. Why do banks share information if there are adverse competition effects? What are the incentives of individuals or firms to disclose information truthfully and completely? What is the effect of information restrictions such as data protection acts? The third generation of models partially answers these questions.

Many of the following models endogenize information sharing. And the role of a credit bureau in credit markets as intermediary, as provider of an inter-generational reputation system and as arbitrator is acknowledged in these models. The first paper that argued for such a type of intermediary was Ramakrishnan and Thakor (1984). The authors did not formalize information sharing itself and hence Millon and Thakor (1985) seem to be the first authors that developed such a model. It explains how "information gathering agencies" are formed in capital markets and the authors hereby refer to credit rating agencies. It is possible for firms to contract a credit rating agency that signals their value to the market. The formation of such an agency leads to a Pareto-improvement. The reason for this is that the expected screening costs for each firm contracting this agency are lower than in the case of independently acting screening agents. The first authors to formalize information sharing in household lending markets are Pagano and Jappelli (1991). Altogether there are only a few other articles that mention the role of the credit bureau (Laband and Maloney 1994, Padilla and Pagano 1997, Van Cayseele, Bouckaert and Degryse 1995). Only the main results of these papers will be discussed here. They are helpful to better understand the development of these agencies. Pagano and Jappelli (1993) find that information sharing and the membership in a credit bureau are more advantageous the greater the number of loans, the higher the geographical mobility, the lower the system's operating costs and the greater the number of participants (Pagano and Jappelli 1993: 1696). They further indicate that in adverse selection markets, information sharing expands the volume of lending by reducing asymmetric information. This creates simultaneous causation, "an increase in the size of the credit market may generate information sharing, which may in turn lead to more lending activity." (Pagano and Jappelli 1993: 1694). This problem of endogeneity plagues all theoretical analyses in this field and it will be discussed in the empirical part of this book. The authors are primarily interested in the question how information sharing can arise endogenously. They assume that banks lend to heterogeneous households, where safe households repay with a higher probability than the risky ones. The authors discuss three settings: (A) banks as local monopolies; (B) information sharing; and (C) competition. Of interest to us is the information sharing scenario. In this situation banks agree to set up a credit bureau with some fixed costs. First, the authors assume that all banks are becoming members and agree to share information. In the adverse selection situation of the model the exchange of data among lenders is a Pareto-improvement. Borrowers that are unknown to the bank now receive credit. Without information sharing, this access to credit would not exist. Data sharing can improve welfare in thin credit markets and the gain from eliminating informational asymmetries rises with the uncertainty about borrower quality.

The benefits of information sharing also arise if only a fraction of banks participate in the reporting system. In this case, the gain from information sharing is a fraction of the benefits compared to the case in which all banks join. Network effects show that the benefit from joining the system rises with the number of participants. This important insight was discussed in the section on information markets. The authors are not only able to formalize the increase in benefits from more participants (a positive network externality on the demand-side), but also to illustrate the tendency for the system to encompass the whole market, "non-members derive a net benefit from joining and incumbents have an incentive to let outsiders join." (Pagano and Jappelli 1993: 1701). The credit bureau seems to be a natural monopoly. In addition to the above results, the authors show that information sharing benefits are reduced with the contestability of the market, because the activity tends to increase the intensity of competition. As experience in different countries shows, lenders hesitate to share information. This may also depend on the size of the bank, since larger banks have lesser incentive to share data with smaller banks. This seminal model sparked further theoretical innovations by Jappelli and Pagano (2002), Laband and Maloney (1994), Padilla and Pagano (1997, 2000), Van Cayseele, Bouckaert and Degryse (1995) and Vercammen (1995). Laband and Maloney (1994), for instance, are concerned with explanations of seller financing and indirect lending. In their setting there is a seller, a buyer and a credit bureau acting as "arbitrator." The purpose of the authors' model is to find an optimal contract that solves opportunistic behavior of the buyer. Sellers compete for buyers and offer finance for them to enable them to buy their goods. In the optimal contract, installments vary over time and the buyer spends on maintenance costs for the good. It is assumed that the incentive to default increases with the maturity of the contract. Through seller financing, it is possible to split risks and a credit bureau can improve the situation, as credit reporting is a reputation system that raises the costs of default for the buyer.

One of the few papers dealing with a regulator's role is Vercammen (1995). He analyzes the welfare consequences of reputation effects in credit markets with moral hazard and adverse selection. Making payments that are due provides borrowers with future benefits, if lenders base their interest rate on the credit history (risk-based pricing). The rewards are lower interest rates for future credit. How can these reputation effects be sustained over time? "Reputation effects are strongest when the lenders are the most uncertain about a borrower's type since it is at this point that lenders are willing to adjust their beliefs the most when new information arrives." (Vercammen 1995: 462). Thus, reputation effects could decrease with decreasing adverse selection (that is due to decreasing asymmetries) and lead to lower welfare. The author indicates that there might be a role for policy to endorse the reputation effects. Vercammen's reputation game with repeated interaction assumes risk-averse Bayesian updaters. The borrower takes into account that a default in the current period affects the future credit history and thus future expected utility. The lender, on the other hand, is able to observe the credit history. Here, reputation effects arise endogenously and the borrower invests extra effort to lower the probability of default. This effort as well as the corresponding change in the costs of capital and the stream of higher expected utility is defined as reputation effect (Vercammen 1995: 468). Reputation effects can reduce welfare losses that exist in their absence:

> *"The logic is that as a lender collects an increasing amount of information about the borrower in the form of longer credit histories, her distribution of beliefs will become increasingly precise for each borrower she interacts with. Therefore, new information in the form of whether the borrower defaulted or paid in the previous period will cause less of a shift in this distribution."* (Vercammen 1995: 471 - 472)

If credit histories are too long or too short, they will be inefficient. Very long records diminish informational asymmetries over time and lead to a decrease in adverse selection. A decrease in adverse selection it was argued reduces the feasibility of the reputation system. Short histories, on the other hand, do not set any incentive to build up a good history. "Short and long records" denote the time period for which the data are stored. This varies around the world and depends on the type of information stored. The choice of a time frame for the storage of information has distributional consequences. Good borrowers prefer long histories and bad borrowers short ones: "The optimal credit history restriction should therefore also depend on the relative weight that low and high-quality borrowers receive from the social planner." (Vercammen 1995: 473). The author argues for a certain degree of asymmetric information that is warranted to sustain reputation effects. This is done by restricting credit bureaus from selling information that is older than a certain time period and this can be observed in credit reporting regulation.

Van Cayseele, Bouckaert and Degryse (1995) analyze the topic of information sharing from another angle. In a two-periodic overlapping generations model they formalize a credit market with banks, consumers and different kinds of credit bureaus. Of major interest to them is the evolving equilibrium credit market structure in the presence of a positive or a negative credit registry. I summarize the most important results. There are two scenarios: a market with a positive register and one with a negative register. Banks maximize the expected profit by choosing the optimal number of outlets (Cournot competition). "Since every bank in the case of a black register bears the burden of all young charlatans and, in addition, every bank has more outlets, (...) less banks can enter the market." (Van Cayseele, Bouckaert and Degryse 1995: 138). In markets with a positive register, an extra outlet attracts both types of risks (high risk borrowers and low risk ones). Moreover, more banks can enter the market as compared to the negative registry. Padilla and Pagano (1997) show that information sharing Pareto improves the outcome. In their model multiple subgame-perfect equilibria arise, one of them being market collapse (banks do not communicate with each other), but also some in which positive effort levels on the side of the borrower Pareto-dominate the collapse result (if banks communicate). In this case, the credit bureau becomes a viable reputation mechanism, but only if its costs are below a critical level and the sharing of information is sustainable over time. The set-up of a credit bureau certainly involves positive start-up costs that are equally shared among members. It is assumed that the credit bureau can perfectly monitor the reports provided by the information suppliers and detect if a bank misrepresented information.[21] Padilla and Pagano (1997) state that their model is qualitatively unaffected if misreporting is not detected with absolute certainty. This would reduce the parameter region in which the credit bureau is sustainable, just like the increase in the costs of verifying the truthfulness of the members' reports. For the credit bureau's existence, membership fees as well as the costs for verifying information have to be below a critical level. The authors find that in information sharing environments, interest and default rates are lower and the volume of lending may increase. There is a Pareto-improvement in the market, because banks not only increase their own profits, but also raise the customer's welfare along with their own. In a later paper (Padilla and Pagano 2000), they stress the disciplinary effect of information sharing, which increases the borrower's incentive to perform.

There are only few papers on the interaction of credit information sharing and competition in the banking industry and this research has only started to thrive in the 1990s. Gehrig and Stenbacka (2001) state that information sharing among banks can serve as a collusive device. Sharing agreements tend to increase the intensity of competition in future periods and, thus, reduce the value of informational rents in the current period. The reduction of informational rents in their model reduces intensity of competition in the current period and moves it to the future period. They conclude that across a range of economic environments a *ban* on information sharing would be welfare increasing.

---

[21] This is an incentive that has to be corrected. After the borrower reveals the true profitability potential, the bank could be inclined to not report this information or to misstate it to avoid the poaching of this customer.

In the adverse selection model of Bouckaert and Degryse (2004), banks strategically commit to disclosing borrower information. By doing this, they invite rivals to poach their first-period market of good borrowers. Disclosure of borrower information increases the rival's second-period profits. This dampens competition for serving the first-period market. Further, Gehrig and Stenbacka (2005) analyze information sharing with repeated banking competition. They model lending to entrepreneurs. In the presence of switching costs the authors find that a mechanism of information sharing renders poaching more profitable in future rounds of competition. The reason is that in future rounds the poaching can be targeted towards the more creditworthy borrowers. However, it relaxes the competition for initial market shares.

Finally, Bouckaert and Degryse (2006) observe that in many countries, lenders share information voluntarily. This, however, happens not always on reciprocal basis. Lenders might have a strategic incentive to release information on a portion of their profitable borrowers. The authors write that the pool of "unreleased borrowers becomes characterized by a severe adverse selection problem. This prevents the entrants from bidding for all the incumbent's profitable borrowers and reduces their scale of entry." (Bouckaert and Degryse 2006: 702). Altogether, the above discussion presented an overview of the theoretical credit market literature. Models that introduce credit bureaus as players have appeared only recently. They are a major step towards a better formal understanding of credit markets. Yet, several deficiencies remain, but not to the disadvantage of the above models as theoretical abstraction is necessarily always incomplete. However, there are several interesting questions that remain unanswered, for instance, about the borrower's incentive to share information. It is primarily assumed that there are good and bad risks and that both share information. It is not taken into account that bad risks might have an incentive to lie or that some individuals are highly privacy sensitive. Additionally, these models do not include many of the insights on information markets such as the economics of correlation and aggregation, negative externalities or incompletely defined property rights. To better understand the microeconomics of information, we have to turn to approaches that explicitly discuss privacy problems as they are central to credit reporting and its regulation.

2.3.2 Microeconomics of Privacy

It is remarkable how persistently economists have ignored privacy as a theoretical problem. Only in the late 1990s, after widespread information technology adoption and increasing discussions of privacy breaches the topic gradually emerged as matter of interest. In the subsequent sections, I will discuss older contributions to the "economics of privacy" as well as recent ones. The intention is to shed some light on some basic interactions between the borrower, the bank and the credit bureau under different regulatory regimes. The earliest contributions to economic reasoning about privacy are found in the Chicago school of law and economics that is in the works of Posner (1977; 1978; 1979; and 1981) and Stigler (1980). However, these articles employed an empirical approach in testing assumptions about privacy without mathematically formalizing the privacy problem. For comprehensiveness, however, they are included, because the arguments are more theoretical ones. Stigler (1980) approaches the subject from a political economy perspective. He analyzes congressional voting behavior on privacy legislation and the constituents that support such legislation. For this matter, he takes voting records as well as variables on income, education and urbanization from the year 1977. He proves that support for privacy laws is positively correlated with urbanization and negatively correlated with education level. The latter means the higher people are educated the lower the support for privacy. He also explains that those that are considered bad risks (because of impaired credit reports or legal convictions) are politically organized. These groups lobby for non-transparency in the market. The higher their percentage per state, the stricter is the privacy legislation. Privacy is in his opinion not more than a welfare distribution from good risks to bad risks, because privacy statues increase non-transparency. At the same time such statutes reduce employment and wages and increase interest rates levels. It is questionable if groups that (according to Stigler) benefit from stricter laws such as ex-criminals or African-Americans are better politically organized than the financial services industry. Posner, on the other hand, suggests that the economic dimension of privacy is the concealment of information: "By reducing the amount of information available to the buyer in the labor market (...), it reduces the efficiency of that market." (Posner 1981: 405) Sellers and buyers have an incentive to conceal deficiencies. The social costs associated with this fact of life are additional searches and plain mismatches. This "more information is better" doctrine is still held by many economists and policy makers. It is due to the fact that in undergraduate economics the orthodox model of complete markets is taught. Many students believe that more information will always lead to a more transparent market–an argument that can be easily turned upside down. It is true up to the point where information overload kicks in, blurs better options and leads to a retreat from further search. Restrictions in information processing are also taken into account by behavioral economics. Newer approaches in economics, however, show that there is an optimal amount of information that is disclosed in the equilibrium. In addition, in his pioneering work, Sims (1998, 2003) models a macroeconomic situation where agents act under information processing constraints as their capability to process information is limited. This is also called "rational inattention." For a discussion of this macroeconomic literature, the reader is referred to Luo (2004) and Sims (1998, 2003).

Posner (1981) predicts the effects of privacy laws on the state and federal level. He focuses on the legal provisions for non-disclosure of credit reports or criminal records. Like Stigler, he suspects that political pressure from groups with more arrests, convictions and poorer credit reports than the average population is the driving force behind these statutes. He notes that although these groups are not cohesive enough to form political coalitions, they strongly overlap with ethnic groups such as African-Americans and Hispano-Americans: "Given laws that forbid discrimination against members of these racial and ethnic groups, it may be in their interest to press for passage of laws that also forbid 'discrimination' against people with poor credit records and lengthy criminal records." (Posner 1981: 407). Such laws initiate "(...) a redistribution of wealth from whites to members of these racial and ethnic groups." With regressions, Posner attempts to underpin these assumptions. The dependent variable is the privacy law that is regressed on proxies for minorities, interstate migration, per capita income, and tax burden. The author finds the minority variable is positively significant, income is significant only in two specifications, migration is never significant and the tax variable is significant, too. The regressions (and assumptions) come with a number of problems. For instance, it is not explained why some variables are insignificant and other important factors are ignored that might prove the correlations spurious (such as GDP per capita, technology and banking regulation). The contributions of Posner and Stigler remained for some time the only ones in this field. They are therefore a landmark and the first step towards a formal treatment of privacy as economic problem. "Private information" has been explored in numerous articles in information economics, where players do not know each other's payoff functions (*incomplete information*) or are ignorant about the other's moves (*imperfect information*). With the introduction of the "revelation principle" private information has played a prominent role in auction theory. In a given incentive-compatible Bayesian game, the revelation principle assures a so-called "truth-telling equilibrium." Since each

Bayesian-Nash equilibrium can be represented as an incentive-compatible direct mechanism, this principle can be extended to non-auction games as well.[22] The "ratchet effect" in dynamic adverse selection models without commitment stresses the problem of information revelation. These approaches are principal-agent models where an uninformed principal learns information early in the game that she can exploit later to the disadvantage of the agent. This entails that the agent becomes increasingly unwilling to reveal information about his type, because the principal primarily uses this for the shifting of surplus to her advantage. The longer the relationship between both partners exists, the more expensive becomes the activity of inducing information revelation (Freixas, Guesnerie and Tirole 1985). At a certain point, revelation can be undermined completely or lead to bribing of the agent by the principal for revelation. Game theory provides some very good tools for analyzing the problems that arise in information sharing environments. It is a reasonable approach for analyzing strategic information problems. I have already presented the property rights approach to privacy. Through privacy legislation, property rights are divided between data subject and data controller or collector. This division has consequences for market efficiency.

Kahn, McAndrews and Roberds (2000) provide an interesting approach: Imagine a consumer, a firm and an annoying marketing company. The consumer and the firm transact and the marketing company would like to know if transactions took place, but this revelation affects the payoffs of the other parties. Three situations are considered: (1) Public information regime (the marketing company always receives the information); (2) Private information regime (it never receives the information); and (3) Private property regime (where the firm has the decision rule over the release of the information). The authors show that there are several conditions under which inefficiencies in the first scenario might arise that could be negotiated away if contracting with the marketing firm would be allowed. In this case, the consumer and the firm could be compensated for the value of information. In (2) the transaction only occurs when its payoff is greater or equal to 0. Inefficiencies may arise, if there is a social benefit from information release, but the information remains undisclosed. In (3) two subclasses of games are considered, one with the commitment by the firm to withhold the data, the second without this commitment. In the non-commitment game, the information is released if the payoff to the firm is positive. Otherwise the firm and the marketing company engage in bar-

---

[22] The message the agent sends is a truthful reflection of the characteristics of the agent, no misrepresentation and cheating is involved. This is called "direct mechanism."

gaining. In the commitment situation, the consumer and the firm can negotiate the release. Thus the surplus from information disclosure could be
split between the consumer and the firm. Efficiency is only attained if the
firm and the marketing company compensate the consumer to the full
amount of informational payoff. The authors give a mixed summary. Assigning rights to one or the other player might facilitate transactions that
are not feasible otherwise. However, were contracting is limited, inefficient release or inefficiencies from non-disclosure might occur. The authors assume that bargaining power is equal here, but property rights in information are likely to move threat points and change bargaining power.
They also assume that property rights are clearly defined, something that is
not always the case. But the model's strength is the focus on property
rights. These rights are assigned by data protection regimes, which will be
discussed further below.

Taylor (2002, 2003) has proposed several new ideas. In his 2002 contribution, the set-up of the multi-periodic game of incomplete information is
as follows: a continuum of consumers is facing two monopolists that each
sell a distinct good. The demands for the goods are positively related such
that the consumer's decision to purchase at firm 1 is valuable information
to firm 2. Two privacy settings are analyzed: one in which the firm is not
allowed to compile and sell a customer list (anonymity regime) and one in
which this is possible (recognition regime). The welfare comparison shows
that it is crucial if consumers can anticipate the sale of their name or not. If
consumers are myopic in the recognition regime, firm 1 has an incentive to
post high prices and sell the data. The recognition regime then seems to be
preferable for firms. Social welfare can be both under this regime: higher
or lower depending on the average price resulting from price discrimination. Consumer welfare, however, is reduced by the high prices charged
and this loss out-weights the value of information obtained by the firms. If
consumers are sophisticated, however, some interesting welfare effects
arise. Consumers with high valuations of the product strategically reduce
their demand for good 1 if the producer sets a high price. This behavior
undermines the market for data and it leads to a more elastic demand for
good 1. In this case, the firm would weakly prefer an anonymity regime or
a self-binding privacy policy to mitigate the problem. In the second paper
(Taylor 2003), personal privacy is studied in the context of a competitive
product market. The author asks why firms tend to aggressively accumu-
late excessive amounts of data. He shows that under certain conditions, the
policy of acquiring information and of selling to the qualified consumer
dominates other solutions such as totally abandoning the market. To leave
further technical details aside, in the unique sub-game perfect equilibrium,
firms post the lowest prices–consistent with zero economic profit. How-

ever, the low price–in an environment where information collection levels are not contractible–is an incentive to acquire excessive amounts of data about the applicants. The author states that consumers would be better off *ex ante*, if firms posted higher prices and collected less information. Moreover, an aggravating factor is that firms having the opportunity to sell customer data eventually exacerbate the inefficient violation of privacy. To preserve their privacy, consumers demand inefficiently low levels of output. A final result is that if rejected consumers are allowed to continue to apply for the good at different firms, adverse selection results, which may undermine the market and generate a situation in which all parties would be better off if no information was collected at all. Some of the stylized conclusions aside, the model captures some of the most important features of banking or insurance markets, but there is no information intermediary included.

Kleinberg, Papadimitriou and Raghavan (2001), present a coalition game in which individuals are able to control their personal data and have to be compensated in case of the release of this information. The authors state that possession of information stemming from a transaction with the consumer is a by-product for which the consumer is usually not compensated. Often, the decision of further dissemination of the information is made by the data-collecting firm without any consultation nor appropriate compensation of the consumer as rightful owner of the information: "We believe that it is this externality that lies at the root of the privacy problem." (Kleinberg, Papadimitriou and Raghavan 2001: 2).[23] The authors evaluate the value of private information to determine adequate compensation. The solution concepts serve as principles for adequate compensation and fair surplus division. For instance, in the coalition game there is an identification mechanism (Shapley value) that points at a reasonable and unique outcome that is a compromise between the players. It ensures that players share the surplus. The Shapley value suggests that each agent is awarded her average contribution.

Bandulet and Morasch (2003), on the other hand, work with a signaling game (a Salop circle where the consumer's position is her private information). They ask how a consumer's control over information release interacts with a monopolist's strategic price-discrimination, whereby the monopolist may misuse the data to gain a larger share of the total surplus. The authors list positive and negative effects of information revelation: personalization may enhance the value of a product, but at the same time rent-

---

[23] This is an observation also made by Varian (1996) and Laudon (1996b) and I have discussed it in the sections on information markets.

shifting is possible. As discussed in the sections on information markets first-degree price discrimination leaves the consumer with zero surplus. In the model, consumers only reveal information partially in some cases to avoid shifting of the total rent to the monopolist. In other cases, the monopolist must commit to his price menu that is a function of the amount of information disclosed. A pure strategy separating equilibrium exists where types with a high willingness to pay get a personalized product at a relatively high price while low valuation consumers provide no information and obtain a standardized, but much cheaper product. Calzolari and Pavan (2003) introduce a direct mechanism game with revelation. The authors assume two principals that sequentially interact with a common customer. They compare the contracts that are possible under disclosure and non-disclosure regimes. It is stated that information release can reduce downstream distortions that arise due to information asymmetries. This may lead to a Pareto-improvement. Conclusions about welfare should be drawn carefully: "since it also influences upstream decisions, disclosure may as well have negative effects on the agent and the downstream principal's surplus so that its net effect on welfare is in general ambiguous." (Calzolari and Pavan 2003: 4). Acquisti and Varian (2003) are interested at which point a monopolist can profitably engage in second-degree price-discrimination. It was argued that increasing information collection induces firms to discriminate. The case is that a seller can condition his prices on the prior purchase history and group consumers according to this history. In the first case, consumers are myopic, they decide on the price they see today, without taking into account that this influences future prices offered to them. In this environment conditioning has the effect of increasing overall welfare, but the surplus wholly accrues to the discriminating monopolist. In the second case, all consumers are sophisticated–they know that their purchase history affects future prices offered to them. For instance, some customers recognize that buying at a high price is not the best strategy, because the future price offered will be even higher. If there is only a fraction of myopic consumers (or the monopolist can offer increased service to high-value customers), profitable conditioning is possible.

It is not always possible to derive clear-cut welfare effects from the discussed models. The generalization to n players or n periods often changes the results. There are monopoly and duopoly models as well as competition. Consumers might be privacy-sensitive and sophisticated or plainly myopic. Although there are valuable insights into rent-shifting under different disclosure regimes, a number of important questions remain unanswered. For instance, what happens if–in sequential bargaining–property rights are moved and with them threat points? What about the limits to information sharing? Which role do data protection acts play? Most models are incentive-compatible: Cheating, lying and errors do not exist, but they are a plain fact of everyday life. They are especially sensitive and controversial when it comes to credit reporting.

Above I discussed information goods, information markets and the economics of privacy. Information has peculiar characteristics: it can be an endowment or information good or simply a by-product so to say. To understand information transactions, networks economics is helpful as well as the insights into competition strategies of firms that are active in the information market. These strategies are price discrimination, versioning and bundling–all of them have very interesting implications when it comes to personal information as product. The discussion would not be complete without insights from information economics. Although information economics has been around for more than 30 years, and private information has been included in many models, but privacy restrictions were largely ignored. Only recently, a number of models appeared. Conclusions from this literature are mainly varying welfare implications that are not robust. However, game theory helps to understand some of the basic incentives n credit reporting, where three players interact: the agency, the consumer and the bank. There are some interesting insights into the movement of threat points and negotiation power by moving the property rights to information from one party to another. One of the conclusions drawn from this exercise was that the location of the property rights will determine if (positive or negative) externalities appear. In addition, locating these property rights either at the consumer or the bank might be sub-optimal. Property rights should be shared to a certain extent, something that has developed in reality if we look at data protection regimes. However, the location of property rights is under constant challenge and more and more rights have been located at the consumer in the past. Altogether credit reporting has welfare improving effects, but only when properly regulated. If a credit reporting agency is in the market and consumers are aware of its existence, they have the incentive to say the truth. In addition, the bank will have the incentive to lend to them, because there is the (relative) security that a bad credit risk that is lying will be detected. This is especially the case in societies where positive and negative information is shared and where coverage rates approach coverage of the total economically active population. The next chapter describes how credit reporting agencies evolved from small informal exchanges among tailors to large, multinational corporations that collect and process data on millions of borrowers. It will also show the problems existed in the market for personal information which led to industry regulation on both sides of the Atlantic.

3 Overview of Credit Reporting Systems

There are several different types of information intermediaries in financial markets such as rating agencies, commercial reporting agencies or public credit registries. Standard & Poor's, Fitch or Moody's are rating agencies in capital markets that evaluate large corporate borrowers or even countries (see Estrella et al. 2000, Hickman 1958, Sylla 2002). In most cases, these agencies rely on publicly available information that is evaluated quantitatively and qualitatively. The historical research on these agencies is more advanced than that on consumer credit reporting agencies. For this matter, these types of information intermediaries are excluded from the following discussion. Another type of registry is the commercial reporting agency that collects information on firms. Madison (1974) identifies the English Guardians Society for the Protection of Trade against Swindlers and Sharpers of 1776 as predecessor of such agencies. The Mercantile Agency, a commercial reporting firm, opened its doors in 1841 in New York (Madison 1974: 164). Before this kind of service arrived, gossip among bankers as well as relationship lending prevailed. These companies are also excluded from this analysis as there are already many accounts on these types of intermediaries (Kallberg and Udell 2003, Madison 1974, Norris 1978, and Olegario 2003). There are three different types of credit reporting systems identifiable:

➢ Dual systems: public credit register and private credit bureaus;
➢ Private systems: only private credit bureaus; and
➢ Public systems: only a public register.

What path a country takes in terms of the development of a credit reporting system depends on historical factors that will be explained in greater detail below. In general, it holds that public and private credit registers are in many cases complementary and do play different roles. As will be clearer below both are different in terms of their institutional design–for instance with regard to reporting institutions, the thresholds for reporting or how the information is used. Some notes of caution: it would be wrong to assume that public credit registers do play the same role across countries. There are large differences in their design even in a relatively homogenous group of countries such as the EU-27. As stated, the reasons are historical, the institutional design of a public credit registry is based upon the problem perceived to exist in the market at the time it was designed and established. For instance, some credit registers were developed as tool to monitor systemic risk (Germany, Austria or Italy), whereas others have the purpose to prevent overindebtedness of consumers (Belgium or France).

3.1 History of Credit Reporting Agencies

The knowledge about the historical development of credit bureaus is fairly limited. There are some shorter overviews such as in Hunt (2005), Jappelli and Pagano (2003) and Jentzsch (2003a), but more research exists on commercial reporting agencies. The following sections provide a brief overview of the historical development of credit reporting agencies on both sides of the Atlantic. These sections are of introductory character and are not intended to give a full-scale and complete historical account. This has to be left for further research. In general, there are three stages identifiable in the development of credit reporting agencies: (1) Local reporting; (2) establishment of national reporting networks; and (3) internationalization of the business.

The World Bank's survey shows that by 2004/2005, there were 84 countries with private registries. The institution recorded data on bureaus themselves in 33 countries where it got responses to its survey. 66.7% of the bureaus surveyed distribute information on firms and individuals, whereas 16.7% list only individuals and roughly the same fraction only firms. Some of these agencies occupy small niche segments to provide reports to employers or landlords (so-called "tenant screening"). Others operate in the field of medical information or insurance data. In the following the U.S. credit reporting history is presented as well as European developments (with emphasis on Germany, Great Britain and France). The latter three countries are important, because they cover the biggest consumer credit markets in Europe and represent very different systems: UK is a private system, Germany is a dual one and France is a public system with no private bureaus. In the early stages of development, credit reporting agencies have primarily been unregulated. This is the reason why some officials from international institutions think it would be best to only lightly regulate the industry in developing countries. However, one should not forget that the establishment of a credit reporting agency nowadays involves the immediate set-up of computer systems with a capacity to store millions of people. Worldwide more and more public and private credit registries are founded. As mentioned above, these systems differ from country to country, but they do have their origin in the European nations. Anglo-Saxon countries usually only have private credit bureaus operating in their credit markets. The U.S., Netherlands and United Kingdom, for instance, have no public credit registers. Other countries follow the opposite path, as of 2006, there were no private consumer credit reporting agencies active in France and Belgium.

3.1.1 Credit Reporting in the United States

The evolution of the financial system is of significant importance for the economic development in every country. This is a lesson that can be learnt from international surveys (Rousseau and Sylla 2001; Sylla, Wilson and Jones 1994). There are robust correlations between financial indicators and economic growth spanning three centuries. However, distinctive features of the U.S. banking system such as limited competition on a nation-wide scale contributed to the growth of credit reporting. Banks are more inclined to share information if the markets they operate in are not contestable. Odd as it seems, but until the 1990s, the U.S. had not developed a truly national banking market. In the early days, colonial markets were agricultural and local. The first bank in the U.S. was the Bank of North America founded in 1782. Banking regulation largely originated in the states from 1810 on. Yet during the 19th Century, the system was plagued with financial crises and bank runs, contributing to growing popular dissatisfaction. The original American credit reporting agencies were an attempt to manage the risk of trade credit. This type of credit developed because of the capital scarcity in the country. But there were also other factors which contributed to the development of credit reporting. Due to high mobility of Americans and influx of immigrants, informational asymmetries between borrowers and creditors increased. Letters of recommendation by suppliers or respectable members of the community were often not sufficient as quality signal as they were almost impossible to verify. The guarantors were in many cases distant suppliers with whom an individual had previously done business. Some large mercantile houses (for instance, Baring Brothers in Great Britain) hired agents to conduct credit investigations on their U.S. customers. But this was a costly arrangement. The first to be founded in the U.S. was a commercial reporting agency. During the 1830s, businessman Lewis Tappan handled the credits in his brother's wholesale silk business and developed extensive credit records stemming from their line of business in Manhattan (Sylla 2002: 23). Tappan recognized that this information could serve many suppliers, not only his own firm. In 1841, he founded the Mercantile Agency. Tappan contracted with agents and correspondents throughout the country to collect information on solvency and character of local business owners. The Mercantile Agency later became known as R. G. Dun & Co., and merged in 1933 with Bradstreet Company to form Dun & Bradstreet, which dominates the field of commercial credit reporting even today. Twenty years after the establishment of the first mercantile agency, the first consumer credit reporting agencies were established. At that time, business was primarily local: "Product and service choices were limited to what was available in a consumer's neighborhood, the local main street, or perhaps a nearby city." Zuccarini (2001). Some retailers sold on credit, but those that did limit it to well-known and good customers. These creditors kept their own accounts and engaged in information exchange with other local creditors by sharing lists of names that were considered to be bad credit risks. Especially in larger cities, retailers saw the need to exchange information about their customers. One of the first known accounts of a credit bureau in the U.S. is a firm established in Brooklyn in 1869, as the Consumer Data Industry Association reports.

The early days of credit reporting were not without problems. Once consumer data was collected, agencies maintained them as private property. This was no easy task as competitors were interested in copying or stealing data. Additionally, information was shared with all kinds of parties, even those without particular business interest. Olegario (2003: 131) describes that the agencies experimented with different methods of secrecy protection, such as reference books with locks. After the banking panic of 1873, several states legislatures proposed regulation of bureaus in order to punish them for reporting erroneous data. Because none of the measures were enacted into law, courts emerged as early "regulators" of the industry as they had to settle disputes. A specific annoyance to the public was that credit bureaus sometimes distributed erroneous records, intrusive characterizations and prejudiced or biased reports. Information such as solvency, prospects, and personal character of local businessmen was not uncommon. To make matters worse, credit bureaus behaved secretive and tried to avoid contact with consumers.[24] The agencies also soon included contractual disclaimers about the accuracy of the information they provided to avoid lawsuits. One of the major agencies in the U.S. has its origin in these early days. In 1897, the Chilton Corporation was founded. Lawyer James Chilton started to collect customer credit information from local merchants in Dallas, Texas. He noted past due payments and other negative information in a little "Red Book". Gosselin (2003) reports, that a "handful of small

---

[24] This attitude changed only recently, namely in the 1990s. Now many credit reporting agencies regard the consumer as their customer.

companies began collecting consumers' debt-paying histories. The customers for those histories were local merchants who wanted the information to determine which shoppers would be allowed to buy on credit." In 1899, another major firm was founded in Atlanta, Georgia. The "Retail Credit Company" of Cator and Guy Woolford decades later became known as Equifax, Incorporated, one of the largest credit reporting companies today.

Although at the beginning, information sharing was primarily local, banking regulations facilitated information-sharing arrangements between what could have been competitors. It created entry barriers and limited expansion due to the dual banking system and restrictions on branching.[25] By 1900, an estimated 50 bureaus existed in the U.S. with some interesting side effects: Olegario (2003) describes that credit reporting agencies had an effect on U.S. business culture, as they transmitted business values of large commercial centers to nearly every American community. In February of 1906, the Associated Credit Bureaus (at that time called "National Association of Retail Credit Agencies," NARCA) was founded. In the following years up to 1915, its membership increased from 6 to 120 agencies. The association had the tasks of information exchange and standardization. An Inter-Bureau Coupon System was introduced as a simplified method for exchanging credit inquiries and payments. By 1918, 250 agencies were members. In the 1920s, the number of credit reporting agencies exploded due to the credit boom. The credit reporting division of National Retail Credit Association now counted 1.058 members. In the 1920s, the expansion of financial innovations such as installment credit, hire purchase or deferred payment facilities fuelled consumer demand for durables. Murphy (1995) explains the expansion of installment credit with advertising: "(a) critical precursor to this revolution was a transformation of the prevailing consumer attitudes towards incurring debt, and particularly a removal of the stigma against buying on installments." Automobile companies also started to offer the sale of cars on installments. One of the reasons for the Great Depression was that the population spent far more on goods than they could afford which contributed to widespread over-commitment and bankruptcy. The activities and coordination between credit bureaus raised suspicion of the U.S. Department of Justice. It was claimed that binding agreements existed according to which the members allocated territories. The U.S. District Court for the Eastern District of Missouri handed down a Consent Decree in 1933 that led to an institutional makeover of the industry. From 1934 on, bureaus had to pay a fee to use the inter-bureau coupon

---

[25] The fragmented banking system was based upon the National Bank Acts of 1863 and 1864 and the branching restrictions of the McFadden Act of 1927.

system. In the 1940s and 1950s, the organization/association of credit bureaus worked for a further standardization of the system. Later it was restructured as non-profit Associated Credit Bureaus of America, Inc. (Associated Credit Bureaus, ACB). Its main purposes were the set-up of interbureau reporting rules and telegraphic codes as well as education and training of members. Moreover, the ACB also published a Code of Ethics.[26] With rising wealth and increased consumer spending in the pre-war years, the industry experienced a boom. In the early 1950s, credit bureaus were still focused on local markets or a specific region and they primarily served one creditor, exchanging primarily negative information (Furletti 2002: 3). Also, up until the 1960s, credit reporting was mainly industry specific. Banks, retailers and finance companies sponsored credit bureaus, but there was no inter-industry exchange. Furletti (2002: 5) reports, the industry stopped reporting personal information such as promotions and marriages only after the passage of the Fair Credit Reporting Act in 1970. Also, only after the passage of the act, the industry started to focus on objectively verifiable and credit-related information, including positive and negative information.

It is obvious that mainframe computers and inventions such as credit scoring in 1956 had an enormous impact on credit reporting. Gosselin (2003a) notes credit reporting spread to banking in the 1950s: "Before that, bankers knew their customers and could make lending decisions based on first-hand knowledge or repayment histories logged onto 3-by-5 note cards on file in the local branch." Computers proved to be the catalyst for modern credit reporting. By the end of the decade, the first electrified filing system for credit bureaus went into operation in Oklahoma City (Associated Credit Bureaus 1981: 31). The introduction of credit cards created another source of revenue: screening and marketing. Department store cards were around since the 1930s, but only in 1950 the Diners Club card was introduced. Another major innovation in 1951 was the "invention" of revolving credit by the Franklin Bank of New York. But one of the most important discoveries was credit scoring. In the 1950s, Bill Fair and Earl Isaac founded the company Fair-Isaac. The initial response from banks was not overwhelming. In 1960, the first model for a bank credit card was developed, in the mid-1970s, scoring was also introduced in Europe. The first score for a credit bureau followed in 1981. In the 1960s, national credit grantors started to centralize their files, but credit bureaus were still regionally oriented and paper driven. Banks, however, demanded a na-

---

[26] To unify the system, the organization advised the smaller bureaus to use a name such as "Credit Bureau of..." and the city of location. These names are still in existence today.

tional system, therefore the ACB adopted a "National System for Reporting Information" which allowed members to get data from 85 national credit grantors. Already in 1961, the members of ACB issued more than 62 million reports. In 1964, ACB initiated cooperation with IBM to study the feasibility of computer employment in the business. This cooperation involved the Credit Bureau of Greater Houston, Credit Bureau Services in Dallas and the ACB. The purpose was to show that computers could facilitate data collection, storage and sales. The organization adopted a new computer language and introduced statistical programs such as the Index of Credit Reporting and the Index of Collections.

During these days, credit bureaus had largely operated in anonymity; their main clients were banks and retailers, not consumers. Occasionally a lawsuit was brought against them and, as stated, courts proved to be the main regulators. The situation changed dramatically in 1968 as will be discussed in more detail in the sections on legislation. Federal plans to centralize databases sparked a public debate on privacy, an unintended side effect was that credit bureaus also moved into the spot-light. Congress initiated a series of hearings to focus on the new "informational privacy" as compared to physical privacy defined by Warren and Brandeis in 1890 (see Smith 2000: 312).[27] The public debate showed that thousands of consumers were dissatisfied with the credit reporting system and started to demand a right to know about their files. This resulted in the Fair Credit Reporting Act of 1970. The act and its implications will be discussed in the sections on regulation.

When the industry started to employ IT, database concentration facilitated industry concentration. In the 1970s, there were 2.250 credit bureaus in the U.S., the number decreased to 1.833 bureaus in 1997 according to the U.S. Census Bureau. The large market players could afford the expensive data-processing equipment, but smaller bureaus were either sold or contracted automated services from one of the automated bureaus. Five agencies offered such services: TransUnion, TRW (that later became Experian), Equifax, Chilton Corporation and Pinger Systems. The larger bureaus brought smaller bureaus into their computer systems to access their local data collections. The smaller agencies, on the other hand, used the computer processing power and network of the larger companies. They either became affiliates to one of them or remained independent as resellers

---

[27] "Informational privacy" is what Europeans mean with the term "data protection"–the protection of personal information.

of credit reports.[28] The information was co-owned by both the repositories and their local affiliates, consumers were not considered to be the rightful owner of the information.

Figure 3.1

Household Credit, Consumer Confidence and Unemployment

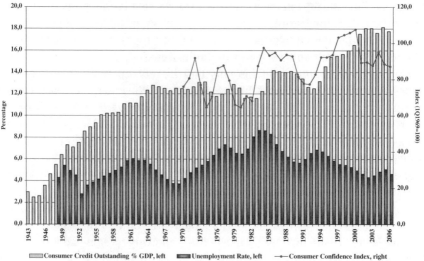

Source: Federal Reserve Bank and U.S. Bureau of Labor Statistics

Figure 3.1 presents consumer credit outstanding as percentage of GDP as long-term time series (1943-2004). It shows a strong increase of out-standing credit/GDP until the 1960s, where it levelled off somewhat. The ratio also reflects the economic boom during the Reagan years (1980s) and the Clinton years (1990s). Unemployment rates and consumer confidence are important variables in the household's credit decision. Unemployment rates reflect economic fluctuations and influence the consumer's future financial perspectives. Consumer confidence is a leading indicator for consumer credit. Over the course of history, an oligopoly emerged within the industry. The Chilton Corporation, for instance, merged with TRW in 1976 and Pinger Systems was sold to the Computer Science Corporation (CSC). To reach national coverage, the companies established a network of affiliates. This leads to more recent developments in credit reporting.

---

[28] Resellers order credit reports from the big bureaus and sell them. Some of them add value by adding further information to the report.

3.1.2 Competition in U.S. Credit Reporting

The following sections review the competition among credit reporting agencies in the 1990s. In that decade, the major credit reporting agencies in the U.S. evolved to large-scale information oligopolists: TransUnion, Experian and Equifax each store files on more than 200 million U.S. consumers. The industry structure in the U.S. is an oligopoly of these three companies that intensively compete in credit reporting.[29] These companies serve different market segments: commercial reporting, consumer reporting and credit scoring services or marketing services. A dominant position in consumer reporting does not automatically mean that the company is also dominant in other segments. Experian (1996: 3) states: "The company believes that it is one of the two largest providers of consumer credit information and the second largest provider of business credit information in the United States." In the commercial reporting market D&B and Experian are the dominating firms. Experian competes with a range of other companies in marketing (Abacus Direct, Acxiom Corporation, etc.). The triad companies also compete in markets for credit scoring services. Since 2002, Fair Isaac directly competes with them as the company provides FICO scores and score simulators directly to consumers. This move was not welcomed by the other agencies as Fair Isaac provides scoring models to all three of them. In addition, the company regularly updates a list on its website which states what interest rates of loans are associated with the credit score.

Table 3.1
U.S. Market Leaders in Credit Information Provision

Year	Position	Company	Revenues (US-$)
2006	1.	Experian	3.1 billion
	2.	Equifax	1.55 billion
	3.	D&B	1.53 billion
	4.	TransUnion	n/a
2001	1.	Experian	1.5 billion
	2.	D&B	1.4 billion
	3.	Equifax	1.1 billion
	4.	TransUnion	1.0 billion

Sources: Numbers are from Electronic Information Report. The estimate for TransUnion for 2001 is from CoolSavings, Inc. (2001), the number for 2006 was not available.

---

[29] Sometimes also a fourth company, Innovis Data Solutions, is mentioned. Here it is only referred to the three largest ones.

There is also a significant number of smaller credit reporting agencies in the market, but they either act as resellers or niche players. Some of them are still credit reporting agencies in the original sense, but the reports are more in-depth consumer inquiries, because these firms cannot compete with the methods and business processes of large credit reporting agencies. Table 3.1 presents the largest providers–industry officials estimate that these companies serve 95% of the U.S. consumer credit information market. The Table also shows that the business is growing–all of the companies could increase revenues, although the relative positions for some of them changed (for instance, for D&B and Equifax). The industry structure is explained in Figure 3.2. In the field of mortgage reporting, industry is three-tiered: (1) Triad oligopoly of Experian, Equifax and TransUnion; (2) approximately 40 resellers that are affiliated with the dominant firms; and (3) 185 independent resellers. In 2002, Experian announced that it bought three affiliate credit bureaus (the company had 38 affiliates) and that it intended to buy additional ones until 2005 (Experian 2002c). The prediction is that most of the affiliates will be bought sooner or later. TransUnion, for instance, has only one affiliate left, Equifax an estimated 15.

Figure 3.2
Structure of the U.S. Credit Reporting Market

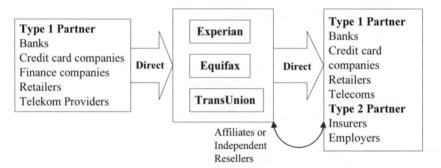

Smaller players occupy niche markets, e.g. tenant screening, employment or mortgage reporting. This is due to the competitive advantage enjoyed by the large companies with regard to national financial service providers or retailers. Independent resellers differ remarkably in their size. The largest ones are First American Credco, Chase Credit Systems, LandSafe, InfoOne, Advantage Credit, The Credit Network and approximately 179 smaller resellers (Foer and Rubin 2003). They get credit reports from the repositories at wholesale prices, then update and correct data and provide re-scoring services. Sometimes they add further data or merge reports from different agencies. But small reporting agencies also add value by concentrating on their local markets and this information is then delivered to the big agencies. Table 3.2 shows the concentration ratios of the 4, 8 or 20 largest credit information providers.

Table 3.2
Concentration in Credit Information Provision

Year	Concentration ratio (CR 4, 8, 20)	Receipts (in Percentages)
2002	CR 4	63.7
	CR 8	76.1
	CR 20	83.6
1997	CR 4	53.2
	CR 8	68.0
	CR 20	75.9
1992	CR 4	21.5
	CR 8	28.2
	CR 20	36.5

Source: U.S. Census Bureau of 1992 and 1997 for the category of "consumer credit reporting agencies" (NAICS Code: 5614501), for 2002 for "credit bureaus," later data was not available.

More and more national retailers deal directly with one of the big companies. "Independent" resellers, on the other hand, do not carry out their own information collection. Term "independent" is misleading in this respect. Instead, they buy credit reports from the repositories and merge them. In the niches such as tenant reporting, small bureaus collect data about potential tenants from public sources such as courts, but also from private ones such as previous landlords or big agencies. Landlords have the duty to inform tenants as to whether they turned them down, because of an adverse credit report. In addition, employers in the U.S. are also allowed to get a report on prospective employees. This is forbidden in other countries and is associated with severe problems for indebted people that might be locked-out of the job market. The employee report also lists financial information such as loans. The main users of such reports were companies in the pharmaceutical and financial services industries, but also in defense and chemical industries. This practice has spread throughout the economy as creditworthiness is considered to be a sign of the (professional) integrity of a person. However, in the 1990s, regulators moved to prohibit getting a report without the explicit, written consent of the consumer.[30] Another niche is medical reporting that serves hospitals and doctors or insurance companies. The U.S. Medical Information Bureau (MIB Group, Inc.) records 20% of U.S. consumers. Since its inception in 1902 it has grown into an association of 500 U.S. and Canadian life insurance companies. The intention is to protect its members from fraud in underwriting of life, health, disability, and long-term care insurance. This intermediary only collects information from the insurance industry, not from doctors and hospitals directly.

Nowadays credit reporting is highly concentrated. The more sources are connected to the network, the more detailed becomes the credit profile and the more precise is risk prediction. Credit bureaus compete in several dimensions: price, coverage rates, data quality, credit risk advise, scoring services and coverage of market segments such as demographic and marketing data. Approximately 2 billion credit profiles are sold per year in the U.S. (Pratt 2003: 3). In this context, it is worthwhile to describe the triad players.

Equifax was founded in 1899. Today it is established in 13 countries, worldwide it has more than 400 million consumers and businesses in its files. In the UK alone, the company has over 30 million consumers in its databases. In 2002, it generated US-$ 1.1 billion in revenue. Together with Experian it is one of the two publicly traded credit reporting agencies that is obligated to report more information than non-traded companies. The firm incorporated in 1913 and became traded over the counter by 1965; it was listed at the New York Stock Exchange in 1971. By 1970, all the files of the company became automated and in 1975, and the name was changed to Equifax. In the 1990s, Equifax started a series of acquisitions in the U.S. as well as abroad. From early on, the company internationalized. As of the mid-1990s, it expanded into Latin American countries and European countries. For a quite some time, Equifax was only interested in dealing with its corporate clients. Only in 2001, under public pressure in the U.S., the company moved forward to sell reports to consumers, a year later the first consolidating 3-in-1 report followed.

Another major player in the credit reporting industry was founded in 1968 when the Chicago Union Tank Car Company (a railcar leasing operation) created TransUnion as its parent holding company. The company, which has roots in the Rockefeller family and its oil fortunes, bought the Credit Bureau of Cook County in Illinois which by that time had 3.6 mil-

---

[30] The Consumer Reporting Employment Clarification Act of 1998 will be discussed in the sections on regulation.

lion card files (Gosselin 2003b). TransUnion grew over the next 30 years into a massive intelligence business. In 1981 it was added to the Marmon Group, one of the largest conglomerates in the U.S. and owned by the Pritzker family. The family is one of the wealthiest in the U.S. with an estimated $-US 15 billion fortune. Penny Pritzker, one of the 12 grand children of industry tycoon Abraham Pritzker, is Chairman of the Board. Tritsch (2003) describes some of the family's history. Member companies of the Marmon Group operate independently in 40 countries. Today, the company is based in 24 countries, but has its own or affiliated offices in 50 countries worldwide. It owns 200 million files that map nearly every credit-active consumer in the U.S. TransUnion accomplished a number of partnerships and cooperation in the late 1990s such as with Acxiom, a data giant in Arkansas (Corporate Library 2003). Both companies agreed on joint marketing of products and it was planned to provide packages that combine demographic and credit data (Fickenscher 1999). TransUnion has followed an aggressive merger and acquisition strategy it bought almost all of its affiliates to eliminate these "middlemen." By 2002, TransUnion had acquired 72 of its 74 affiliates. Internationally it has expanded to Europe, Latin America and South Africa. In 2005, it was announced that TransUnion is spun off from the Marmon Group and there are rumors that the company either goes public or is sold through a merger.

The third company in the triad is Experian, the only agency which is British-American and has headquarters in the UK, the U.S. and Monaco. There are several companies which later became a part of Experian, for instance the Chilton Corporation (established in 1897) and the Michigan Merchants Company, founded in 1932 (later called Credit Data Corporation, CDC). The main player in Experian's history, however, was TRW. In 1996, the birth year of Experian, TRW sold its complete Information Systems & Services Division to an investor group which in turn sold it to the British Great Universal Store PLC (GUS PLC). This retail conglomerate in the United Kingdom later merged TRW Information Systems & Services with CCN. The new holding company was named Experian. Today, the company has offices/affiliates in 22 countries. In the U.S. it has more than 240 million consumers on file. It has followed an aggressive acquisition strategy around the world and entered markets in many European countries and even in South Korea and South Africa. It also established an office in France and tried to pair up with a German company. The latter market, however, is dominated by a local player. In October 2006, Experian became an independent company traded on the London Stock Exchange after a demerger from GUS. Altogether the three agencies are the largest ones on earth, although there are new players such as Creditinfo in Eastern

Europe and CompuScan in Africa. The big three agencies are under intense competition pressure in the U.S. and this contributes to the high volumes of credit reports sold to the industry and increasingly also to consumers. Figure 3.3 shows estimated sales.

Figure 3.3
Number of Credit Reports Sold in the U.S.

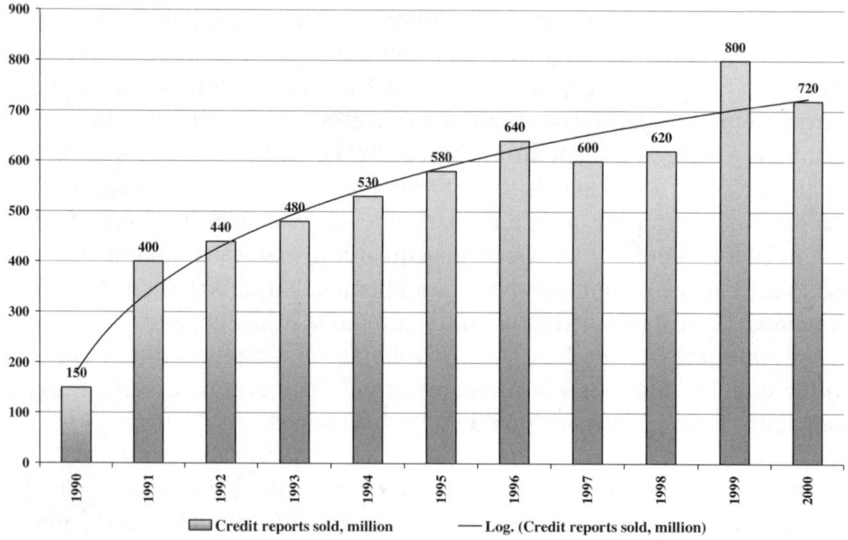

Source: Estimates are compiled from different newspaper and industry sources.

The estimates are compiled from different sources as credit reporting agencies typically do not disclose how many credit reports they sell or how many inquiries they record as they regard this as sensitive information and business secret. However, some indications can be found in newspaper articles or government reports. Another company well worth mentioning is Fair Isaac Corporation.[31] In the past, this firm has provided credit scoring models to the three credit reporting agencies. Equifax uses Beacon, Experian uses the Experian/Fair Isaac Risk Model and TransUnion Empirica. Still, many lenders use their own scoring models, which is especially the case for banks that have a large customer base. Industry officials state that Fair Isaac's move to sell merged credit reports in the U.S. sparked tensions among the business partners. As stated, the company was founded in 1956

---

[31] The firm was formerly known as Fair, Isaac & Co. Incorporated. In 2003 the firm was renamed into Fair Isaac Corporation.

and after providing scoring models to banks, it introduced the first credit bureau score in 1981. Six years later it was already listed at NASDAQ. In 1993 insurance scores followed and in 1998 small business scores. Until the 1990s, credit scoring was rarely used in mortgage lending, where it is far more widespread now. In 2002, the firm started to sell its FICO scores directly to consumers.

Figure 3.4

Credit to Disposable Income and Consumption Expenditure

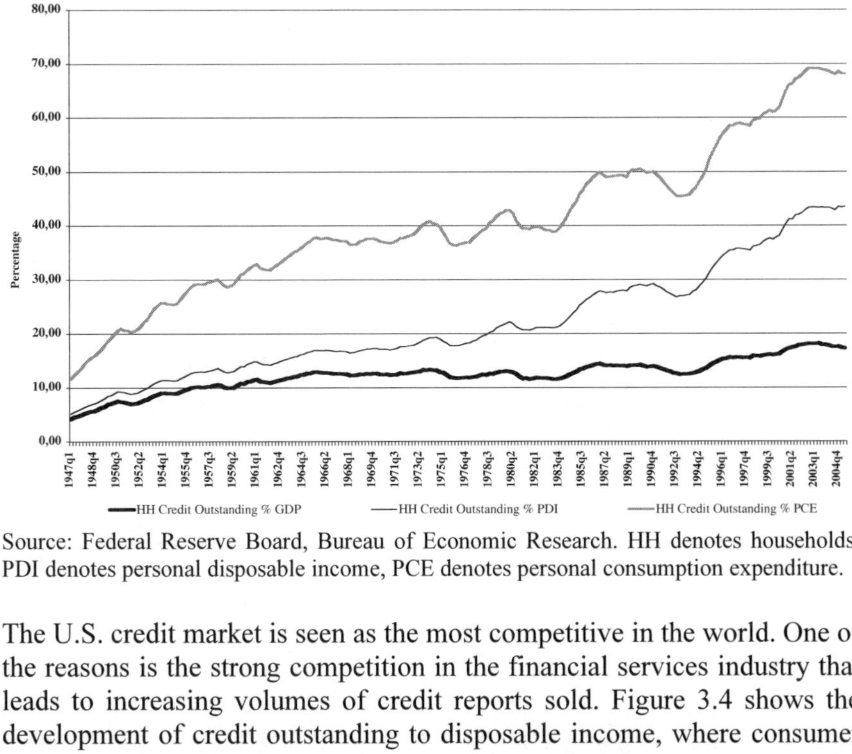

Source: Federal Reserve Board, Bureau of Economic Research. HH denotes households, PDI denotes personal disposable income, PCE denotes personal consumption expenditure.

The U.S. credit market is seen as the most competitive in the world. One of the reasons is the strong competition in the financial services industry that leads to increasing volumes of credit reports sold. Figure 3.4 shows the development of credit outstanding to disposable income, where consumer loans and mortgages are summed up. It also shows the increase of credit outstanding to disposable income. However, it gives no indication of financial and non-financial wealth accumulated by U.S. households, which is far higher. Figure 3.5 shows the total financial obligations ratio (FOR): these are the recurring monthly costs of financing debt. One of the most hotly discussed issues with regard to the U.S. credit market is as to whether indebtedness developments are sustainable and if households can keep up with debt financing. A good measure to look at is the household debt-service ratio–the sum of the minimum and interest rate payments on debt as percentage of the household's total disposable income. The Federal

Reserve Board has revised the measure in 1990 (U.S. Federal Reserve Bank 2001a). It also collects statistics on charge-offs and delinquencies (U.S. Federal Reserve Bank 2001b). A more detailed explanation of the data is given in the Glossary in the Appendix. These obligations seem to fluctuate with economic activity, there is no clear upward trend discernible over the past 20 years (Figure 3.5). The financial services obligation ratio for homeowners (total homeowner FOR, see figure) seem to not have increased, there was a noticeable increase in the financial services obligation ratio for renters starting from 1992 on (total renter FOR).

Figure 3.5
Financial Services Obligation Ratios

Notes: FOR denotes financial obligations ratio. Source: Federal Reserve Board

In 2001, households spend more than 30% of their disposable income on debt obligations. Note that interest rates on personal loans have not increased to a major extent during the 1990s. Altogether, the increasing financial services obligation will render these households more vulnerable to interest rate movements. In addition, the 1990s have been the longest boom in U.S. post-war history. The period was marked by a decrease in unemployment, comparably high GDP growth rates, stock market boom as well as housing market boom. Despite these positive fundamentals, there was a remarkable increase in consumer bankruptcies (chapter 7 and 13 procedures), see Figure 3.6. Bankruptcies are due to a number of influences such as changes in bankruptcy laws or changes in social stigma among other things. Often, there are several factors that contribute to a desolate financial situation. However, it is an undeniable fact that the filings hit record peaks in the 1990s and surpassed 1.4 million cases in 2001. Over the past decades an exponential function can be fitted to the bankruptcy filing numbers.

Figure 3.6
Increase in U.S. Consumer Bankruptcy Filings

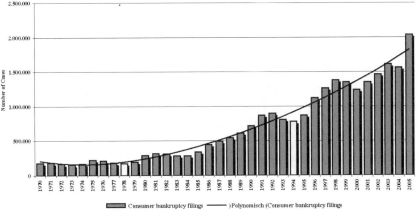

Sources: Administrative Office of the U.S. Courts

In Figure 3.6, the two light grey bars (the data points for 1978 and 1994) denote years where major reforms of the bankruptcy legislation were introduced. Although the figures show long-term trends such as that of credit outstanding and total financial services obligations, nothing can be said about co-integration or causality. For such analysis, time series econometrics must be applied. The credit reporting industry has been mentioned several times as one contributing factor for the expansion of credit. The industry developed from small local bureaus and national credit reporting agencies to international information giants. Today three major players dominate and small players survive in niches. However, the past also brought regulation into play. Through insufficient definition of property rights in information, consumers could not exert basic rights. This led to abuses and to regulation as will be discussed further below in the sections on regulation.

3.1.3 Credit Reporting in Europe

The following sections provide an overview of the history of credit reporting agencies in Europe. These sections are not intended to provide a complete historical analysis, instead they are meant to provide a roadmap of the most important developments in three quite different credit reporting systems (Germany, Great Britain and France). It is wrong to assume that credit reporting enables consumer credit and without such a system, no lending is possible. Credit has developed much earlier. Gelpi and Julien-Labruyère (1994) trace it even back to ancient times. Philosophers such as Plato and Aristotle criticized interest on credit on the grounds that it was "unnatural." In their view, money was an exchange medium and not something that could bear fruits. These views were later rediscovered in the Medieval Age.[32] The Old Testament forbade interest on credit and usury rates were also condemned. The church adopted these rules. The argument was that usury interest would cause poverty, misery and despair and enrich only a few wealthy people. With the rise of the bourgeoisie and the rural, economic and societal transformations, pragmatism spread (Gelpi and Julien-Labruyère 1994: 58). I will not go into detail about the historical development of consumer credit, the point to be made here is that its history dates back far longer than that of credit reporting. Credit extension was for a long time guided by relationship lending or kinship. Knowing each other reduced the risk of default and strengthened social control. Today this is implemented as group lending schemes in the developing countries, where members guarantee for each other. Prior to the arrival of credit reporting agencies, networks of merchants as well as chambers of commerce distributed information on creditworthiness (Olegario 2003: 118). The first known credit information exchange was operated by a group of English tailors as a cooperative venture for their mutual protection in 1803, the so-called *Mutual Communication Society of London* (Associated Credit Bureaus 1981: 10). Its members had discovered that some individuals purchased from them repeatedly without paying (Connelly 2001: 23). Also some of these individuals would repeatedly cheat on fellow tailors. Therefore, these businessmen started to pass along negative information about the bad credit risks they knew. In other countries, similar exchanges developed: in Austria a bureau was founded in the 1860s and in Germany in the 1870s (Jappelli and Pagano 2001: 2025). Reporting in these early times was mainly focused on local markets, in many cases the information was

---

[32] Even over-indebted borrowers are mentioned in early times. During Solon (367 b.c.) the "XII Tables" provided measures for over-indebted borrowers to pay back the amount overdue in three years (Gelpi and Julien-Labruyère 1994: 33)

only provided to members ("closed user group principle"). In Europe, most private credit bureaus were founded much later, in the 1960s and 1980s. Public credit registers that are operated by national central banks are one characteristic of credit information sharing in Europe. I have briefly mentioned these institutions in the introduction to this chapter. These registers are mandatory reporting systems and all financial institutions under the supervision of the central bank have to report to it. I discuss dual systems in sections further below.

In contrast to their U.S. counterparts, European credit bureaus in the past primarily focused on local and national markets, therefore they will be treated in separate sections. Due to the increasing economic integration Europeans witness an intensification of competition in the second half of the 1990s as well as increasing merger and acquisition activity due to market entry of major U.S. players. The operations of private credit bureaus in Europe range from exchange of large volumes of positive and negative data (Great Britain, Germany and Sweden) to medium scale exchange (Finland and the Netherlands) and finally to only rudimentary exchange (Portugal and Greece in 2004). In France, however, there exists only a negative information exchange and in Belgium there exists a regime that is transformed from a negative to a positive regime without private sector credit reporting (see Table 3.3).

In 2002, the population coverage rates of private credit bureaus (not reported in the Table) differed from about 50-60% in Great Britain and Ireland to nearly 80% in Germany and, remarkably, to virtually no coverage of the economically active population in France. The latter is a negative only regime that records no positive information on consumers. However, as discussed below, the competition among those companies in Europe will lead to higher coverage rates and might have effects on the credit-granting industry. In addition, there is increasing information exchange in the new European Members States, where especially the Icelandic company Creditinfo is active. Coverage rates in these countries are currently lower and in some markets there is only negative information exchange, although it is planned to also share positive information. Coverage rates in general depend on the maturity of the credit market and if there is a credit bureau which has been active for years. It does not necessarily depend on competition: Germany with one dominant company has one of the highest coverage rates in Europe. Although Germany, Great Britain and France are reviewed in-depth further below, an overview of the European countries is also presented.

Table 3.3

European Credit Reporting Systems

EU	PCR est.	CB est.	PCR pos. info	PCR neg. info	CB pos. info	CB neg. info	Limit ind. (PCR) €	Limit ind. (CB) €
AUS	1986	1941	Yes	No	Yes	Yes	350.000	35
BE	1967	—	Yes	Yes	—	—	200	—
BU	1998	1995	Yes	No	Yes	Yes	510*	0
CY	—	2001	—	—	Yes	Yes	—	0
CZ	1994	2000	Yes	Yes	Yes	Yes	0	0
DN	—	1971	—	—	No	Yes	—	130
EST	—	2001	—	—	Yes	Yes	—	...
FI	—	1961	—	—	No	Yes	—	0
FR	1946	—	No	Yes	—	—	500	—
GER	1934	1927	Yes	Yes**	Yes	Yes	1.500.000	100
GR	—	1993	—	—	No	Yes	—	0
HU	—	1990	—	—	Yes	Yes	—	0
IR	—	1963	—	—	Yes	Yes	—	200
IT	1962	1989	Yes	Yes	Yes	Yes	77.500	0
LV	2003	...	No	Yes	Yes	Yes	150	...
LT	1996	2000	Yes	Yes	No	Yes	14.500	
LU	—	—	—	—	—	—	—	—
MT	—	2002	—	—	No	Yes	—	
NL	—	1965	—	—	Yes	Yes	—	125
PT	1978	1996	Yes	Yes	Yes	Yes	0	50
PL	—	2001	—	—	Yes	Yes	—	0
RO	1999	2000	Yes	Yes	Yes	Yes	...	...
SK	1997	2003	—	—	Yes	Yes	—	...
SL	1994	...	Yes	Yes	...	...	0	...
SP	1962	1967	Yes	Yes	No	Yes	6.000	n/a
SW	—	1890	—	—	Yes	Yes	—	0
UK	—	1960	—	—	Yes	Yes	—	n/a

Source: World Bank, Jappelli and Pagano (2002) and the author. PCR denotes public credit register, CB denotes credit bureau, est. established, neg./pos. info is negative and positive information and ind. denotes individuals, "..." denotes "unknown," "—" denotes non-existent. *threshold for overdraft on debt cards, "limit" is the reporting threshold. **data are stored but not distributed to institutions.

Table 3.3 provides an overview of years of establishment, the information sharing regime as it existed in 2005/2006 and the threshold for reporting individuals (not corporate borrowers) to the registry. The variation of system may constitute a problem for cross-border reporting in Europe. Also industrial organization is very different from country to country.

Austria: This country has a public credit registry (founded in 1986), private credit bureaus and an association that shares information. The KSV in Austria was founded in 1870 as the association for the protection from insolvencies *"Creditorenverein zum Schutz vor Insolvenzen."* In 1941, this association was renamed to *"Kreditschutzverband von 1870"* (KSV). Members of the KSV (banks, insurance and leasing firms) exchange positive and negative information. There are altogether more than 700 members. The KSV has a information sharing database, but also a fraud database. This information sharing mechanism is not for profit. The Österreichische Nationalbank runs the public credit register which has the purpose to serve banking supervision (Basel II) and at the same time the industry. The public register has a relatively high threshold for credit or lines of credit (350.000 Euro in 2006) so that there is no substitutional role as the register concentrates on large credit exposures. This explains why there is only a small number of consumers stored. In addition, this register only collects overall outstanding indebtedness and not negative information. This means that Austria is a dual regime with a public and a private information sharing mechanism, where there is a labour division between them.

Belgium: Belgium is an example where public credit reporting crowded out private credit reporting. The National Bank of Belgium runs two registers: (1) the central corporate credit register (founded in 1967)–a positive register for large credit exposures of corporations; and (2) the central individual credit register (*Centrale des crédits aux particuliers* founded in 1987) with a threshold of 200 Euro for consumer loans and none for mortgages. The latter is a positive-negative sharing mechanism. In the past, the central bank has successively expanded its coverage of the market: in 1991 it covered all forms of credit and further expanded in 1993 (National Bank of Belgium 2005). In 2005, it stored 4.4 million borrowers at an annual cost of 3.7 million Euro. Until recently, the Union Professionelle du Crédit (UPC) shared data though its *Mutuelle d'Information sur le Risque* (MIR). This private mechanism was transferred to the central bank in September 2004 and continues there as "Unregistered Registrations" database. When the central bank announced plans to start to take prevention measures (by collecting data about accumulation of debt) in September 2003, it was clear that MIR was not sustainable in the long run (Union Professionelle du Crédit 2004). The industry in the country has criticized that this will make information sharing more expensive. By 2005, there were no private credit bureaus in the country.

Bulgaria: The Bulgarian National Bank set up a register in 1998. According to the regulations, it is a positive register with a threshold for specific types of credit such as overdrafts on debt cards. This is not regarded as sufficient among banks. In 2005 the Icelandic Creditinfo Group established Creditinfo Bulgaria by starting with a negative information sharing mechanism. The company is collecting information on both companies and individuals respectively. Due to the fast growing consumer lending business in this country, it is planned to include non-bank lenders in the information sharing. Experian has also announced to open an office in Bulgaria.

Cyprus: The knowledge about Cyprus' credit reporting system is fairly limited. The central bank in the country runs a register for bad cheques which does not qualify as credit register for bank supervision purposes. It is allowed to establish credit bureaus in the country and to collect positive and negative information. In 2003, the Creditinfo Group acquired Delos Creditinfo, a local company that conducted commercial reporting since 2001. With this acquisition the focus of the company was shifted to consumer reporting. Creditinfo Cyprus currently implements positive-negative information sharing. There are around 170 subscribers. In addition, the Group also acquired stakes in Mecos in 2005, a company with extensive activities in the Middle East. It primarily collects information on companies.

Czech Republic: The Central Register of Credits is a non-profit information sharing register at the Czech National Bank. It shares positive and negative information, but only on individual entrepreneurs and legal entities. There is no threshold applied in this exchange between public and private commercial banks. This leaves information sharing about individuals to the private sector, where now a number of bureaus compete, despite the fact that the country has relatively strict data protection laws (such as opt-in for negative information). There are several providers in the Czech credit information market, for instance the Czech Credit Bureau (CCB) established in 2000. This bureau has two databases, one for banks and one for non-bank institutions and both are outsourced to the Italian bureau CRIF. CCB also provides marketing services and risk control services. CRIF is the only other bureau with increasing activity in the region. The Icelandic Creditinfo has also entered this market, in 2004 it established Creditinfo Czech Republic. Another market player is Solus that collects information from telecom and other companies. The credit bureaus in the country exchange positive and negative information.

Denmark: The country does not have a public credit registry, but only private credit bureaus. One of the largest ones is the RKI Kredit Information A/S, which was founded in 1971 and a competitor is Experian A/S Denmark. In Denmark it is legally limited (by the Act on Processing of Personal Data, Act No. 429 of 31 May 2000) what types of negative information can be passed on–for private credit bureaus the amount must exceed 1.000 DKR (approximately 134 EUR). Both credit bureaus only register negative information compiled from their clients and the Danish Official Gazette. The exchange is voluntary.

Estonia: Estonia does not have a credit register at the national bank. However, there are many companies in the private sector active to collect data. For instance, in 2001 Estonian banks established a credit register which is administered by Krediidiinfo. It collects positive and negative information on individuals and companies. This company belongs to the Experian Group and it is also active in Latvia and Lithuania. Another company in the market is Creditreform Eesti OU which is also active in other Eastern European countries but primarily collects information on companies.

Finland: There is one dominant credit bureau in the country, the Suomen Asiakastieto Oy Finska, which has been licensed by a government agency as for-profit institution. It is only supervised by the central bank, but it is not considered to be part of the central bank's organizational structure. This bureau was founded in 1961 and banks and other financial institutions own part of it. Suomen Asiakastieto Oy Finska collects only negative information and applies no threshold; there are no legal obligations for banks and other financial institutions to share information with the bureau. The other private credit bureau operating in the country is D&B Oy providing commercial reporting services.

Greece: The Greek central bank administers a register with bad cheques and it is required for financial institutions to consult this database. The country has no full-scale public credit registry, only private credit reporting agencies. One of the larger private for-profit agencies, the Tiresias SA, was founded in 1993. The institution is in ownership of national banks and other financial institutions. This information sharing mechanism is a negative one with no thresholds for loans. Banks and other financial institutions are not required to provide data to the credit bureaus. The two other bureaus, Creditinfo Hellas (in the market since 2005) and

Icap primarily collect information from non-bank institutions. Creditinfo Hellas holds records on more than 1 million borrowers.

Hungary: Hungary does not have a public credit register at the Magyar Nemzeti Bank. But the central bank has already recognized the advantages of introducing a credit register, in a report of 2005 it stated that the introduction of a positive register for household lending activities could ease asymmetric information and lead to a better assessment of lending conditions. But there are a number of credit reporting and debt collection agencies active in the country. For instance, in commercial reporting, there is D&B Hungary, Creditreform and Intercredit. BISZ Interbank Informatics Service Ltd is a company that is active in consumer reporting. It is allowed to share positive and negative information in the country.

Ireland: Ireland has a similar credit reporting system to the UK in terms of not having a public credit register. However, the private credit information market seems to be not as competitive as the UK one. Since the 1960s, the country has had a dominant for-profit private credit bureau, the Irish Credit Bureau (ICB) which was established in 1963. It is in ownership of Irish banks and finance companies. ICB collects positive and negative information and applies a threshold of 200 Euro for inclusion in the database. Other competitors in the market are Experian Ireland Ltd which also collects positive and negative information and the Italian CRIF. Becoming a client of a credit bureau is voluntary.

Italy: The country has a public credit registry at the central bank, which was established in 1962 as Central Credit Register (*Centrale dei Rischi*) with a focus on monitoring systemic risk. There is a high threshold of 77.500 Euro. It registers bank loans and informs participants about the aggregate indebtedness (Banca d'Italia 2005). But there are other information sharing mechanisms in the country: Centrale Rischi Finanziaria (CRIF) and Consorzio per la Tutela del Credito (CTC).[33] Whereas CRIF is a for-profit institution, CTC is non-profit and collects only negative information. Otherwise, the Italian system is one of positive and negative information sharing. CRIF connects 440 financial institutions (CRIF 2005) and manages over 30 million credit files. The company has expanded European-wide in the 1990s and has even entered the U.S. market. Across the Atlantic, in Mexico, it pairs up with TransUnion. CTC is a creation of the association of Italian financial service providers, particular car finance. The database is more focused on non-banking institutions,

---

[33] The name means "Consortium for the Protection of the Credit."

whereas CRIF focuses on the banking industry. A third player in the market is Experian Information Services S.p.a. in Rome–this credit bureau of Experian in Italy was founded in 1995. In 2004, the company acquired 100% ownership of Equifax Italy SRL. The latter was founded in 2000 when Equifax acquired the company SEK but then exited the market as the competition apparently made it unattractive.

Latvia: The Bank of Latvia manages the Register of Debtors. This register has been set up in 2003 and there is only negative information compiled in the database. The reporting to it is obligatory if outstanding payments exceed 100 Lats (roughly 150 Euro). The register is currently not member of the Memorandum of Understanding of European credit registers, therefore it has no cross-border agreements with other credit registers. There are also private companies in the market, for instance, Creditreform Latvija SIA which was established in 2001 and processes positive-negative data on individuals and companies. Another player is Krediidiinfo, a company that belongs to the Experian Group.

Lithuania: The Bank of Lithuania manages the Loan Risk Database based upon rules that have been published in 1995. The database itself was established in 1996 and compiles information on individuals and businesses. Commercial banks are required to provide information to it to be able to receive data in return and in general, there is a reporting requirement for supervision purposes. Banks share positive and negative information through this database and the minimum loan size is 14.500 Euro. The Creditinfo Group was also on shopping tour in this market: in 2003 it bought Infobankas UAB (a database on individuals and businesses) and in 2006 it acquired a stake in ZIA (credit management and debt collections). Currently Creditinfo only shares negative information, but it is intended to implement positive-negative information sharing. It competes in the market with Krediidiinfo.

Luxembourg: Luxembourg has neither a public not a private credit register. It has a data protection act (*Protection des personnes à l'égard du traitement des données à caractère personnel*) which implements the European Data Protection Directive just like in other European countries, but the market seems to be to small to have private credit bureaus. There are over 160 banks in the country for a population of 470.000 people. There are providers outside of the country that also cover the Luxembourg market. For instance, Equifax lists Luxembourg as one of the countries it can provide reports on.

Malta: The country has no public credit register and the author has no information about other databases such as for bad cheques. However, there is some private sector activity in the country. Creditinfo Malta has been established in 2002–it provides information on the Maltese market to D&B and distributes D&B products there. It manages a database of all companies of Malta as well as of individuals (Defaulting Debtors Database). In 2005, the information exchange was primarily negative, however, it was planned to introduce a new platform that enables positive-negative information sharing.

Netherlands: The Netherlands is (like Finland and Ireland) another example of a country that has one dominating information sharing system in the private sector, but no public credit register. The Bureau Krediet Registratie (BKR) was founded in 1965 and is actually a foundation (Stichting Bureau Krediet Registratie)–a non-profit institution. It collects positive and negative information and applies a threshold of 125 Euro for negative information and 500 Euro for loans. The database covers more than 8 million people in the country. BKR has also some cross-border relations, for instance with the Schufa Holding AG in Germany. A majority of banks and financial institutions contribute data to the registry.

Poland: Poland has no public credit register at the central bank. However, there is private-sector activity in the country. For instance, the Biuro Informacji Kredytowej S.A. which is in ownership of different banks collects positive and negative information, no threshold is applied to the loans or default information collected. Banks are required–once they contribute data–to share complete information. Consent of the data subject is only required for positive information. Other commercial services providers in the country are KSV Information Services and Coface International that collect information on business entities. The Italian CRIF also entered the market in 2007.

Romania: In Romania, the Central Credit Register and the Overdue Credit Register have been implemented with a regulation dating back to 1999. The company Delos Creditinfo operates since 2000 in Romania. It is is one of the larger companies that provides information on businesses in the country. In 2005, Creditinfo increased its stake in the company to over 60% and renamed it Creditinfo Romania. In addition, it purchased a former local D&B correspondent (Alfacredit). By 2005, the company offered information on 1 million companies and 3 million individuals. The company provides verification and scoring services. There is also another player in the market owned by banks. In addition, Experian bought a company with negative information on businesses. Some commercial service providers are also active in the country such as Creditreform as well as Coface International.

Portugal: The Banco de Portugal has registered credits since 1978, when its PCR was established (*Serviço de Centralização de Riscos de Crédito*). It is part of the supervisory functions of the bank and contains information on credit extended by participants to individuals and organizations. The collection and processing of positive and negative aggregated information on individuals only started in 1993. The threshold of this register is relatively low: if the total liability of a borrower is above 50 Euro, financial service providers are mandated to send the data to the registry (Banco de Portugal 2005). There is also a market where credit reporting agencies compete. A major player is the *Associação das Financeiras para Aquisição a Crédito* (ASFAC), Portugal's Association of Financial Companies. It was established in 1991 and encompasses almost the total Portuguese consumer finance market. The association monitors the indebtedness of consumers. In 1995, ASNEF-Equifax announced the establishment of a joint venture with ASFAC, called Credinformações, which is now the dominating credit bureau in the country that distributes positive and negative information. ASNEF-Equifax is holding 75% interest in the company and ASFAC the remaining 25%. The members of ASFAC contribute the data to the databases of Credinformações.

Slovakia: The National Bank of Slovakia has set-up a register in 1997. Its so-called Registry of Bank Loans and Guarantees collects only information on firms, not individuals. There are also some private entities that collect information. In 2003, several banks founded the Slovak Credit Bureau (SBCB), a year later they laid out the terms of the bank client information system and a cooperation was founded of the Czech Credit Bureau, CRIF and the SBCB. There is a competitor in the market which is Creditinfo Slovakia that started to operate in 2004.

Slovenia: In Slovenia, the public credit register (Kreditni portfelj bank) has been set up in 1994 at the Slovenian Central Bank. This register collects positive and negative information. According to World Bank information access to the register is open to private credit bureaus. There is no minimum loan size. The number of borrowers stored by 2006 was roughly 27.000 according to the World Bank. No information on private credit bureaus was available to the author as the market seems to be at an early stage of development.

Spain: Since 1962 the Bank of Spain manages the public credit registry *Central de Información de Riesgos*. The primary intention of it is to provide financial institutions with data required for the optimal analysis of credit risk (Banco de España 2005). The registry collects positive and negative information on the credit exposure of borrowers and the reporting to it is compulsory above the threshold of 6.000 Euro. It is banks, saving banks, credit cooperatives and specialized credit institutions that report the information to the PCR. In 2004, 14 million borrowers where stored in the database. It issued more than 210 million records in 2003 (Banco de España 2003: 53). However, Spain has a competitive credit reporting market as well. In 1994, Equifax set up a joint venture with the *Asociación Nacional de Establecimientos Financieros de Crédito* (ASNEF), the national federation of credit finance companies that had existed since 1967. The joint venture ASNEF-Equifax was established for the provision of positive and negative data. The database records more than 50 million online consultations per year (CEOE 2004). Altogether it manages data on more than 38 million individuals in Iberia. Experian is also in the market and collects information on legal incidences or from the financial sector (Experian 2003). Spain has a relatively rigid competition policy. The operation of credit bureaus is only allowed if the companies get the authorization from the Competition Court. In Spain it is considered that credit bureaus constitute a "form of trust" between firms of the same industry and that this is likely to influence competitive strategies. Therefore, the practice is forbidden if not explicitly allowed (San Jose Riestra 2002: 11). There are several decisions by the Court concerning credit reporting.[34]

Sweden: The country has the same system as the U.S., UK and Ireland with no public credit registry. This in one of the few countries that have a data protection law and an extra Credit Information Act. The industry in Sweden is competitive, credit bureaus have been founded as early as the 1890s, some credit bureaus are AAA Soliditet, D&B, CreditSafe or the Upplysningscentralen (UC). The bureaus collect positive and negative information, primarily from publicly available sources such as taxable income and wealth or property owned. This information is *not* publicly available in other countries, Sweden is therefore an atypical case! UC manages a database, where banks and other financial institutions exchange positive and negative information. There is no threshold applied to the data exchange and participation is entirely voluntary. However, the databases can only be accessed if data is contributed (principle of recip-

---

[34] These decisions are published in Spanish on the website of the Competition Court: http://www.tdcompetencia.org/index.htm (section Informes y Resoluciones).

rocity). It is estimated that more than 6.5 million negative entries are stored in the database. All in all, the above discussion shows how different credit information markets are in Europe: some countries do have no public register, others have one but it is only a database on bad cheques, whereas some countries have public registers that mimic private credit bureaus. There is even a country without any type of register: Luxembourg. In addition, the industrial organization varies. Some countries are dominated by one large provider, others have had competition for years. Again some countries (especially in Eastern Europe) only start to build up systems. In the following, three case studies are discussed in depth: Germany (dual system), Great Britain (private regime) and France (public register).

3.1.4 Germany: A Dominated Market

Credit cooperatives developed in Germany in the 19th Century (Besley 1995). These cooperatives typically borrowed from a bank or the government and distributed the funds among their members. They used local knowledge and enforcement for this kind of activity. Relationship networks aside, informal groups such as associations and mutual protection societies usually exchanged knowledge on customers. One of the first agencies founded in Germany was the Verband der Vereine Creditreform (in the following, the short form "Creditreform" is used). It was established in 1879 to protect its members from the defaults of their borrowers. Nowadays, Creditreform mainly provides commercial reporting services, but is active internationally. Only recently it has teamed up with Experian to provide consumer data services. There are a number of credit bureaus in Germany, in 2001 an estimated 20 firms. The dominant one, however, is the Schufa Holding AG. Although some credit cooperatives had developed in Germany, consumer spending only picked up after World War I and credit became more widespread. Retailers in the rural areas typically extended credit to clients that were known to them (so-called "*anschreiben*") and lending was primarily local.

According Schufa Holding AG (2002), utility provider Bewag in Berlin sold energy on credit as well as durable goods such as vacuum cleaners and fridges. The sales people in the company could ask the department in charge for energy sales for names of slow or late payers. Some costumers were already known in that department as bad risks, the information only needed to be shared within the company. This system was soon expanded to include outsiders such as banks, financial companies and retailers with whom information was shared. The participants, however, were asked to trust each other and to also transmit addresses of good customers (Schufa

2002: 5). In 1927, a group of businessmen founded the *Schutzgemeinschaft für die Absatzfinanzierung und Kreditsicherung, e.V.*, an association that compiled lists of customers for speeding up the process of credit granting and utility provision. Only two years later they had compiled 1.5 million index cards. This successful idea spread throughout Germany and 13 regional associations were created. During the Hitler regime (1933-1945), National Socialists abused the collections of information in the German bureaucracy - an experience that profoundly influenced the German and European awareness for data protection. I discuss this point in greater detail in the section on privacy regulation. In World War II the Allies bombarded Berlin and destroyed the main building of the Schufa together with its data collection. In 1934, the central bank of Germany (*Deutsche Bundesbank*) founded its public credit register (*Evidenzzentrale*), because the Great Depression proved the severity of systemic risk arising from incomplete information with respect to borrowers.[35] With the boom after World War II, banks and finance companies saw the need for an information hub that protected them against defaults. Installment credit, but also the mail-order business began to pick up. In 1952, the Bundes-Schufa e.V. was founded as an umbrella association of the regional associations that were re-established. By 1965 it already sold 10 million credit reports (Schufa 2002: 7). Just as in the U.S., the arrival of the computer marked an end to the capacity restrictions posed by manual file systems. The adoption of IT systems by government and firms raised public suspicion, based upon the aforementioned historical experience. Maybe this is the reason, why Germany was the first country worldwide to adopt a data protection act. One of the driving forces in Germany for legislation was a conflict between local communities and the state administration concerning the power stemming from large IT systems. But this was not the only dispute:

> *"There was also a conflict between the legislative body and the executive body because of the different use they could make of power-enhancing data processing. The legislature was afraid to be cut off from information if it disappeared in the bureaucracy of the executive."* (Burkert 1999: 45)

In addition, there was a dispute concerning state power and civil rights. The first data protection law by the state Hesse addressed these questions. It established confidentiality clauses and an independent data protection officer to control the administration.[36] Other countries such as Sweden and

---

[35] The exchange via the Evidenzzentrale is based on the Law on the Credit Industry, Federal Data Protection Act and associated guidelines.

[36] The law was enacted on the state level and is the Datenschutzgesetz of 07.10.1970, a federal law followed later.

France followed. The U.S. introduced its first industry-specific law on October 26, 1970. The first industry to be regulated was the credit reporting industry when Nixon signed PL 91-508, the Fair Credit Reporting Act, into law. I will discuss this extensively in the sections on credit reporting regulation. In the 1970s, the Schufa digitized its index card system and in 1975 it introduced the "*Selbstauskunft*" (access to information for data subjects). At that time no law was in place that controlled the private sector (Schufa Holding AG 2002: 11). The actual rush by consumers to see their reports did not happen, many did not know about it, others were not interested or found access too expensive. In general, Germans only contact the Schufa when there is a problem with getting credit. The Schufa clause in credit contracts that releases creditors from bank secrecy and enables them to send information to the credit bureau is often signed by consumers without really being read. In 1977 German Federal Data Protection Act (Bundesdatenschutzgesetz) was enacted. This constituted the first legal regulation of the private sector.

Figure 3.7
Lending to Private Persons in Germany

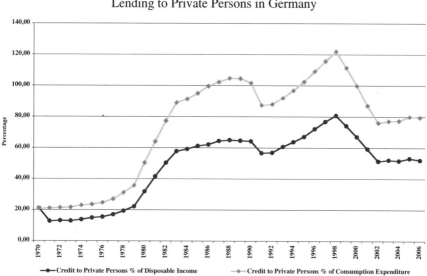

Sources: Deutsche Bundesbank and Statistisches Bundesamt Deutschland

Figure 3.7 shows that lending has increased rapidly since the 1970s when measured as percentage to disposable income or as percentage to consumption expenditure. It also shows the boom after the reunification, when the Berlin Wall came down in 1989. From 1998, there is a reversal of this trend partially due to the end of the "reunification boom." The household debt-service burden calculated by Deutsches Institut für Wirtschaftsforschung (DIW) from the socio-economic panel shows a burden of 14-17% of households in West-Germany, where it was somewhat lower for East Germany in the years 1997-2001. The debt-service burden is smaller for households that are not poor compared to the poor ones. From the evidence available, the gap between the household debt service burdens in the East and West of Germany in the second half of the 1990s. Whereas this burden was somewhat lowered for Western households, it increased for the Eastern ones.

By the 1980s, information exchange with the Bundes-Schufa had become a routine for German creditors. They informed consumers about their data sharing practices via a clause in the credit contracts. However, some changes were soon to come. The Consumer Protection Association of Berlin analyzed the clauses and initiated a lawsuit that even went to the Federal Court (*Bundesgerichtshof*). The court decided in 1985 that the "Schufa Clause" in credit contracts had to be modified. The judgment is important, because it stated some fundamental principles concerning information practices–this will be discussed further below. The clauses were changed and applied throughout the industry. By 1985 the Schufa sold 23 million credit reports per year, the demand from mail-order businesses, credit card and telecommunication firms increased annually. For some time the Schufa–as a non-profit association–was sheltered from competition.

Table 3.4

Schufa Holding Indicators

Indicators	2001	2002	2003	2004	2005	2006
No. of persons stored (mio.)	57	59	62	62	63	64
No. of data items stored (mio.)	299	317	343	362	384	407
Inquiries and updates (mio.)	66.4	65.5	69.5	72.3	77	82
Inquiries with scores (%)	48	37	36	43	53	55
Inquiries by individuals ('000)	857	827	879	984	1.069	1.172

Source: Schufa Annual Reports

The Table 3.4 shows some business indicators that are publicly available from several annual reports of the firm. Schufa more or less acted as a monopoly in the market as the biggest players from the financial services industries were members. Small niche players in credit reporting were unimportant. Schufa introduced the scoring service *Auskunfts-Scoring Service* (ASS) in 1995, later than the major companies in the U.S., where credit scoring was developed. This might be due to the high competitive pressure under which the U.S. credit reporting agencies operate.

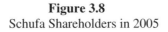

Figure 3.8
Schufa Shareholders in 2005

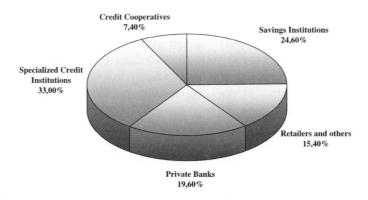

Source: Schufa Holding AG

Banks and other credit institutions are still the major shareholders (see Figure 3.8). In 2000, the 61 Bundes-Schufa partners, mainly companies from the banking industry as well as the retail and mail order industry, decided to restructure the non-profit as for-profit company which is now called Schufa Holding AG. For this matter, the stakes of eight regional credit bureaus were transferred to the Holding which took over management and supervision. With this new legal status, Schufa could enter competition. Another major player in the market is the Vereine Creditreform e.V. that is primarily providing business information. This changed in 1998 when the firm founded a joint venture with Experian (Creditreform Experian GmbH). It brought the company into direct competition with the Schufa Holding AG. Experian had been active in Germany for nearly ten years and in 1998 also bought the Directmarketing GmbH, a database of 28 million addresses. With the acquisition of Cards Direkt Experian became the market leader in the processing of customer cards in Germany. Other fields of activity are scoring products, risk management, advise and loyalty solutions. Other smaller players in the German market are KQIS-Group and Bürgel. The former has its roots in the mail-order industry.[37] The database includes approximately 68 million customers in Germany and creditworthiness information for 21 million consumers (Karstadt Quelle Information Services 2005). Bürgel Wirtschaftsinformationen

---

[37] KQIS is the abbreviation for Karstadt Quelle Information Services.

stored data on 32 million firms and consumers.[38] All credit institutions and even some public administration offices in Germany are obliged to report borrowers who are in debt exceeding 1.5 million Euro at any point in time during the last quarter to the public credit registry. Quarterly, all creditors receive references relating to the overall indebtedness of their clients. Private credit bureaus do not have access to the database which is for prudential supervision. The Bundesbank states that due to the high reporting threshold there is no competition with private credit bureaus (Deutsche Bundesbank 2002). However, there is an increasing number of individuals reported in the database: in 2000 there were approximately 47.000 profiles of individuals reported. Further information on the register is available from Deutsche Bundesbank (1998, 2001) and Estrella et al. (2000).

Figure 3.9

Company and Consumer Insolvencies in Germany

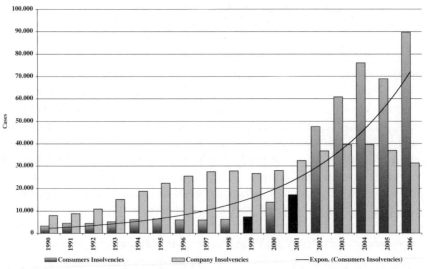

Notes: Numbers for consumers refer to the category "consumers and others" used by Creditreform. The number for 1990 is estimated by the author. Source: Creditreform.

Figure 3.9 shows the trend in consumer and firm insolvencies in Germany for the 1990s and beyond. An exponential function can be fitted to the number of consumers who become insolvent. The annual average growth rate of the figure for consumers is 28.63%. The years 1999 and 2001 are marked with black bars: in these years, major legislative and regulatory

---

[38] During the research phase, the company did not make separate estimates available to the author.

changes took place. In 1999, legislators introduced a new bankruptcy law.[39] This law intended to provide consumers with a fresh start: Consumers who were not able to finance their debt must get debt counseling and they are obliged to find a compromise with their creditors. If the parties do not agree, the process continues in court, where the consumer can ask for an exemption from the rest of the burden. Shortly after the introduction of the law it became clear that legislators had made a mistake: Not many over-committed individuals used this option due to the relatively high costs (!) of the judicial process that had to be paid by the already overindebted consumer. Legislators had to change this measure once more in 2001. Figure 3.9 shows the large increase in 2001-2002 after the change. Schufa Holding AG (2003) reports, financial problems were especially concentrated in the age bracket of 20-34 year old people. And they were primarily recorded in the banking sector, but increasingly also by telecommunication services. The latter contributed to a major extent to the rising numbers of bankruptcies in the second half of the 1990s. Altogether, Germany is a well-developed credit market with a pervasive information structure. However, over the 1990s the growth rates in consumer credit have not been extraordinary. This is paired with rising numbers of consumers who go bankrupt.

3.1.5 Great Britain: Intense Competition

Credit reporting originated in Great Britain. The earliest account available to the author is the *Mutual Communication Society of London* operated by a group of English tailors as a cooperative venture for their mutual protection in 1803 (Associated Credit Bureaus 1981: 10). During this time, gossip among tailors prevailed, however, the Society proved to be a more formal information exchange as its members regularly shared the names of people that would cheat on them or not pay amounts due. These businessmen started to pass along negative information about bad risks they knew. Over the course of the century, Great Britain developed a highly competitive market due to relatively low data protection restrictions and no public register. In addition, the Executive branch set up a centralized system of collection of judgments that could be accessed by the agencies. This appears to be lowering the costs of operating in the market as this activity would have to be done by agencies themselves. In fact in other countries, credit reporting agencies still have to collect such information from courts in an often decentralized judicial system. The circumstances in the UK

---

[39] This is the so-called Verbraucherinsolvenz-Gesetz.

were very favorable for the development of the companies. Today, there are several credit reporting agencies in the market, the coverage rate is more than half of the economically active population. Only with the implementation of the European Data Protection Directive, Great Britain started to have a regime of data protection that is stricter than in the past and provides a higher level of consumer protection.

Figure 3.10
Total Financial Assets and Liabilities of UK Households

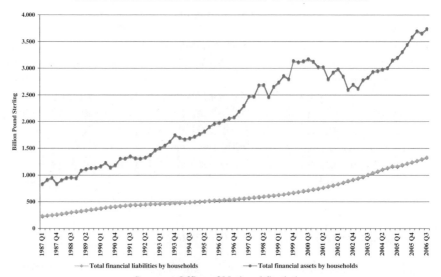

Sources: Office of National Statistics

Figure 3.10 shows the total financial liabilities and assets of UK households since the end of the 1980s as well as the record levels reached after 2005. This has led to the discussion as to whether current levels of borrowing are sustainable. Per capita indebtedness of UK consumers is among the highest in Europe. In terms of credit reporting, Great Britain's market resembles that of the U.S., because there is no public credit register administered by the central bank. However, the Registry Trust Ltd., an independent organization that was established by the Lord Chancellor's Department holds the statutory register for all county court judgments. It was set up by parliament in 1852. Registry Trust (2004) states that the original Act provided for the registration of all county court judgments of £10 (roughly US-$ 17) in England and Wales. A county court judgment is an official claim by a creditor or a number of creditors against a borrower for money that is owed. This claim has to be done through the county court system and is registered there. Money plaints, on the other hand, describe the seizure of goods to recover money owed to the creditor after other measures for recovering have failed.

Figure 3.11
Judgments and Money Claims in the UK

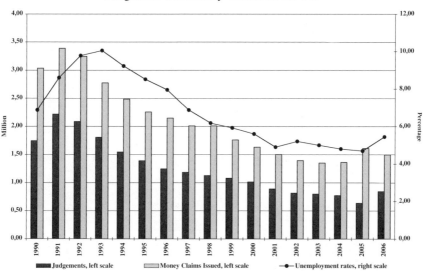

Sources: Department of Trade and Industry, Registry Trust, Office of National Statistics.

Figure 3.11 shows a downward trend in the judgments and money plaints after peaking in 1991. This is in co-incidence with a decreasing unemployment rates in the 1990s. Again, this does not give evidence for possible co-integration. The early Registry was more a source for trade data than for consumer data. Goods of mass consumption such as the Singer sewing machine where sold at a price below the threshold, therefore many consumer transactions remained unregistered. By 1874 some 25.100 register entries were made. For some time the system of registration remained unchanged until costs became an issue in the 1980s. By that time, the register also included consumer judgments. Costs started to exceeded profits and the main question was as to whether the registry should be closed or the threshold increased. After intensive lobbying from the industry, the Lord Chancellor agreed to hand over the operations to a non-profit organization. In 1965, the number of entries had reached 450.000. Under the Register of County Court Judgment Regulations 1985, the Registry receives judgments, satisfactions and cancellations daily from all the county courts in England and Wales (Registry Trust 2004). Access to the register is public, therefore also credit reference agencies can withdraw data. This is compiled together with positive data which can be collected after the consumer has provided consent. Consumer enquiries have grown continuously throughout the 1990s according to the Citizens Advise Bureaux Annual Reports in the UK. The larger part of these enquiries is concerning consumer credit and other issues, while a smaller part is about mortgages. The above numbers are also influenced by increasing awareness of advise services, therefore they are only indicative and cannot be seen as evidence for an increasing number of consumers in debt problems. There has been a long and controversial debate in the UK concerning overindebtedness and how it should be measured. The measurement will determine the scale of the problem. In 2007, the European Commission decided to develop a common operational definition of overindebtedness.

Figure 3.12
Number of Bankruptcies and Voluntary Arrangements

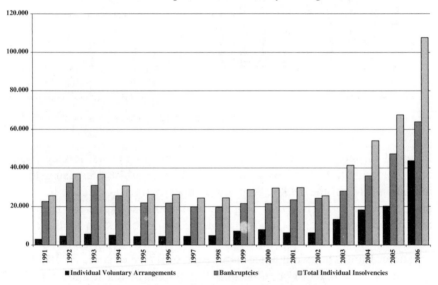

Source: Department of Trade and Industry

Figure 3.12 shows the number and trend of individual insolvencies. This number aggregates bankruptcy orders and individual voluntary arrangements. Proceedings for bankruptcy usually commence at county courts with the appropriate jurisdiction. In such procedures the control of financial matters is transferred to a trustee. Individual voluntary arrangements are agreements between debtors and creditors and can be made if the amount of debt does not exceed £5.000 (approximately US-$ 9.880). Application for such an arrangement must be made at the court. Over the

1990s, there is no clear trend in the number of individual insolvencies. The British Task Force on Tackling Overindebtedness at the Department of Trade and Industry encourages the industry to share data: "Lenders should seek to share all currently permissible data, both positive and negative, with other lenders. This should include outstanding credit balances, credit limits, open credit lines, history of repayments and amounts borrowed." (Department of Trade and Industry 2001: 35). The Task Force also encourages all non-credit organizations that regularly take payments from consumers to register them and especially defaults. There has been an increase in the number of individual bankruptcies (including consumers and entrepreneurs).

Figure 3.13
UK Household Liabilities as Percentage to Expenditure and Income

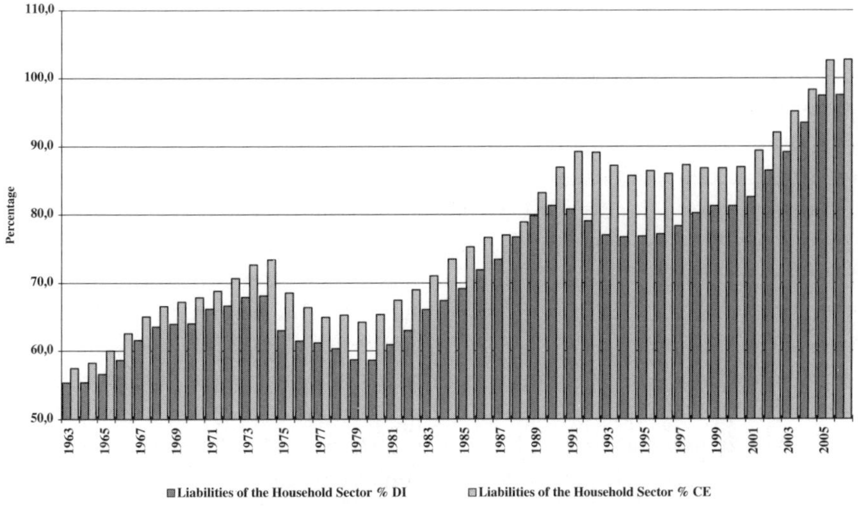

Notes: DI denotes disposable income, CE consumption expenditure. Sources: Office of National Statistics and Bank of England

Figure 3.13 shows that in the past years, new record levels were reached, something that politicians found alarming. Figure 3.13 shows the outstanding liabilities of households measured as percentage of disposable income (DI) and consumption expenditure (CE). Not pictured are the assets, households accumulated during the same time. As stated, the British credit market is regarded is the most competitive and innovative market in Europe. It comprises loans secured by dwelling as well as unsecured lending such as credit cards, mail order, hire purchase, store cards or home equity withdrawal. One aspect contributing is the credit reporting industry.

The industry of Great Britain is highly competitive, too, and there is a lot more merger and acquisition activity than in Germany. Since the beginning of the 1990s, a number of takeovers have taken place. Just like in the U.S., there is an oligopoly market structure with three dominant players: Callcredit Plc., Equifax Plc. and Experian Ltd. In 2001, a new web-based credit reference agency was created, a partnership between the American D&B and the British Skipton Building Society (Callcredit Plc). In 2004, the company stated to have data of 30 million consumers on file. Equifax is also active in the market, in the past the company bought four other firms and invested in founding Equifax Card Solutions.[40] In 1994, Equifax won the bidding contest for UATP Infolink against TransUnion. In 1999, the Office of Fair Trading gave the green light to the acquisition of a minority stake in the company Choicepoint. Altogether the company holds data on over 30 million consumers in the UK. Experian has one headquarter in the UK.[41] In the sections on competition in U.S. credit reporting it was explained that this company was bought by the British Great Universal Stores Plc (GUS). GUS paid more than US-$ 1.7 billion for the company. Since its establishment, Experian has been on an equally aggressive expansion course as the other two major credit reporting agencies. Its typical strategy is to first establish a joint venture and then to acquire the other firm completely. In the UK, Experian bought ICD and the CCN Group among others. The company holds also data on the lifestyles of 13.5 million British consumers. According to numbers of the British Bankers' Association, the number of total cards held by the British population rose from 28.6 million in 1989 to over 55 million in 2001. Remarkable as the economically active population is only 58 million people. Decreasing interest rates in the 1990s (especially the base rate) made debt more affordable. Altogether, the British Market is certainly one of the most competitive ones in Europe in terms of credit reporting and in terms of lending to consumers. Great Britain stands in stark contrast to France.

---

[40] These four companies are: UATP Infolink, Grattan, Check-a-Cheque and CCI Group.
[41] To be precise the company has three headquarters, one in Costa Mesa (U.S.A.) one in Nottingham (United Kingdom) and one in Monaco.

3.1.6 France: Public Credit Reporting System

The French consumer credit market is one of the slowest growing among the European nations–but it grows despite a public credit register with only negative information. Figure 3.14 depicts the growth of consumer credit as percentage of private consumption expenditure and as percentage of disposable income in the 1990s. Consumer credit as percentage of GDP has slightly trended upward since the beginning of the 1990s, but in general hovers around 5-10% (not displayed). The amount of consumer credit in relation to disposable income is increasing and reached over 12% in 2002.

Figure 3.14
Consumer Credit as Percentage of GDP and Consumption

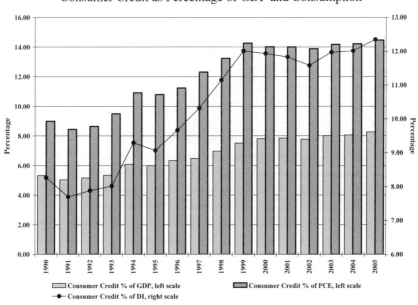

Note: GDP is Gross Domestic Product, PCE denotes personal consumption expenditure and DI denotes disposable income. Source: European Credit Research Institute

This slow and gradual increase of lending has been the trend for the past 20 years and is in general explained by interest rate caps among other regulations as well as the stiff privacy rules in the country that only allow sharing of negative information. In fact, France has a distinct information sharing regime considered the other credit reporting systems in Europe. It is centralized, non-competitive and structured along strict public policy lines. In addition, it is a negative information only regime. The Banque de France hosts several data bases, the so-called Fichier National des Chèques

Irréguliers (FNCI), the Fichier Centrales des Chèques (FCC) and the Fichier Bancaire des Entreprises (FIBEN). Since we do not analyse fraud or rating of enterprises, the only database of interest here is the Fichier National des Incidents de Remboursement des Crédits aux Particuliers (FICP), the National Register of Household Credit Repayment Incidents. The FICP was created by the Neiertz Act of 1989 (also called the Act on Preventing and Resolving Personal Debt Problems). And there are details of data collection and transmission described in several regulations that accompanied the act. The FICP is also governed by the French act on data protection. The Neiertz Act of 1989 mandated the Banking and Financial Regulatory Committee (Comité de la Réglementation Bancaire et Financière, CRBF) to create and regulate a national database on repayment incidents. Its purpose is to centralize and distribute two kinds of reports:

1. Incidents in connection with credit granted to individuals for non-professional purposes; and
2. Repayment schedules drawn up by the French overindebtedness commissions outside court-settlement procedures as well as recommendations after judicial review (Banque de France 2001a: 6).

Altogether the records contain the identity of the borrower, incidents on all types of credit granted for non-professional purposes, including overdrafts and repayment schedules drawn up by overindebtedness commissions in out-of-court settlements. The Banque de France has the sole right of collecting information on judicial measures except for cases in which a bank is directly involved in the case. Credit institutions are free to consult the FICP, but access is granted only to credit institutions, the financial service business of the Post, overindebtedness commissions and the judicial authorities (Banque de France 1994: 102). Again this is a stark contrast to other countries in Europe, where more sources may access credit information databases, among them insurers, telecom providers or even landlords who might check the information for screening purposes. It is in turn obligatory for financial institutions to report the data to the register (Banque de France 1994: 101). The French system can be characterized as an exclusive reporting scheme that allows only the aforementioned institutions to use the information. Furthermore, the financial institutions are not allowed to transfer the reports to other parties in any form whatsoever (Banque de France 2002b: 5). This means tertiary transactions on the side of the bank are forbidden. Privacy is strictly guarded in the French system and France is ranking among those countries with the highest data protection standards in the world. This will be discussed in greater detail in the section on the regulation of credit reporting.

Figure 3.15
FICP Files, Payment Incidents and Overindebtedness Dossiers

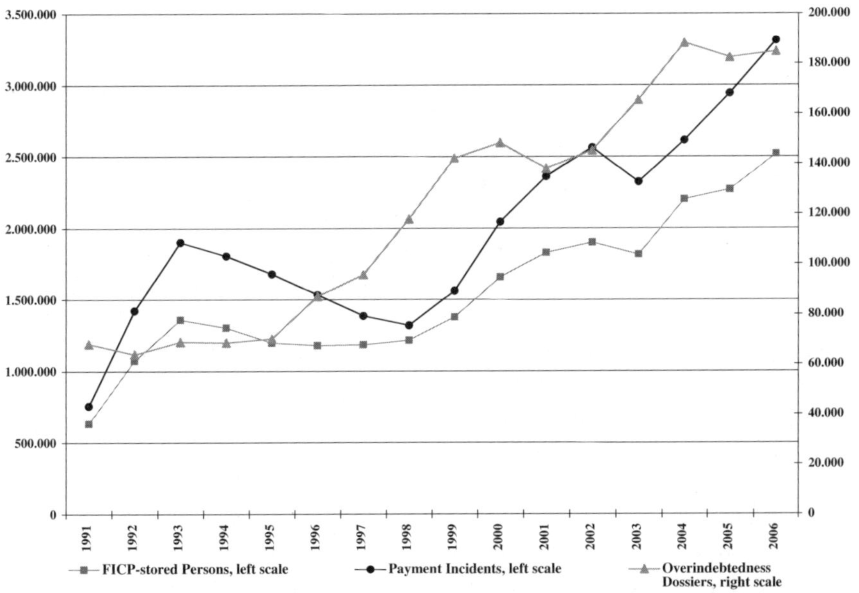

Notes: Number of FICP files for 2006 and of incidents (2004-2006) are extrapolated.
Sources: Banque de France, INSEE, World Bank

Figure 3.15 shows the trend in numbers of debtors that have been reported to the Banque de France since database inception in 1990 (data therefore start at 1991 only). There is the number of incidents reported, but also the total number of persons affected, some of them having multiple incidents. The persons that are stored in the FICP as well as the incidences that are recorded at the credit register are on the left scale as total number. Noticeable are the strong increases in all three time series after 1998. Roughly 4% of the population in France is affected by over-indebtedness if the numbers of overindebtedness dossiers is taken into account. By 2007, there was no common definition of overindebtedness in Europe, therefore, defining over-commitment was and certainly remains a controversial issue. The threshold for incidents and overdrafts is about 500 Euro (Banque de France 2002b). An incident is not reported to the Banque de France until one month has passed, because this period allows a borrower to pay the amount due. Also, this allows for situations where the borrower has simply forgotten to pay the amount due without the intention to default strategically. However, if the liability remains unpaid, it is mandatory for the financial service providers to report the information. This is also the case where no other solution with the borrower was found. However, the reporting institution must inform the borrower about the inscription in the database (Banque de France 2002a: 3). In 2001, the highest percentage of incidents is the category of personal loans. Housing loans, on the other hand, usually show a low rate of defaults, they are less risky compared to personal loans. The data in the FICP are listed for different time periods that have changed several times in the past. Judicial measures and repayment plans were originally stored for three years without erasure in case of repayment (Banque de France 1994: 102). In 1993, the CRBF decided to extend that period to five years and in 2000 it issued a new regulation that expanded the period again, this time to eight years.

The Banque de France (1994) describes the main characteristics of the registered FICP as follows: (1) the file is "legal," because it establishes an equal system of access; (2) it is "non-monopolistic," because individual creditors can hold their own internal files if they wish; (3) it is a publicly administrated database justified on the guarantee of objectivity, impartiality; and (4) it is justified that the Banque de France administers it as it has experience with large, national databases (Banque de France 1994: 99). Another critical feature is the exclusive collection of negative data–only payment incidents are stored. The Banque de France explains that the system does not function as an overall indebtedness registry but as an incidence registry (Banque de France 1994: 99). What is the rationale for it? There is apparently no explicit legal prohibition for sharing of positive information in France, but the Neiertz Act also does not explicitly authorize positive files. The attitude of data protection officials in the country is that only if the law explicitly authorized it, positive records would be allowed. The Banque the France explained that this legislation did not intent to create a positive file, but rather a negative database (Banque de France 2002b). The French Data Protection Authority CNIL states that positive information is susceptible to being diverted from its original purpose, because the richness of the data might lead to usage for other purposes such as marketing or employment screening.[42] These worries are not unfounded as experience from countries as diverse as the U.S., China and South Korea shows, where the data are in fact used for credit-unrelated purposes. While one could easily switch from a negative regime to positive-negative reporting, once positive data are collected it is difficult to return to a negative-only regime (Leclercq 2000: 20). This is one of the examples for path dependence, once an initial decision is made such as the sharing of positive-negative information, it will later be virtually impossible to reverse this decision. The CNIL states that it is not worried about the credit risk: in

---

[42] The abbreviation CNIL stands for *Commission Nationale de l'Information et Libertés*. I will use the common French abbreviation.

comparison with the U.S., the percentage of payment incidents in France is lower. A working group in the French Senate expressed consent for refusing positive information. However, the same group stated that it was important to improve the efficiency of the FICP (Senat 1997). The group wanted to extent the FICP to unpaid taxes, unpaid bills registered by French telecommunication providers and unpaid premiums registered by the French insurance industry. Of course this would have posed questions about access and cost sharing.[43] The system does not function without problems, as the CNIL has been addressed by many consumers that have complained about their banks for inscribing them into the FICP without a justification or for transmitting other erroneous information.

There are also private companies in the market that provide information services, but they either belong to the marketing industry (such as Claritas, Consodata and Cofinoga) or the business reporting industry (Bürgel, D&B or Graydon). There are also three credit reporting agencies in the market, Experian, Equifax and CRIF, but they do not provide credit reporting services in the common sense. These companies are active in the field of cheque processing or risk-management.

It is important to note that the outsourcing of file management is allowed, but only for internal uses (Commission Nationale de l'Informatique et des Libertés 2002). The CNIL does not authorize the collection of positive files by credit reporting agencies, although there has been substantial lobbying in the country by those firms. Altogether the resistance of French authorities against private sector credit reporting and their conviction that positive files were not the intention of legislators is the reason why there is no private credit reporting service in France. Nevertheless, there is some activity in the French credit services market. Also, here, Experian was on shopping tour: in 1998 it bought the card and cheque processing firm SG2 from Société Générale and one year later DMC Informatique, another cheque processing firm. According to its website, Experian collects in fact information on individuals as well as on companies and sells scoring services and other risk-management products to the financial industry in France (Experian 2001: 5, 2002b). The company verifies credit demands of individuals by analyzing their annual telephone bills, files of the postal service (in case they move) and files of clients. Together with non-existent private credit reporting, the coverage of the population in France is low. The FICP coverage rates tend to be rather small, in the second half of the 1990s it was about 2.2% of the total population. In addition, as stated above, there is a relatively low growth rate of the main credit aggregates.

---

[43] In 1997, the whole system's costs were about 16.5 million Francs or 2.5 million Euro by that time (Senat 1997).

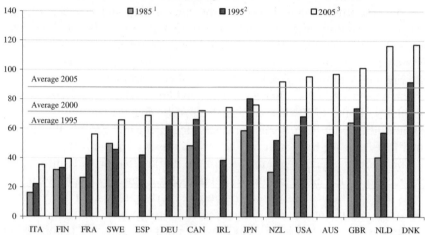

Figure 3.16
Household Debt as a Percentage of GDP in OECD Countries

Notes: [1] indicates 1987 for the United Kingdom, [2] indicates 1999 for Ireland and [3] marks 2004 for Australia, Germany, Denmark, Spain, Finland, United Kingdom, Italy and Japan.
Source: OECD

From the above discussion, it is clear that credit information markets in Europe differ, some are competitive such as that of the UK and Sweden, others develop rather slowly and some do currently not exist such as in France, Belgium or Luxembourg. Figure 3.16 shows a comparison of household debt as percentage of GDP, showing low levels of indebtedness in Italy, Finland and France. There has been considerable discussion how credit constraints can be lowered and on what circumstances they depend. The intensity of competition in a credit market as well as the regulatory environment are contributing factors. For instance, interest rate caps could reduce the amount of credit granted in the market. Incomplete risk assessment might also contribute as lenders hesitate to lend to parties, where risk is not at least semi-transparent. Such credit rationing affects disproportional small companies and micro-entrepreneurs as well as consumers. Credit rationing does not usually affect big companies or wealthy borrowers with extensive bank relationships and extensive credit history. Through information sharing as well as improved regulations such constraints can be lowered. Per capita indebtedness also differs greatly. Countries such as Italy and Portugal range on the lower end, France and Spain in the middle field and UK and Netherlands have the highest indebtedness per inhabitant. Again, by only focusing on the indebtedness side, the picture is incomplete as the household budget also contains financial and non-financial wealth (which is not discussed here in detail).

3.1.7 Cross-border Reporting in Europe

As of 2006/2007, credit reporting across European borders was virtually
not existent. The reason is as simple as this: there is no demand for cross-
border consumer credit and the migration of borrowers is still too low. Although one could argue that this hampers credit market integration in
Europe, one could turn this argument around–lack of credit market integration hampers the development of one common credit information market.
The lack of cross-border exchange of data is especially a problem for internationally mobile workforce. Three types of cross-border data traffic
must be distinguished:

- ➢ Exchange among public credit registers;
- ➢ Exchange among commercial reporting agencies; and
- ➢ Exchange among consumer reporting agencies.

Whereas there is some development in the international information sharing among public credit registers, and commercial reporting is fairly advanced, there is little progress in consumer reporting. In the following, the
three types of exchanges are discussed. Altogether 14 countries in Europe
have a public credit register. Most of them do collect data on natural persons (except for the Czech Republic and Slovakia), but with greatly varying reporting thresholds. In addition, as discussed above, there are two
countries where only public credit registers exist and no private credit bureaus (Belgium and France), and there is one country, Luxembourg, where
nothing exists. In Belgium, the register has the explicit purpose of tackling
over-commitment of consumers and in France the register was set-up for
the same reason and to increase security in the lending business. The data
exchange among PCRs in Europe is *currently not legally regulated on the
EU-level*,[44] but there exists a Memorandum of Understanding between a
subgroup of registries.[45] In mid-2002, only a few countries (Belgium, Italy,
Portugal and Germany) had laws in effect that allowed the international
exchange among public credit registers (Deutsche Bank 2002). But this has
changed. As of October 2006, seven EU countries (Austria, Belgium,
France, Germany, Italy, Portugal and Spain) had signed this agreement and
the registers from the accession countries were invited to join. The memorandum covers data on corporate borrowers as well as on private persons.
The PCRs have agreed to provide each other with data on borrowers if the

---

[44] The October 2005 Consumer Credit Directive draft contains a provision stating that a
Member State shall ensure non-discriminatory access to the databases in its territory.

[45] Memorandum of Understanding on the Exchange of Information among National Central Credit Registers for the Purpose of Passing it on to Reporting Institutions (20 February 2003), available from the European Central Bank's website.

indebtedness of the borrower exceeds 25.000 Euro. Data on borrowers that are resident in the receiving PCR's territory are exchanged regularly, but also in ad hoc requests from the reporting financial institutions, insurance companies and investment firms. *Ad hoc requests* must always be transmitted through the national PCR, which has to check compliance, and as to whether the creditor has an established credit relationship with the borrower or intends to establish one. The national PCR therefore acts as *clearing house for requests and replies*.

The content of the information exchange is currently limited to the total amount of indebtedness of the borrower. In other words, if a bank wants to know the total indebtedness of a borrower in its home country and in another Member State, it must request both types of information from its national PCR. For the indebtedness in the other Member State the PCR requests the information from the PCR in that other Member State. According to the MOU, PCRs may use the information they have received for banking supervision purposes and internal research, banks, on the other hand can use it for credit risk evaluation of the borrower. The current business practice is that only information on corporate borrowers is exchanged, however, after gaining experience with this practice, the participants will decide if they also exchange information on individuals. The amount of cross-border exchange of information is relatively low at the moment. Commercial credit reporting (the exchange of information on companies) is further developed than the exchange of data in other areas. In Europe it is organized via networks of competing credit reporting agencies such as BIGNet, Eurogate and EurisConnect. Users of BigNet are commercial agencies, while Eurogate is a net of credit reporting agencies in Austria, Belgium, Germany, Spain and Great Britain and EurisConnect is a net one of several European credit bureaus (among them Schufa and CRIF) that provide a European standard report for consumer credit profiles. Other large providers of company information are Coface International and Creditreform which have had international reporting networks for years. The international networks are increasingly in competition with one another, an area where there has been very little research in the past. Consumer credit reporting is now starting to become more feasible. There are two possible ways to develop such cross-border services: either to pursue a merger and acquisition strategy (employed by Equifax, Experian, and Creditinfo) or to negotiate cross-border contracts (pursued by Schufa, BKR and others). The *Association of Consumer Credit Information Suppliers* (ACCIS), the European industry association of credit reporting agencies, has developed a standard contract that can be used among companies to exchange data on private individuals. Under this contract there are two possible options for accessing credit information in another country. The first is direct access: Creditor from country B can directly be linked up to the credit bureau in country A. The problem then is the reciprocity provision: creditor B must transfer data on consumers in his own country to the credit bureau in another country–data on consumers in country B would be stored in country A. In principle, this is possible due to the harmonisation of data protection regimes. However, this kind of link-up is rather rare, because formats and technical systems differ. The second option is a bilateral cross-border contract between a credit bureau A and credit bureau B. Bank B in country B asks credit bureau B, for credit information on borrowers in country A. Credit bureau B then approaches credit bureau A and requests this information. Credit bureau A delivers. Credit bureau B transfers it to bank B who requested it. Credit bureau B acts as *circuit*–it transfers the information, but does not store it for commercial purposes. If a country has only negative information all that credit bureau A can deliver to credit bureau B is negative information.

Table 3.5

International Presence of Credit Bureaus in Europe

Entity	Country Presence
Experian	Austria, Denmark, Finland, France, Germany, Greece, Ireland, Italy, Monaco, Netherlands, Norway,[*] Spain, Sweden, United Kingdom
Equifax	United Kingdom, Ireland, Spain, Portugal
Creditinfo	Bulgaria, Czech Republic, Cyprus, Greece, Lithuania, Malta, Slovakia, Romania, Iceland,[*] Norway[*]
CRIF	Italy, United Kingdom, Czech Republic, Poland, Slovakia

Source: Experian Annual Reports, Equifax Annual Reports, Creditinfo Annual Report, CRIF, company website. [*]denotes EEC countries.

Some companies pursue the strategy of merger and acquisition; two companies are outstanding in this sense: the British-American Experian and Icelandic Creditinfo Group, the latter is a newcomer that was virtually unknown five years ago. Both companies have pursued an aggressive expansion policy, whereas Creditinfo expanded to Eastern European countries, Experian tries to expand in more mature markets. Equifax is employing a strategy in between: there are joint ventures on the one hand, while the company is also considering bilateral cross-border contracts. Presence in a country must not always mean that consumer reporting is conducted–in many cases it is the acquisition of a commercial reporting agency or of ancillary services such as card processing or credit scoring. However, it is clear that the primary intention of such expansion strategies is to become Europe's dominant credit reporting agency. For this matter, the international agencies employ the same platforms in the subsidiaries in the different countries to be able to exchange information across borders. In addition, it is observable that companies such as Experian or CRIF increasingly lobby in Brussels. Although cross-border data exchange is possible as all European members have implemented the EU Data Protection Directive, this traffic is in its infancy as stated. As stated, there are several other factors that hamper the demand for cross-border traffic such as lack of consumer demand, language and cultural differences and lack of interest on the side of the banks. Due to the differences in reporting standards and the cross-border character of services, it is maybe just a matter of time until the European Commission will act on the matter and probably even draw up a directive.

3.2 Design of Credit Reporting Systems

Public credit registers serve public interest purposes, whereas credit bureaus serve private profit interests. This is one of the main differences between these institutions: credit bureaus are profit-maximizers, public credit registers provide a public good such as stability of the banking system. In the next sections, both institutions will be discussed with regard to the following design parameters: laws and supervision, funding sources, reporting thresholds, services provided to clients, reporting institutions, information items and frequencies as well as coverage ratios and price structures. This discussion allows conclusions about the roles both information intermediaries play. Over the past years, there have been discussions at the World Bank and International Finance Corporation as to whether they play a substitution role or if they are complementary. As we will see, it depends on the institutional design of the register–public registers might be designed in a way that private credit reporting is not feasible or crowded out. Only logically, the more the public register is designed like a private credit reporting agency, the more its role will be substitutional. A public register that mimics private bureaus might be an entry barrier so that private sector activity will not develop in the long run. However, if designed in a way that allows private credit reporting, both institutions can become complementary.

Public registries are typically monopolies–this has advantages and disadvantages. Consumers deal only with one register and not with several that are in competition. Regulators also deal only with one entity. However, a public register that mimics a private bureau is likely to be slow in innovation, it might be more inefficient and more expensive, because there is no competitive pressure. In addition, know-how implementation will be also quicker in private bureaus. It differs from country to country what came first: the credit reporting agencies or the public credit register. For instance, in Belgium, Italy, Portugal and Spain, the public credit register was founded first. In Austria and Germany, private credit reporting came first. The World Bank has compiled information on credit reporting systems around the world (World Bank 2004). Most of the public credit registries have been founded in the 1980s and 1990s with some notable exceptions. The register in Germany was founded in 1934, because the Great Depression showed the disastrous impact of systemic risk. France set-up its register in 1946, the Turkish register was founded in 1951 followed by Spain (1962), Italy (1962) and Belgium (1967). During the 1980s, there was a wave of establishments: Austria (1986), Chile (1986), Malaysia (1988) and Bolivia (1989). In the 1990s, there was a second wave and more registers were founded in Latin America (Colombia, Costa Rica, or Ecuador), but also in Eastern European countries such as Lithuania and the Slovak Republic. In the Asian countries, the Asian financial crisis of 1997-1998 showed the need to keep track of the credit behaviour of large companies, but also of the increasing indebtedness of households. Therefore, public credit reporting agencies were established for supervisory purposes. In the past 5 years there has been an increasing activity of founding such entities in African countries, sometimes as public registers in the original sense and sometimes as microfinance registers.

Overall, credit bureaus developed earlier as public credit registries as noted elsewhere in this book. At the beginning, credit bureaus were locally or regionally focused and they often constituted non-profit information sharing mechanisms within industry associations. But the number of credit bureaus around the world has increased rapidly in the past, especially with the increasing employment of information technologies. In the 1980s and 1990s, innovations such as credit scoring, small business scoring and risk-based pricing were introduced. There is the hope that credit reporting can help to build up reputation of borrowers that have no assets and increases their access to finance. In addition, there are increasingly discussions how credit reporting can help to link informal lending arrangements with formal ones. The history and international activities of credit reporting agencies have been discussed in other sections in this book (the reader is referred to chapter 3). At this point it can be noted that the establishment of a public register must not prevent the entry of private players into the credit information market.

3.2.1 Laws, Supervision and Funding

Public registers are either operated by the central bank, the supervisory authority or they are contracted to a private sector entity. In Europe, all public registers are operated by the central bank, there are twelve countries that have public registers (Cyprus also has one but one that only collects information on bad cheques and Luxembourg does not have a register), see Table 3.6. The central bank might even manage several different databases–one for bad cheques, one for indebtedness monitoring of households and one for the monitoring of large corporate borrowers. This information is valuable from a supervisory point of view. In the overview of credit reporting systems and competition in the EU markets some of the features of public credit registers were explained. In the following, the design is discussed in greater detail. The central bank is typically collecting large amounts of (statistical) information on the banking industry, therefore knowledge how to handle such volumes is "institutionalized."

Even in countries that do not have a public credit register, central banks try to collect indebtedness information on large borrowers, which is part of the information requirements of a central bank and derived from its supervision function. The majority of credit bureaus are for-profit entities, as stated, but there are also some that are not-for-profit (consortia of members, foundations or industry associations). In a survey of European registers, DG Competition stated that half of the credit bureaus recorded banks and other financial companies as stakeholders, others where either non-profit or part of a holding.[46] Although there will be an extended discussion of laws and regulations further below, I give a brief indication what laws are applied.

There are different acts that apply to public and private credit registries with areas of some overlap. Laws usually regulate the set-up, the design and the activity of the public credit registry. They lay down the main tasks reporting institutions have as well as the access criteria for withdrawing data form the register. Such access criteria include credit granting activity, banking licence, sometimes physical presence in the country, reciprocity compliance and data protection law compliance (European Commission 2007). The law establishing the public register is either part of the legislation for the banking industry or the central bank act. All institutions that fall under that law have to report data to the register. In turn, only these institutions have access ("reciprocity").

---

[46] The survey did not cover all credit bureaus in Europe, only 19 from 27 (see European Commission 2007).

Table 3.6

Operation of Public Registers in the EU-27

Country	Year est.	Name	Operator
Austria	1986	Grosskreditevidenz	Central bank
Belgium	1985	Centrale des Crédits aux Particuliers	Central bank
Bulgaria	1998	Central Credit Register	Central bank
Cyprus	—	None	—
Czech Rep.	1994	Central Register of Credits	Central bank
Denmark	—	None	—
Estonia	—	None	—
Finland	—	None	—
France	1946*	Fichier National des Incidents de Remboursement des Crédits aux Particuliers	Central bank
Germany	1934*	Evidenzzentrale für Millionenkredite	Central bank
Greece	—	None	—
Hungary	—	None	—
Ireland	—	None	—
Italy	1964	Centrale dei Rischi	Central bank
Latvia	2003	Register of Debtors	Central bank
Lithuania	1996	Loan Risk Database	Central bank
Luxembourg	—	None	—
Malta	—	None	—
Netherlands	—	None	—
Poland	—	None	—
Portugal	1978	Serviço de Centralização de Riscos de Crédito	Central bank
Romania	—	None	—
Slovakia	1996	Register of Bank Loans and Guarantees	Central bank
Slovenia	1994	Kreditni portfelj bank	Central bank
Spain	1962	Central de Información de Riesgos	Central bank
Sweden	—	None	—
UK	—	None	—

Notes: Information is from the World Bank and the author; * Consumer reporting was introduced only later.

In addition, where countries do have a data protection act that covers the public and private sector–this act then also holds for the public register. This is the case in most European countries. Data protection acts demand a minimum of consumer protection standards such as access to the data, to have them corrected or deleted if obsolete. Details of information exchange are often regulated qua regulations or decrees. For the private credit registries the main law applicable is the data protection act. A general rule is that there is a data protection law and more detailed regulations designed by either the Ministry in charge or by the Data Protection Officer. There is a very small number of countries, among them Belgium and Sweden that have a general data protection act *and* an industry-specific credit reporting act. Credit reporting acts are introduced if a general data protection act is not feasible in the medium term. Two laws can lead to overlap and conflict in legislation, competing authorities and legal uncertainty. South Africa is a negative example for this: one authority pushed through regulations of credit bureaus while the other at the same time drafted a data protection law and both institutions did not talk to each other.

Sometimes the industry is also regulated by codes of conduct (such as in Italy and United Kingdom) or industry guidelines. The supervisory institution in charge for the public register is in many cases the central bank, for credit bureaus it is the Data Protection Officer or a ministry that publishes regulations. Sometimes the latter function and the enforcement function are separated. The exact design of the legislation will depend on the situation in the individual country. The funding sources for both types of registries differ. Public credit registries are funded by the central bank, participants are sometimes charged a usage fee, but in the majority of cases, public registers do not charge fees for joining or for transactions, because there is no intention to make profit. Rather the activity is conducted in the public interest for increasing the stability of the banking sector, the participation is mandatory. Of course, funding for private credit reporting agency comes from the banking industry and all others that buy reports. As credit bureaus compete, funding comes from volumes of sold credit reports, but also from other services such as scoring and risk management, marketing and consultancy services.

3.2.2 Reporting Thresholds and Services

Another important feature to distinguish both types of institutions is the reporting threshold. This threshold marks what loans are reported to the register (for instance, above 2.000 Euros). Sometimes the threshold also denotes what amount of outstanding indebtedness a borrower must surpass so that his/her name is reported to the register. Therefore, a threshold is fairly important for a country that wants to develop a dual credit reporting system–but it is not the only institutional parameter of importance. A rule of thumb is that the reporting thresholds of credit bureaus are lower than for public credit registers as they cover retail lending and other services such as telecommunication. Some of the EU-27 countries show a relatively high threshold for the public register such as Austria, Germany and Italy. In the medium range is Lithuania and Spain and on the lower end Belgium, France, Latvia, Portugal and Slovenia. There are also several countries that do not have a public credit registry, Denmark, Greece, Ireland, Sweden, UK and U.S. In these markets, private credit reporting agencies are the only players and some of them record loans of any type. The question for policymakers is if they want both institutions or if they want to create a public monopoly. Usually, the market is broad enough that different types of information intermediaries can be sustained. It is not a question of *either* private credit bureaus *or* public registries, but of how to design both. It certainly also depends on the reporting threshold as to whether public and private credit registries are substitutes. But even if the threshold is relatively low (as in the case of Spain and Portugal), this does not automatically mean that private credit bureaus are pushed out of business as there are other parameters of differentiation. Both institutions provide different services to their clients or associated reporting institutions. Whereas the public registry is part of the supervisory structure in a country, the credit bureau is usually operating in a competitive environment. For this reason, the latter provides a wider range of services and develops new products and services for their clients more frequently. The information public registries collect is more comprehensive and more complete (regarding the institutions that report to them) than that of credit bureaus, because reporting is mandatory. Credit reporting agencies, on the other hand, have a wider variety of sources that furnish data–but this is subject to the next section.

All of the public registries provide raw indebtedness data on consumers and on businesses if there is positive-negative information sharing. Such data are also provided by private agencies. Not all public institutions provide credit scores, but private credit bureaus often do. For credit bureaus, score development is a major product line. If clients (i.e. banks) want to merge raw data with their own application data, credit bureaus deliver raw data and if clients want to see the bureau score, they deliver the score only. As stated in the sections on competition in information markets, there is the tendency to bundle and version the information and to sell it for many different purposes.

Scores can be tailored to the needs of the specific industry (banking, insurance, telecoms) or to specific products (consumer loans, mortgages). In addition to the creditworthiness assessment, credit bureaus also provide fraud prevention and tracking services (such as address verification) and marketing services (profitability scoring or customer identification). Especially the latter–marketing–is a major line of income for bureaus that develop customer relationship management programs and all kinds of consultancy services. Public credit register data, on the other hand, are used for supervision purposes such as determining the total indebtedness of individuals or corporations, to identify conglomerates, industry trends or banks that make risky loans. A general rule of thumb is that the group of firms that report to the public register is narrower defined than that reporting to the private registry. In some countries, a higher number of firms provide information to the public credit registry compared to the number of firms providing information to the private credit bureaus (this is the case for Germany, Italy and Spain). Institutions that report to the public register typically encompass public and private commercial banks, development banks, credit unions and cooperatives and finance corporations. If reporting to the registry is mandatory, these institutions *must* use the public register, but they *may* use the credit bureau. There is certainly area of overlap, where institutions report to both. However, some companies do not report to the public credit register, but only to the private credit bureau. These are typically credit card issuers, merchants and retailers, mail-order industry and telecommunication firms which are not under direct supervision of the central bank, but still engage in credit granting and deferred payment services. In addition, the bureaus create value-added by collecting information from further sources such as courts or tribunals. The information collected by private credit bureaus is proprietary and sensitive, however, it is also mixed with public information such as bankruptcies.

Neither in Germany nor in Italy, Portugal or Spain information is shared between public register and credit bureau. To the author's knowledge such arrangements do not exist in Europe. There are only few countries that have such information sharing regimes: Argentina, Columbia, Ecuador, Peru and South Africa. In these countries, credit bureaus can access the information stored in a registry. Majnoni et al. (2004) note that "the existence of a PCR can assist entry into the private credit bureau market by lowering entry costs in making a set of basic credit information available at low cost." This is true, but the "artificial lowering" of market entry barriers may also lead to an inefficiently high number of credit bureaus in the market. South Korea seems to be an example for this. This practice of providing access for credit reporting agencies is rare. Public institutions in Europe sometimes pool information as is the case with the Registry Trust in the UK, a database of court judgements to which credit bureaus have access. While it is a good idea to pool information that is public and to provide access to it, it is not common practice in European countries to provide access to the public credit register.

3.2.3 Information Collected, Delivery Modes and Fees

There are no clear patterns in terms of what information is collected by both institutions. Most credit registers (public and private) collect name and address or taxpayer's ID of the borrower. Also, the name of the reporting institution is collected (but not always disclosed for competitive reasons) as well as the amount and type of loan. Some collect the maturity of a loan, the type and value of collateral or guarantees. Further information beyond the common information categories includes: arrears, income, utility payment records, bad check lists, court judgements and bankruptcy procedures. This kind of information is primarily collected by private credit reporting agencies. The typical updating cycle for most of the public credit registries and private credit reporting bureaus is a monthly cycle. However, it may also be every second month (Spain) or quarterly (Germany). This might be sufficient for supervision matters, but maybe not for consumer credit and mortgage lending, where decisions to grant credit should be based upon up-to-date information. The data are delivered via computer disks or CDs or via written documents. In Germany, Italy, Portugal and Spain this data delivery is done over modems, dedicated phone lines, computer disks or CDs. Private credit reporting agencies, on the other hand also allow different modes of access such as via internet, telephone lines or fax. Private credit registries typically do not disclose how many individuals they have stored. Therefore, only estimates are available. These estimates for individual years or coverage ratios have been compiled by the World Bank. In countries, where the public register has a high threshold (Italy and Germany), the number of private individuals stored in the private register surpasses that of the public register. In countries, where the threshold is lower, it is the other way round. In Portugal and Spain the coverage rates are lower for the private credit registries compared to the public one. There is only limited information on the fee structure of public registries and private credit bureaus. The latter group regards this as trade secret that has to be kept privately. Some general observations can be made here. As explained, many public credit registers do neither demand transaction fee nor annual fee or joining fee. Those public registers that charge for the information services do so according to the size of the bank (based upon balance sheet assessment). Credit reporting agencies have several different ways to charge for their services. Prices are differentiated according: (a) Type of information shared (positive-negative, negative only); (b) Modus of delivery (web-based, paper, telephone); and (c) Volume requested (high volumes justify lower prices). Credit bureaus negotiate with financial service providers the prices and might in some cases induce them to share complete information by offering lower prices. if more data items are shared. If credit bureaus charge different prices for negative and positive information, positive information is more expensive. If they charge according to delivery modus, the most cumbersome paper-based delivery is the most expensive. Altogether the above discussion showed that credit bureaus and public credit registers differ in their design in a way that private and public actors can co-exist. I have discussed these differences with regard to laws and supervision, funding, reporting thresholds, services provided to clients, reporting institutions, data items and frequencies as well as coverage ratios and price structures. Governments that carefully plan the design of their public credit register will be able to also have a sustainable credit reporting industry.

4 Regulation of Credit Reporting

Economic analysis of information yields the power to predict the business partner, the power to negotiate and to set contract terms. In the political realm information collections have been used in the past for political oppression. More and more policy makers are aware that people should not only enjoy protection of their information in the political realm but also in the economic one. Data protection originated in Europe, but around the world more and more countries are adopting data protection laws. In addition, there are several international institutions that deal with data protection, although for now it is not clear which institution will play the leading role in setting standards. In the following I discuss the data protection trends around the world. In addition, four country cases are presented in-depth: U.S., Germany, Great Britain and France.

4.1 International Data Protection Overview

The majority of the countries on earth, do not have data protection laws. However, those that have enacted such laws typically follow the European model for the simple reason of ensuring adequacy of data protection. By August 2005, 24 nations had adopted laws inspired by or based upon the EU Data Protection Directive. This group of countries included not only EU members or accession states in Eastern Europe, but also some nations in Latin America or Hong Kong. Data protection is one of the few fields, where the EU proved to be more successful in exporting its standards than the U.S. One of the reasons is the demanding "extraterritorial principle" in the EU Directive. According to this principle, personal data on Europeans should be only exported to countries that provide adequate data protection. This must not mean similar data protection, but legislation that the EU Commission finds is worth to be awarded the label "adequate." The methodology of awarding the standard is described in the section on extraterritorial clauses. In the following, a short overview over the major regions is presented.

European Union: The European Union has developed a "harmonized regime" that is applied in all EU member countries. It has served as an example for other countries around the world. The protection covers both the public and the private sector. Although the directive remains below the average of rights and duties as implemented in the member states as we will later see, ranks among the highest protection regimes in the world.

Pacific Rim: In the case of the U.S., Australia and New Zealand, data protection is based upon different combinations of common and case law, administrative law and legislative rights. Together, these countries' legislations are based upon the English law tradition. In these regimes, basic data protection rights are granted, but especially the U.S. is a country with lower protection than in other nations. In general these countries grant a lower number of property rights to the individual such as the right to opt-out, to have data blocked or erased.

Asia: In Asia, there is no coherent picture, but these countries seem to be far behind in their development of up-to-date standards. China does not have a data protection law. However, the country has developed some basic standards for its public credit register. Japan, a country with German legal origin has only recently introduced a very incomplete law. Hong Kong was the first nation in the region to enact a law based upon the Data Protection Directive of the European Union, the Data Privacy Law (Ordinance). South Korea has a law on credit reporting which reflects very little understanding and knowledge of the industry and is basically a market entry regulation. Due to major problems in the market, regulators started to discuss revisions of the law. This was also the case in Thailand, a country with an industry-specific credit reporting law. In Singapore there is no general data protection act, but only some provisions in the e-commerce legislation. The ad hoc practices in Asian countries generally provide lower data protection compared to Europe. The protection of financial data is mainly derived from Banking Acts in South Korea and Singapore.

Latin America: With the democratic changes in the Latin American countries, human rights, including the right to privacy, were established. In some countries such as Brazil, Paraguay, Peru, Ecuador or Columbia, the constitution incorporates the so-called "Habeas Data." This is a constitutional right to access all information stored on the individual in public or private records. Several countries in the region grant access to information of credit bureaus as well as correction possibilities as is the case in Argentina, Brazil, Columbia, Chile and Peru (del Villar, de Leon and Gil Hubert 2003). Some of the nations have taken the European regulations as a model. However, the constitutional protection of personal data is new. In European countries the more general right of privacy is protected or indirectly protected. In addition, in a number of countries, international advisers have drafted industry-specific laws and regulations, strongly promoted by international institutions.

Africa: In many African countries no data protection exists and where credit reporting systems are introduced, policymakers prefer ad hoc rules for it. International donors and institutions essentially promote industry-specific laws in the countries or amendment/changes to banking laws. However, South Africa is the first country to adopt credit reporting regulations (under the National Credit Act) and there is a data protection law planned. It is considered to be the forerunner in this respect for other African countries. In Uganda, a relatively incomplete regulation was drafted and in 2007, Tanzania was at the verge of developing new regulations.[47] Malawi and Mozambique reported that individuals have no right to access their data and the same holds for Niger, Nigeria and Senegal. Countries without laws do not guarantee other important rights such as correction and dispute settlement. Most of the African countries such as Benin, Botswana, Burkina Faso, Cameroon or Mozambique do not have laws or develop "codes of conduct."

Middle East: For Syria, Libya and Iran–countries not especially known for democratic traditions–data protection seems to not play any role. In the United Arab Emirates there seems to be the same situation, also in Saudi Arabia. In Egypt a law was drafted that is relatively basic and provides a low standard of consumer protection. By looking at the formal regulation via law the picture is bleak for these countries that grant their citizens in most cases not even the most basic rights. In addition, the public either lacks an awareness or interest in this topic.

From the above discussion, it can be concluded that data protection is directly related to economic development. It is associated with technological progress: countries that have a more developed technical infrastructure are also more likely to have data protection rules.

---

[47] International advise in this field is not always of high quality, as many advisers are covering also related fields (such as microfinance regulation) and have little understanding of credit reporting itself.

4.2 The Regulatory Regime in the U.S.

The first country to regulate credit reporting was the U.S. Credit reporting had developed over the latter half of the 19th Century and affected an ever greater number of people. Consumers did not know about the information sharing, they had no access to credit records and credit bureaus sold the information to who ever had any kind of interest and the system was prone to misuse. Consumers were increasingly disgruntled. The hearings that took place before the first law was enacted in the U.S. are testimony of the negative experiences consumers made with the unregulated industry. Americans did not enact a general data protection law, but instead followed an industry specific approach. In the next sections, I discuss the most important regulations and their changes in the U.S. over the past 30 years. This will provide the reader with some interesting insights about the interaction of credit reporting and its regulation.

4.2.1 Fair Credit Reporting Act of 1970

The Fair Credit Reporting Act was the first law to specifically target an information industry in the U.S. Credit reporting bureaus were the first kind of industry to be regulated in terms of data protection. U.S. politics is often reactive–it needed strong public pressure to convince legislators to act on this matter. The Fair Credit Reporting Act (FCRA) is by far the most important statute in U.S. credit reporting to date. Therefore, I will present the most important rules and how they have been changed. The historical overview turns out to be interesting, because it provides a historical recount of what actually worked in terms of regulations and what created problems in the market. This is an important lesson for other countries that start to regulate the industry. Without the knowledge about the history of credit reporting regulation in the most advances countries it is not possible to judge the quality of laws and regulations drafted by international self-entitled "expert" advisers for developing countries. Put differently: legislators (or their advisers as in many developing countries) draw up an initial distribution of property rights, but this distribution might be sub-optimal and lead to negative externalities in the market. This leads to public pressure and to renew legislation–probably even re-distribution of the property rights to information between data subjects and data collectors. These problems can be circumvented if–from the beginning on–an approximately optimal separation of property rights is implemented. The main rules of

FCRA are permissible purposes for disclosing credit records, procedures for disputing inaccuracies and basic obligations for record users. The law also defines credit reporting agencies.[48] Box 4.1 shows the permissible purposes. In the U.S., credit reporting agencies have lobbied to use the information for many other purposes, unrelated to creditworthiness. In the section on competition in information markets, it was discussed that there is an incentive to version and bundle information. This is exactly the strategy when credit reporting agencies repackage the data or display it in another way to further cover purposes that are not directly related with credit granting. Some credit bureaus sell the data for employment or tenant screening, for profitability scoring or for marketing. Note that some of these practices are forbidden in European countries for very good reasons. In Germany, no employer would ask for the credit record as it is considered to be unnecessary for the assessment of the potential employee and as far too intrusive. This will be discussed further below.

Box 4.1 Permissible Purposes for Disclosure in the U.S.

There are four main purposes for which records can be disclosed according to the FCRA of 1970. That is in connection with:

- A credit transaction;
- The underwriting of insurance;
- Any other business transaction initiated by the consumer; and
- Any other purpose if the report user has a legitimate business need;

The latter is a very general clause that covers any other needs for disclosure and it is a controversial question as to whether credit records should be used for purposes that are essentially unrelated to creditworthiness assessment.

In terms of dispute settlement, the FCRA prescribes that the bureau must verify the disputed data or delete it. Inaccurate information must be corrected.[49] It is important to acknowledge that action concerning inaccuracies can only be taken against credit bureaus, *not against the information furnisher* (the bank, telecom provider or any other company that furnishes in-

---

[48] A "credit reporting agency" is defined as any person who for profit and non-profit regularly engages in the practice of assembling and evaluating consumer credit information for the purpose of furnishing consumer reports to third parties.

[49] If the information is still disputed even after the investigation by the credit bureau, the consumer may file a statement with his/her point of view and this statement has to be distributed with the report in the future.

formation). The latter was not considered to be a credit reporting agency under the law. This rule carried a high price for many consumers as we will later see. But there were more gaps. For instance, access rights were only applied to the agencies and not to the business that obtained the credit report. This means the consumer could only ask the credit bureau to disclose information stored upon him/her, not the credit provider. For the users of such records duties only arose where the consumer experienced adverse action such as the decline of credit or the decline of an increase of a credit line. It is doubtful that this is the most efficient rules as some might assume. In this case, the creditor had to inform the client which agency furnished him with the record.

Figure 4.1
Fair Credit Reporting Act of 1970

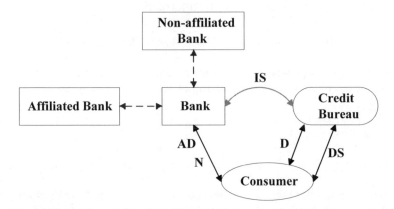

Figure 4.1 maps the rules. The abbreviations denote rights and responsibilities of participants. Bank and credit bureau share information (IS) on the consumer. If the consumer wants to have information disclosed (D), he/she must approach the bureau, also in case of dispute settlement (DS). The bureau was obliged by law to follow "reasonable procedures to assure maximum possible accuracy" (FCRA §607[b]) in compiling information. In case of adverse action (AD), the consumer had to be notified (N) by the bank. [50] The bank did not have to explain to the consumer with whom ever else the information was shared (for instance, affiliates). The figure is an example of insufficient and incomplete regulation of credit reporting. It disregards the network nature of the industry, a network of furnishers, users and data subjects, where the credit bureau is the central exchange circuit.

---

[50] "Adverse action" relates to all business, insurance, credit and employment actions that have a negative impact on the consumer, for example credit denial or promotion denial.

For years this act created problems, because of its incomplete approach. The FCRA did not place any burden on information furnishers: neither were they obliged to provide accurate data, nor did the consumer have the right to approach the bank to see the information they had stored. However, this is a precondition for correcting information. Note that I explain the law in its literal terms–I do not take into account as to whether banks actually offered this kind of service to consumers. What counts here is that they were not obliged by law to do so. Instead, the law placed the primary burden on the credit bureau–the party with the least interest in consumer privacy and the highest costs of information verification (Maurer and Robert 1997). Additionally, legislation demanded for the investigation of disputed information to be only completed within a "reasonable period of time." This proved to be insufficient: in 1991, the U.S. Federal Trade Commission reported that it took an average of 23 months (!) to correct mistakes in credit reports (Reidenberg and Schwartz 1996: 299). Above all the whole system of information sharing essentially remained non-transparent for consumers. This will be also the case in developing countries if regulations are applied that mimic U.S. regulation in the 1970s and 1980s. Consumers had no idea who collected their information and for what purposes it was shared. In addition, they had little understanding of the workings of information markets and that there is profit in bundling and versioning of their information. There was no explicit right to see the predictive score calculated from credit record information. Neither did the FCRA mandate any responsibilities for updating or correcting of data on the side of information furnishers. Mistakes often multiplied and resurfaced over and over again (so called *re-pollution*). Consumers would try to root them out by approaching many institutions, however without information furnishers obliged to correct the information, mistakes would resurface with every new updating cycle.[51] This regime was not changed for more than 25 years, lobbying from the side of the financial services industry and credit bureaus seem to have defeated attempts to change the law. Only in the 1990s, consumer associations had grown much stronger in the U.S. and the pressure increased to change the system.

---

[51] The updating cycles in the industry mean that banks send tapes with their data to the credit bureaus every month. These data are then fed into the credit bureaus' databases.

4.2.2 Consumer Credit Reporting Reform Act of 1996

The first important act to amend the FCRA significantly was signed into law by President Clinton in 1996. It was the Consumer Credit Reporting Reform Act (CCRRA) that went into effect in 1997. Initially, the U.S. Federal Trade Commission was the only body in charge for the regulation of credit reporting, but the new act transferred the oversight also to the Comptroller of the Currency and the Federal Reserve Board–both institutions oversee the financial services industry. What were the most important changes? The law primarily closed the loopholes discussed earlier. Now the credit bureau had to investigate inaccuracy claims, inform the consumer about the results and provide him/her with a free credit report. It was prescribed that mistakes had to be removed within 30 days. The largest agencies are now required to notify each other if items in the report have been changed or deleted. This is done through a joint notification system of national credit bureaus (U.S. Federal Trade Commission 1997a). This is a good idea considered that there are several credit bureaus in the market and the consumer would have to go to each to have mistakes corrected. The re-insertion of inaccurate data was forbidden. For the first time, the CCRRA also established duties and liabilities for information furnishers such as banks. They were now prohibited to disclose information that they know or *"consciously avoid knowing"* is inaccurate. They are also obligated to correct, update and resubmit data. In addition, they have to inform all credit reporting agencies to which they had submitted the data of the corrections. Again, this is necessary if there are several credit reporting agencies in the market. It should be the duty of banks to correct information with all parties that have received the information within a particular time frame. If the information is in dispute between bank and customer, this has to be indicated to the credit reporting agency. Let us have a look at the new structure of the law after this reform. At the first sight, Figure 4.2 shows that much more information flows were introduced among the network participants. Bank and credit bureau now had to notify each other (N) if mistakes were found. The biggest national credit bureaus had to set up a notification system to inform each other of corrections. The consumer could now dispute (DS) the information also with the bank. If a bank wanted to share information with an *affiliate*, the consumer had to be notified (N) and provided with the right to opt-out (O). "opt-out" means that the consumer's consent is assumed until the consumer explicitly forbids the information sharing. This places the burden onto the consumer.

Figure 4.2
Consumer Credit Reporting Reform Act of 1996

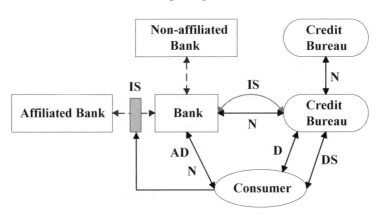

For consumers, the reform introduced the right to update data and to block disputed data. Note that these are again new property rights that are granted to the consumer. This illustrates how negative externalities led to a relocation of property rights as discussed in the theoretical chapter of this book. However, there was still no "opt-in"–a major difference to the European regimes where the consumer in many cases has to give explicit consent for data processing. Also credit scoring was left out of the law, it did not have to be explained to the consumer, nor did the institutions have an obligation to disclose the credit score. The CCRRA allowed affiliates to share credit information, but only after notification and opt-out.[52] With the new act, so-called "experience information" could be shared without limit, this information derives directly from the relationship with the customer. Some other, further corrections were important. Although financial institutions were not legally required to report delinquencies, if they decided to do so month and year of the delinquency had to be included. For the credit bureau this is a reference date for calculating the retention period of the data (Fischer and McEneney 1997: 9). Moreover, if a consumer closed an account voluntarily, this fact had to be indicated as well. Credit report users had to certify the purposes for which they wanted to obtain the report and they had to certify that it was not used for other purposes. If the report served as basis for an adverse action the consumers had to be informed

---

[52] In the past, the regulatory agencies restricted data sharing among members of the same holding and treated them as unrelated third persons. For this reason, they often refrained from information sharing altogether (Fischer and McEneney 1997: 6).

about it.[53] Such a notification had to include the name of the agency and its toll-free number. Creditors and insurers that ask for pre-screening lists had to make a "firm offer of credit" to the listed individuals. In the past, this included the granting of a loan or the opening of an account (Fischer and McEneney 1997: 6). Such an offer could only been withdrawn in unusual circumstances such as that of bankruptcy.[54] An alternative is that firms inform consumers that the offer is no *firm* offer. These details are important as they literally show which problems had to be mended. Also under this law the consumer had an opportunity to opt-out of pre-screening. The majority of these provisions is still in effect today.

4.2.3 Consumer Reporting Employment Clarification Act of 1998

One of the most controversial areas in the law and its amendments is the sale of a credit reports for employment purposes. Employers are in general interested in background checks: they use criminal records, credential verification, other records such as those on motor vehicles or security number searches. In the U.S. it was also allowed to share credit reports for employment purposes. While in general the verification of data in the application is certainly necessary, it is questionable that credit data should be disclosed to employers. This is essentially in contrary to international privacy standards that state that information should be used for the purpose for which it was collected in the first place and not for any unrelated purposes. Employment screening and pre-screening is done in a more pervasiveness manner than ever before, and used for hiring for jobs that require the handling of (even small) amounts of money to government contractors or people who enter homes to provide. It is now even used in the temporary help services industry. What was originally intended to only cover security-sensitive jobs in the financial services industry and in government has now expanded into many other areas of economic life and it creates increasingly problems for consumers that are affected by such information sharing. The Consumer Reporting Employment Clarification Act (CRECA) of 1998 amended the FCRA in stating that no party might obtain a credit report for employment purposes without the explicit consent and written authorization of the consumer. Read: this is opt-in and new property rights assigned to the consumer. Also, any party that intends to obtain a report for

---

[53] The consumer must react within 60 days to get a free credit report.
[54] This event had to occur between pre-screening of the customer and his acceptance of the offer.

such purposes must inform the consumer about it. The FCRA prohibits consumer reporting agencies from providing adverse information that is more than seven years old (or ten years in the case of bankruptcies) for employment purposes. However, there are major exemptions, where the annual salary is more than US-$ 75.000, there are no restrictions upon reporting adverse information for jobs. The act (that had to reverse some of the clauses in the CCRRA) provided for a relaxation of obsolescence restrictions for criminal convictions that are older than seven years for jobs below the US-$ 75.000 threshold. Altogether one may severely doubt that this law is providing consumers with a higher level of protection, although it introduced a clear opt-in. This is again a move of property rights back to the consumer due to the severe negative effects of such information sharing. The main question is if this is really "consent." The reader might ask if he/she would decline such a request in the precarious situation of a job interview. As discussed in the section on versioning and "purpose creep," consumers can be locked-out of the job market as it already happens in the U.S., in South Korea and China. It is only a question of time, until this also happens in South Africa, where politicians rigorously pushed for the allowance of employment reporting, despite being warned about it from several sides. The point is once the problems start to surface in the market they have to be mended by re-distributing property rights back to the consumer–something that should have been done from the beginning.

4.2.4 Financial Services Modernization Act of 1999

In recognizing significant technological changes in the 1990s, President Clinton pledged that he would not allow "new opportunities to erode old and fundamental rights." (Office of the Press Secretary 2000: 1) He emphasized that medical and financial information should receive special protection. The latter was codified in the Financial Services Modernization Act of 1999 (FSMA). The act imposes privacy regulations on financial services institutions, now information flows among financial institutions and non-affiliated third parties were regulated. It is important to note that Congress did not intend to revise the FCRA by approving the FSMA. Instead, the FCRA regulates information sharing among affiliates and with credit bureaus, while the FSMA emphasizes the regulation of sharing arrangements of financial institutions with all non-affiliates. U.S. legislators could have spared themselves and the industry this artificially complex regulatory pattern if they would have applied a general data protection act in the first place.

Figure 4.3
Financial Services Modernization Act of 1999

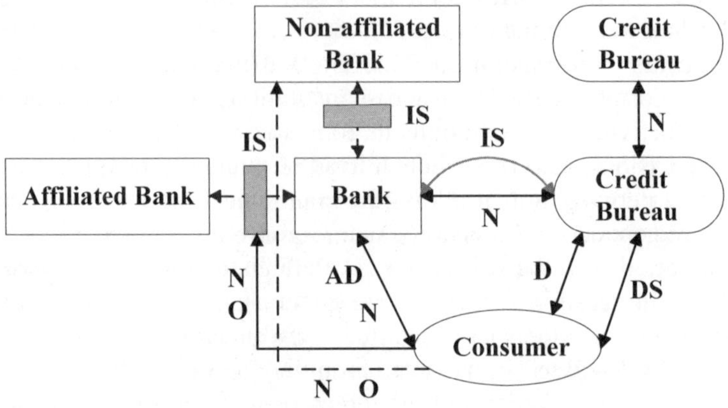

Figure 4.3 shows that the aforementioned rules remained basically un-touched: disclosure (D), dispute (DS), adverse action (AD), notification obligations (N) and information sharing (IS) remained unchanged. How-ever, new obligations for financial service providers that are information furnishers (and users) were introduced. If a bank wants to share non-experience information such a credit reports with affiliated or non-affiliated parties, the consumer now has to be provided with a notice of that sharing (N) and with an opt-out (O) opportunity. Again, new prop-erty rights assigned to the consumer. Formerly only the sharing with af-filiates was regulated. Banks now essentially have to explain their privacy policy to the consumer. This policy statement has to be "clear, accurate and conspicuous" (U.S. Federal Reserve Board et al. 2000: 1). It must be made at the beginning of a customer relationship and afterwards annually, during the continuation of the relationship. This has been said to produce enormous amounts of trash: notices that consumers simply throw away. Second, credit data may not be shared with unrelated third parties unless the institution has provided notice and opt-out and the consumer has not used the latter (U.S. Federal Reserve Board 2001c: 386). The whole set of rules is now even more complex than before: Data received by the bank from other financial institutions or from a credit bureau may be re-vealed to affiliates of the own corporate family or affiliates of the credit bureau. If these members intend to provide the information to another third party, they can do so only to the extent the first user was allowed to do so (U.S. Federal Trade Commission 2001c: 387).

This also holds for information sharing with a non-affiliate. If a bank discloses information to a non-affiliate that party may in turn only disclose the information to other third parties if the disclosure would have been lawful for the bank in the first place.[55] Thus, the receiving party "steps into the shoes" of the financial institution that made the initial disclosure (U.S. Federal Trade Commission 2000a: 33367). This is intended to provide a consistency of privacy policies across institutions despite different privacy rules. The activities of credit bureaus constitute a major exception from the FSMA provisions. The U.S. Federal Trade Commission explained this approach as a permission that allows the continuation of the credit reporting business in general (U.S. Federal Trade Commission 2000a: 33668). Since all information that banks transfer to credit bureaus is considered to be "non-public personal information" and data sharing with non-affiliates is exactly what banks do when they share information with credit bureaus. Therefore, they had to be exempted from the notice/opt-out requirements: "A customer has *no right to prohibit those disclosures or even to know more* than that the disclosures are being made `as permitted by law'." (U.S. Federal Trade Commission 2000a: 33667, emphasis added). Again, an opportunity missed to make the credit reporting regime more transparent for consumers. A rule of thumb is that consumers should always be informed with whom their data are shared. Whereas the FCRA only mandated the power of interpretation of these statutes, the FSMA amended the FCRA in vesting the rulemaking authority in several functional regulators: the U.S. Federal Trade Commission, the Federal Reserve Board, the Comptroller of the Currency and even die Security and Exchange Commission. These agencies have emphasized three main requirements: disclosure, annual notices and opt-out options (U.S. Federal Reserve Board et al. 2000; U.S. Federal Trade Commission 2000b).

"Information remedies are most likely to be the most effective solution to information problems. They deal with the cause of the problem, rather than its symptoms, and leave the market maximum flexibility." (Beales, Craswell and Salop 1981: 413) The FTC acknowledged this rule at the beginning of the 1980s. The agency also realized natural monopoly and free-rider problems in information markets and described market power problems, but only by referring to product markets and advertisement. Beales, Craswell and Salop (1981) state that there are several information remedies that can be introduced when information problems are faced by market participants: the removal of information restrains measures for truthful and complete information and measures that affect disclosures. In general,

---

[55] See FSMA, 15 U.S.C. Section 6802 [c] and U.S. Federal Trade Commission (2000a: 33366).

such insights also hold for credit reporting regulations, where policy makers must identify the origin of problems, before applying regulations. Information problems demand information solutions. Other solutions are second best.

4.2.5 Fair and Accurate Credit Transactions Act of 2003

The version of the FCRA that went into effect in 1997 was temporary legislation due to certain sunset provisions, which are further discussed below. Apart from these provisions, several other problems surfaced in the 1990s: Identity theft proved to be the fastest growing crime in the U.S. and the Fair and Accurate Credit Transactions Act of 2003 (FACTA) was supposed to become a tool for consumers to prevent and fight this crime. For this purpose it added some new sections to the FCRA. One of the main reasons for changing the law yet another time were the aforementioned sunset provisions of the FCRA of 1996 (as amended by the CCRRA) such as pre-screening purposes, adverse action requirements and responsibilities of information furnishers. The provisions were originally set to expire in January 1, 2004 ("sunset"). The renewal, however, came with the Fair and Accurate Credit Transactions Act of 2003 that was signed into law by U.S. President George W. Bush. To improve the quality of credit information, the new act places the main burden of monitoring on the consumer, who now has the right to get a free report once a year. The conference report (U.S. House of Representatives 2003: 47) also states that unemployed consumers (including those on welfare) may request a free credit report once a year from regional and local consumer reporting agencies in addition to a credit report from each national consumer reporting agency. After providing reasonable proof of identity and a police report on the theft of identity, consumers may now block certain information in the profile that resulted from the theft. This ensures that transactions made by thieves do not impair the credit report.

Figure 4.4
The Fair and Accurate Credit Transactions Act of 2003

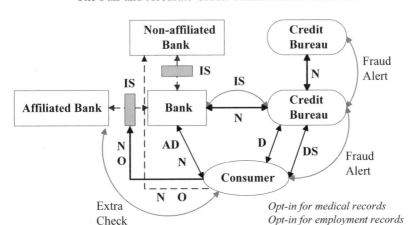

Figure 4.4 shows that the main transactions such as notice (N), opt-out (O), dispute settlement (DS), adverse action (AD) or disclosure (D) remained unchanged and that new obligations have been added. These are explained in the following. Firstly, Congress acknowledged the benefit of self-monitoring and provided the consumer with the right to get one free credit report per year from one of the national credit reporting agencies. If the consumer had been victim of identity theft it was now possible to flag the account (fraud alert). This means that the consumer does not want to have credit extended without special permission. For placing the fraud alert, the consumer must provide proof of identity to the credit bureau. The fraud alert is initially effective for 90 days, but can be extended for seven years. These flags alarm the creditor to conduct "reasonable steps" to verify if it is not an identity thief they are dealing with after receiving an application for credit. Items on the record that resulted from identity theft can be blocked. When a fraud alert is placed, the consumer is entitled to a free credit report. Also, the consumer will be excluded from pre-screening lists for two years. In addition, companies must now truncate full account numbers and expiration dates, one of the main sources for identity thieves. Another aspect is that consumers now have the right to see their credit scores. Upon a "reasonable fee" they have to be provided with the most recently calculated credit score, the range of possible scores, the top 4 negative key factors used, the date the score was created, and the name of the company

providing the underlying file or score.[56] Moreover, the new law grants opt-in for the provision of reports that contain medical information. For the inclusion of medical information in a report as part of an insurance transaction, the consumer's consent is also needed. The new act changed the level of care of furnishers. They may not report information if they have "*reasonable cause to believe that the information is inaccurate.*" As explained by the conference report on the bill (House of Representatives 2003: 44): "This 'reasonable cause to believe' standard is based on actual knowledge of the furnisher of factual information that would cause a reasonable person to believe that the information is not accurate." The furnisher has to follow reasonable practices to ensure the accuracy of data. This does not mean that all data must be accurate. This would hardly be achievable. However, it establishes the new right of consumers to request reinvestigation of the information directly from the *information furnisher*. Furnishers have to set up a system, where consumers can notify them of disputes and they have the obligation to investigate the disputed information within 30 days. The furnisher has to present the results to the consumer and in case of inaccuracies; he has to inform the credit reporting agencies promptly. The credit reporting agency must now reconcile differing addresses by notifying the user of the report that addresses differ. Furthermore, if consumers request their profiles, these reports also have to include the address and contact numbers of the information furnisher as well as those who requested the profile. Also, national credit bureaus have to inform each other about fraud alerts, again this is something that is advisable for countries that want to have a private credit reporting industry. Moreover, the nationwide agencies must establish procedures for referring consumer complaints of identity theft and requests for blocks or fraud alerts to the other nationwide agencies. Let us briefly summarize the development in the U.S. The probably most striking observation is that market developments challenged the existing regulations and led to a revision of the legislation: over the course of the years, more and more obligations have been added for credit bureaus as well as for information furnishers. Consumers, on the other hand, have been assigned *more property rights to their information.* The free credit report set aside, consumers now have opt-in rights for medical and employment. In addition, the law has now made it easier to opt-out of marketing such as pre-screening and to place fraud alerts. Altogether, the misaligned and incomplete regime had to be revised several times–more often than in European countries as we will see. One of the major reasons for this is that from the beginning the U.S. embarked on an

---

[56] Under the Equal Credit Opportunity Act (ECOA) a creditor who made an adverse action is required to disclose the principal reasons that most contributed to the adverse action.

industry oriented regulation path, disregarding some of the features of network industries. This may create problems it was argued above– incompletely informed policy makers (or their advisers) might create such regimes that later have to be revised, because of the problems surfacing in the market.

4.3 Regulatory Regimes in Europe

Approaches to privacy should never be judged without the historical knowledge about the reasons why such an approach developed in the first place. Any critical analysis of privacy laws should include the origin and initial problem that was tackled with these laws. Briefly after the capitulation of Germany and the end of World War II., European nations agreed to define privacy as a fundamental human right. This was proclaimed in the Universal Declaration of Human Rights (UDHR) of 1948, based upon the reasoning that "disregard and contempt for human rights have resulted in barbarous acts which have outraged the conscience of mankind (...)." Article 12 of the Declaration states:

> *"No one shall be subjected to arbitrary interference with his privacy, family, home or correspondence, nor to attacks upon his honor and reputation. Everyone has the right to the protection of the law against such interference or attacks."*

The historical background for this is rarely mentioned. Europe, especially Germany, Italy and several East European countries had experienced dictatorships. "One factor that enabled the Nazis to efficiently round up, transport and seize assets of Jews (and others they viewed as 'undesirables') was the extensive repositories of personal data available not only from the public sector but also from private sector sources." (Samuelson 2000: 1144; Swire 1999). In the Holocaust under the rule of Hitler (1933-1945), the Nazis killed more than 6 million Jews. For this matter they also used personal information recorded in government files such as census data and commercial files including telephone and bank records for tracking down Jews, resistance activists, communists or others. This is one of the reasons why privacy is especially strictly protected in Germany and France (Green 2001). Also, in other countries such as in the Netherlands,

Nazis accessed lists of people and their religious affiliation.[57] In fact, it coined European consciousness so much that it is not only reflected in privacy legislation, but also in anti-discrimination laws. European data protection laws are said to have the "hidden agenda" of discouraging a recurrence of the Nazi Gestapo efforts to control the population, "and so seek to prevent the reappearance of an oppressive bureaucracy that might use existing data for nefarious purposes. This concern is such a vital foundation of current legislation that it is rarely expressed in formal discussions." (Flaherty 1989: 373 - 374) The author also describes this as rationale behind the strict legal regime for all kinds of data collections, public and private, respectively. The right to privacy can only be restricted by a public authority in accordance with domestic law and only inasmuch as it is necessary in a democratic society. Therefore, privacy in Europe is certainly not underpinned by "ideology" but rather by sensible considerations about experience made with regimes that use data collections for prosecution of politically unwanted people. The experience of *perverted uses of data originally collected for other purposed* remains a lasting legacy. Based upon this background it is pure cynicism to state that the Europeans–by protecting privacy–have "learned exactly the wrong lesson from history." (Cato Institute 1997: 189). It is especially cynical if this sensitive issue is linked to censorship in order to justify direct marketing! Privacy is a human right based upon the catastrophic experience with dictatorships in Europe. It is considered to be one measure to avoid that such a catastrophe ever happens again.[58] These lessons found their way into the *Council of Europe's European Convention on Human Rights* that was declared in November 1950 and into other contracts. Among those are the *International Covenant on Civil and Political Rights of 1966*, the *OECD Guidelines on the Protection of Privacy and Trans-border Flows of Personal Data* of 1980, the *Council of Europe Convention of 1981* and the *UN Guidelines concerning Computerized Personal Data Files* of 1990. Even in the reformed contracts of the European Union such as the Amsterdam Treaty of 1997, the right is still explicitly included (see Article 286). Europeans–usually more than Americans–realize "the abusive potential for reuses of personal data that may initially have been provided to a particular entity for a specific, limited purpose." (Samuelson 2000). Privacy is regarded as human right by Europeans (restated in the EU Data Protection Directive) and as a protection of a fundamental right of people. This

---

[57] Even in the 1980s, there were accusations that databases on Jews that had been created by the Nazis still existed. For instance, the CNIL had to investigate Interpol which was claimed to use a database on Jews created in 1941 in France (Flaherty 1989: 208, 218)

[58] Anderson and Seltzer (2000) discuss in greater detail the role of "otherwise benign" databases of the census in times of war.

background is often forgotten by Americans or ridiculed as being an excuse for establishing trade barriers. Europeans are in general suspicious with regard to centralized data collections, but this is based upon the aforementioned background of oppressive regimes and bureaucracies. This also holds for Eastern European countries, one example is the Czech Republic which has also a very strict data protection law.

These fears of oppression were revived in the 1960s and 1970s in the face of the new capabilities in automation, computerization, information storage and processing. It sparked fears of powerful government agencies that stored names of critical and politically active people, for instance. Public pressure to implement legislation increased and many of the technically advanced Western countries started to enact privacy laws. The forerunner was the state of Hesse in Western Germany, as mentioned in the section on the credit reporting system in Germany. The country, where major atrocities had been committed during the Nazi regime, later became the "cradle of data protection." Today it is one of the strictest regimes in Europe. The Swedish Data Protection Act of 1973 followed the Hesse act, but constituted the first comprehensive data protection legislation on the national level. Since then nearly every European country has passed legislation. The development of these laws was inspired or directly influenced by supra-national norm promulgation by the OECD, UN and the Council of Europe.

Table 4.1 presents and overview of laws. Latecomers are especially the new European states that have received EU membership only recently. Especially the OECD proved to be very influential for many national laws with regard to data protection.

Table 4.1

Data Protection Acts in Europe

Country	Year	Title of the Law
Austria	2000	Act for the Protection of Personal Data
Belgium	1992	Law of 8 December 1992 on Privacy Protection in Relation to the Processing of Personal Data
Bulgaria	2002	Personal Data Protection Act
Cyprus	2001	Processing of Personal Data (Protection of the Person) Law of 2001
Czech Rep.	2000	Act on the Protection of Personal Data
Denmark	2000	Act on Processing of Personal Data
Estonia	2000	Personal Data Protection Act
Finland	1999	Personal Data Act
France	1978	Loi 78-17 du 6.1.1978
Germany	1990	Federal Data Protection Act
Greece	1997	Law on Protection of Individuals with Regards to the Processing of Personal Information
Hungary	1992	Protection of Personal Data and Disclosure of Data of Public Interest
Ireland	1988	Data Protection Act
Italy	1996	Protection of Individuals and other subjects with regard to the processing of personal Data
Latvia	2000	Law on Personal Data Protection
Lithuania	1996	Law on Legal Protection of Personal Data
Luxembourg	2002	Protection des personnes à l'égard du traitement des données à caractère personnel
Malta	2001	Data Protection Act
Netherlands	2000	Personal Data Protection Act
Poland	1997	Law on the Protection of Personal Data
Portugal	1998	Act on the Protection of Personal Data
Slovakia	2002	Act on Personal Data Protection
Slovenia	1999	Personal Data Protection Act (1999)
Spain	1999	Organic Law 15/1999 of 13 December on the Protection of Personal Data
Sweden	1973	Personal Data Act
Slovenia	1999	Personal Data Protection Act
UK	1984	Data Protection Act

Notes: Table contains the latest version of the law the author could find.

Most of the basic principles and guidelines developed by these bodies can be found in all data protection laws in Europe. They are summarized in Box 4.2.

> **Box 4.2 Basic Data Protection Rules**
>
> The must basic data protection rules as incorporated in a wide variety of laws and guidelines are:
>
> - Right to notice before collection takes place;
> - Right of access to the data;
> - Right to have the data corrected or deleted;
> - Right to object to certain data processing methods; and
> - Right to not have variables on race, religious beliefs, etc. recorded.
>
> One of the most basic principles is that an individual is informed about the collection of data and that no data collection might take place secretly.[59]

Although there are considerable problems associated with comparing national privacy regimes, there is a "core" of similar standards in national laws, often based upon the OECD principles. Most laws apply to the public and private sector. Secondly, they include manual as well as automated data processing and exclude data collected for solely private purposes (such as address books). Despite such similarities, there are still many differences. Some of the laws include articles directed specifically at health or credit information, some include specific time frames. In the past, it has been argued that different privacy regimes create barriers to the free flow of information and that they increased regulatory drifts between countries. In beginning of 1992, when the discussion about data protection in Europe intensified, only 10 of 18 countries had ratified the *Council of Europe Convention for the Protection of Individuals with Regard to Automatic Processing of Personal Data (Convention 108).*[60] Several factors account for the inconsistencies:

(1) Different legal traditions and regulatory approaches;
(2) Various legal reforms and varying transposition phases; and
(3) Diverging interpretation of supranational norms.

One of the first legally binding international instruments in data protection was the Council of Europe Convention 108 of 1981 that required the signatories to transpose its principles into national law. The Council of

---

[59] I invite the reader at this stage to think about the American context, as I have discussed it in the sections on the history of credit reporting regulation.

[60] By 1997, all fifteen EU Member States (except Greece) had privacy legislature consistent with the Convention.

Europe (COE) states that it drew its inspiration directly from the European Convention on Human Rights and Fundamental Freedoms (Council of Europe 2004). The Convention 108 is open to any country, even those that are not member of the Council of Europe. It is necessary for countries to enact adequate legislation *before* becoming a party otherwise they cannot enter the contract. By 2005, the Convention was ratified and entered into force in 34 states.

It soon became clear, however, that this would not provide efficient protection across countries considering the fast technological progress. In the 1960s large-scale mainframe computers where introduced by private companies and public administrations. Therefore, it was decided by the Council to lay down basic principles for avoiding unfair and unlawful collection and processing of personal data. Furthermore, the signatories of the convention already constituted something like a *"free information zone"* in guaranteeing the free flow of information among the states that signed the convention. There are only two cases in which states can intervene in the international transfer of data:

(1) Where there is no equivalent data protection provided; and
(2) Where the data are transferred to a third state which is not party to the Convention.

A committee consisting of representatives of the signatories administers the Convention. Similar to what will be discussed for the EU Data Protection Directive, the administrators worked on facilitating international data flows by setting up a model contract between Convention members and third countries.[61] The national Data Protection Authorities interpret the principles of the convention. Since it is only a minimal standard, the signing states rely on non-binding recommendations for governments for specific sectors. In the past, a number of recommendations were published, such as on medical databanks (1981), direct marketing (1985), employment data (1989), financial payments and related transactions (1990) and the protection of medical and genetic data (1997). Unequal data protection standards across countries created potential obstacles to the free flow of information in Europe. At the beginning of the 1990s, the European Commission started to regard this as a serious impediment to the development of a harmonized internal Market. Therefore, in 1990, the Commission of

---

[61] In 1999, the Committee of Ministers of the Council of Europe adopted an amendment to the convention. It was intended to strengthen the cooperation of the EU with the COE. This could potentially strengthen the COE position towards third party countries.

the European Community issued the first draft of a European directive on data protection. During the lengthy debate about the draft, members of the European Union were far from agreeing on a single approach. While Great Britain considered the regulations to be to strict compared to their own statutes, Germany and France, on the other hand, criticized that their high protection standards might be reduced by the European legislation. Moreover, Great Britain, the Netherlands, Ireland and Denmark put forth that a ratification of the European Council Convention would be sufficient (Charlesworth 2000: 256). Directives by the European Commission only apply to problems within the competence of the Union and one of the most important tasks is the establishment of the Single Market and its four freedoms (movement of goods, services, capital and people), which apparently included the free flow of information implicitly. In the past, the Commission's competence has been successively expanded and it received a greater scope for regulating consumer protection issues, too.[62] The Commission seeks to minimize differences in national laws: "The right to privacy of citizens will therefore have equivalent protection across the Union." (European Commission 1998)[63] After several years of discussion, a compromise on this issue was eventually reached in the Council of Ministers in 1995, and the Directive could be adopted in October of the same year.

The Member States had three years to implement the directive into national law (deadline: October 24, 1998). This process, however, took far longer than expected. By 2001, most of the countries had finished the implementation process, while others were in the middle of the legislative process (Germany, Ireland, and Luxembourg) and one country (France) was still discussing a draft. Although it is commonly assumed that the directive is a "minimum standard," this is not the case. The regulation is primarily supposed to *harmonize* the regimes, not to *minimize* data protection. Based upon the historical background, there are several preconditions that have to be fulfilled to make data processing legitimate. The most important features are listed and described in the Box 4.3.

---

[62] This is codified in the Treaty of Amsterdam of 1996 (Article 153) effective in 1997.
[63] It has to be noted that the Directive only regulates activities that fall under the scope of EU law, this excludes public safety, defence, state security and the activities of the state in areas of criminal law. (Carey and Russell 2000: 5).

Box 4.3 Preconditions for Lawfulness of Data Processing in Europe

Under the European Data Protection Directive, several pre-conditions must be met to make the data processing lawful. Otherwise the processing of personal information remains unlawful. Article 7 (a) states:

- The data subject must unambiguously give consent to data processing;
- The processing is necessary for the performance of a contract concluded in the interest of the data subject;
- The processing is necessary for the public interest;
- The processing is necessary for the vital interest of the data subject; and
- Data can be processed whenever the controller or a third party has a legitimate interest in doing so and this interest is not overridden by the interest of protecting the right to privacy of the data subject.

European legislation has a clear separation between purposes, but also balances the rights of an individual to privacy with the legitimate interest of other parties. How this balance will ultimately be determined is left to the decision of courts.

The rules establish that controllers must disclose certain information to the data subject. In Europe, anyone has the right to know the identity of the controller and the intended purposes of the data processing. Additionally, the consumer has the right to be informed about any (potential) recipients of the information and the existence of the right to access and rectification. This is a very important: If the individual is not informed to whom the information was transferred–as is often the case in the U.S.–how is it possible to exert rights such as access and correction? The Directive also limits secondary uses of data. It states that information may only be processed for *legitimate purposes* and *not further in any way incompatible with those purposes* (Directive 95/46/EC, Article 6, 1[b])

Another important feature is the processing of a specific kind of data category, so-called "sensitive information:" racial or ethnic origin, political, religious and philosophical beliefs, trade-union membership or health or sex life.[64] This prohibition can be overridden by a data subject's explicit consent. Data about criminal convictions must be processed under the control of an official authority or a private body, but in the latter case only if the national law grants specific security provisions. There are also provisions of confidentiality and security of data processing (Article 16, 17) and

---

[64] Directive 95/46/EC (Article 8, 1.).

notification duties on the side of the data controller.[65] For instance, the authority has to be notified before any automatic processing of personal data is carried out. According to Article 19, there are several aspects that controllers have to disclose to the authorities when they register: the name and address of the data controller, purposes of processing, description of data categories, the recipients of the data, and proposed transfers to third countries. Moreover, it is explicitly mandated that the processing operations have to be publicized: "The register may be inspected by any person." (Directive 95/46/EC, Article 21, 2.). Data subjects, on the other hand, do have the specific right to access the information of controllers. Apart from the aforementioned disclosure rules, the right to access "means that anyone is entitled to approach any data controller to know whether he processes personal data relating to him or her, to receive a copy of the data, and if need be, to ask for the correction or erasure of the data." (European Commission 1998). The disclosure has to occur without excessive delay or expense. Everybody is also guaranteed the right to block or rectify data if they are incomplete or inaccurate; this means consumers have the right to settle disputes with all data processors.

Similar to the U.S. legislation in the 1990s, third parties that previously received the incorrect information have to be informed by the initial data processor of any data blocking, rectification or erasure. A second important right assigned to consumers is the right to objection. At a minimum, the states are obligated to grant an individual right to object to data processing if the processing is necessary only for the "legitimate interest" of the data controller. This right can be exercised at any time. Consumers also have the right to object if the data is used for direct marketing purposes (Directive 95/46/EC, Article 14 [b]).

How does the European picture compare to the American one? Figure 4.5 shows that consumers can approach any party: the bank, affiliates, non-affiliates and the credit bureau and ask anybody for disclosure of information (D). The consumer has to right to dispute the information (DS) at anybody who has stored it. He or she can also object to information sharing (IS) by banks with other parties. If the consumer stops it, data controllers have to notify each other of this matter (N). It took the Americans more than 30 years to approximately reach this level of protection, where rights are far more equally distributed and the efficiency of the system is increased through higher transparency.

---

[65] In the European context, "notification" relates to the notification of supervisory authorities, not of the individual as discussed in the U.S. legislation.

Figure 4.5
EU Data Protection Directive of 1995

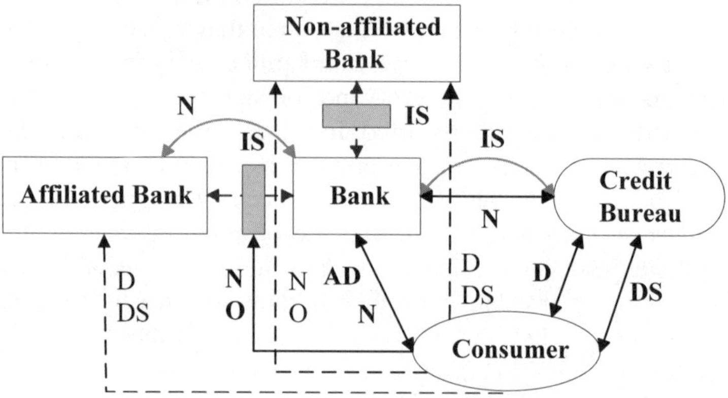

In the case of transfer of negative data from the bank to the credit reporting agency the consumer cannot really opt-out as it is usually argued that the stability of the banking system is a higher-ranking public interest than the individual's interest in personal privacy. Therefore, in Great Britain as well as in France and Germany, the consumer is merely informed about the data transmission. One innovation, however, is the right of not being subject to a purely automated decision in cases were it has great (legal) impact on individuals. This is the case in credit or insurance scoring. Automated processing is allowed when entering or performing a contract: "In this case the data controller must adopt suitable safeguards such as giving the possibility to the data subject to express his or her point of view if his or her requests are not satisfied." (European Commission 1998). Finally, Article 22 and Article 23 provide rights to judicial remedies and compensation.

4.3.1 Germany: Informational Self-determination

Germany has been the leading country in the field of data protection, for the reasons discussed above. At the same time, Germany certainly ranks among those countries with the strictest data protection laws. It established a bureaucratic and legalistic approach. The first data protection law in the world was enacted in the state of Hesse in 1970. The law later served as an example for the federal law. This section discusses the most important laws in Germany which enacted its first federal law in 1977 (Federal Data Protection Act). This law established the Federal Data Protection Officer

(*Bundesbeauftragter für Datenschutz*) and granted many rights to individuals such as access, rectification, blocking or erasure of data. The laws in the individual states had to be amended after 1983, the year the Federal Supreme Court ruled in the census case that citizens have a right to "informational self-determination" (*informationelle Selbstbestimmung*). In its short version, this means that every person has the right to know who, what and were personal data is stored. In the decision the Federal Supreme Court elaborated on self-determination:

> "*This fundamental right guarantees the power of the individual insofar as to decide oneself about the disclosure and use of one's personal data. Limitations of this right of 'informational self-determination' are only permissible if there is a higher-ranking public interest.*"
> (Bundesverfassungsgericht 2004, translated by the author)

Note that there is the balance between private interests and interest of the public. The German Supreme Court unambiguously granted the property rights to information to the individual in cases where there is no higher-ranking public interest.[66] It is intended to create as much freedom for the individual with as little restrictions as possible, while the individual remains the central focus of the legal consideration. Although this was probably not anticipated by German Supreme Court Judges, but with this rule they established an efficient separation of property rights to information (as discussed in the section of basic interactions in credit reporting). The separation is in so far efficient, as individuals have no control over negative information and cannot prevent the sharing of it, while they have full control over any other information sharing which is not overruled by a public interest. The German law terminology even influenced Europe, for instance by using the term *data protection* instead of *privacy protection*.[67] The negative default rule was established which meant "processing of personal data was seen as interference, per se, that needed legitimating." (Burkert 1999). This is a major difference to the U.S., where data processing is seen as legitimate and does not need extra authorization. Moreover, persons subject to the processing could access their information anywhere without putting forth any special reason. The Hesse act regulated the public sector only, but it covered the whole public sector. This set the stage

---

[66] In Germany, this right is derived from Article 2, Section 1, General Freedom of Action, in connection with Article 1 Section 1 Grundgesetz, Guarantee of Human Dignity (Virtuelles Datenschutzbüro 2004).

[67] As Burkert (1999: 46) describes, this was a misnomer: what was meant was not the protection of the data but of the rights of the individual to whom the data belonged.

for an equally comprehensive regulation at the national level, meaning the whole public sector plus the private sector:

> *"The Hesse Act expresses the regulative philosophy which is very common in Germany and perhaps also in some other European countries: If you establish regulation that seeks to influence behavior, you cannot (exclusively) rely on litigation to establish that behavior as a pattern. Litigation is associated with burdens, particularly when this litigation is supposed to be directed against the state. One needs institutions, an organizational back-up to take care of one's interests, even if this body by way of its own infrastructure is close to the infrastructure of the state."* (Burkert 1999: 46)

In Germany three phases of data protection legislation can be identified (Lutterbeck 1998): (1) The Federal Data Protection Act provided a common ground for the individual states (*Bundesländer*). It applied a comprehensive approach applying to the private and public sector; (2) the second phase began in 1990, when the Data Protection Act had to be amended to bring it in line with the census case of the German Supreme Court, the informational self-determination as explained above; and (3) the third phase is characterized by the Data Protection Directive and its implementation into national law. Altogether the German law situation in the 1990s can be described as a phase of transition. The transposition of the EU Directive in Germany followed two steps: The first was intended to implement the essential adjustments, while the second was to establish a comprehensive overhaul of the data protection laws (European Commission, 1999: 6). In May 2001, the new Federal Data Protection Act of 2001 went into effect, marking the first step in the implementation of EU law. In the aftermath of the Act, six German states adopted new privacy protection laws.

Table 4.2 shows the data protection laws and their amendments.[68] The 1990 law states that everything that is not explicitly allowed by the data protection law is prohibited. Only where there is a legitimate interest, personal data can be used or processed under consideration of the data subjects' individual interests. In charge for the enforcement of the data protection acts are the Federal Data Protection Officer (the so-called *Bundesdatenschutzbeauftragter*) and the *Bundesländer* have their own data protection laws and authorities, the latter are in charge for supervising

---

[68] During this research, my research assistant Nadine tried to get a complete list of laws from the authority in charge in Berlin. The authority replied that there have been "many changes" and that they had lost overview. Therefore, I cannot guarantee that this Table is complete.

credit reporting agencies (*Aufsichtsbehörden*). Here, especially the "Düsseldorfer Kreis," an association of officials from the Ministries of the Interior and the Data Protection Officers of the *Bundesländer.* They are in charge for negotiation with the private industry.

Table 4.2
German Data Protection Laws (Amendments)

Year	Law
1990	Federal Data Protection Act
1991	Law of December 1990
1994	Law of December 1993
1994	Law of September 14, 1994
1997	Law of December 17, 1997
2001	Federal Data Protection Act of May 18, 2001
2001	Law of June 26, 2001
2002	Law of December 3, 2001
2003	Law of December 20, 2001
2002	Law of July 19, 2002
2002	Law of August 21, 2002

In Germany, the first Federal Data Protection Act was introduced in 1977, as stated above. From 1970 - 2003 altogether 5 modifications of German legislation are of importance, the others relate to fields that are not relevant for our subject matter. There are also several guidelines that hold for data protection on the federal level.[69] In Germany, data for creditworthiness can be processed only with written consent of the data subject. It is common business practice of credit-granting institutions to include a clause in contracts that enables them to transfer positive data to a credit register. This is necessary, because in the case of creditworthiness information, the "legitimate interest" of the bank covers only the transfer of negative data. Box 4.4 gives an example for the Schufa clause for financial service providers. Similar clauses with modifications exist for other industries. Note that the clause in Box 4.4 is a complete briefing of the consumer about credit reporting.

---

[69] An example of such a regulation is the *Telekommunikationsdienstunternehmen-Datenschutzverordnung (TDSV),* a data protection guideline for telecommunication firms. However, there are no guidelines for credit reporting in Germany.

Box 4.4 Schufa Clause for Financial Service Providers

I herewith confirm that the credit institute (*name of the institute*) transmits to the credit reporting agency (*name of credit reporting agency*) data about the application, opening and termination of this account. Independently from this, the credit institute (*name of the institute*) will also transmit data about contractual incompliant behavior (for instance, fraud). According to the Federal Data Protection Act, this report may only occur according to the balancing of all concerned interests. Insofar, I also exempt the credit institute (*name of the institute*) from bank secrecy. The (*name of credit reporting agency*) stores and transfers the data to contract partners in the EU internal market, to provide them with the creditworthiness data on natural persons. Contractual partners of (*name of credit reporting agency*) are mainly credit institutes as well as credit card and leasing companies. The (*name of credit reporting agency*) also reports to retailers, telecom providers and other firms that provide services based upon credit.

The (*name of credit reporting agency*) only provides personal data if there is a trust-worthy justified interest in the individual case. For locating debtors, their addresses are provided. When providing credit reports, the (*name of credit reporting agency*) may also report a score calculated upon its databases for the evaluation of risk by its contractual partner (scoring). I can access the personal data related to me stored at the (*name of credit reporting agency*). Further information about (*name of credit reporting agency*) reporting and scoring is given in a brochure available at the contractual partner of (*name of credit reporting agency*).

(Translated by the author, 2004)

This briefing is done with more or less 10 sentences. Anyone disputing that the consumer can be fully informed due to cost considerations obviously does not account for the efficiency with which this can be done. In the past I came across a couple of industry officials and policy makers who stated that the introduction of an opt-in right would result in a breakdown of the credit reporting system. This is a wholly unfounded claim: consumers who are eager to get credit, usually "sign everything" and data protection considerations do not play a greater role in this decision. In many cases consumers do not even bother to read the clause! However, it is in cases of dispute, where the above rules are becoming important. Of course, the borrower must not be asked for consent in the case of negative data, because the stability of the banking system is in the higher-ranking public interest compared to the borrower's right to his privacy for negative data (Sosna 2002: 22). Altogether, Germany is among the countries with the highest data protection on earth. It applies a somewhat bureaucratic and inflexible approach, but consumers are fully informed (if they wish to learn more) and they have re-dress possibilities as well as institutional back-up in form of the data protection officer. Although Germany is an opt-in regime for positive information, there is no such requirement for the transfer of negative information. These strict privacy rules do not constitute a mar-

ket barrier. As described in the discussion of competition in credit reporting, Germany has one of the highest coverage rates of the economically active population and despite these strict rules there is competition in the
market.

4.3.2 Great Britain: Stricter Data Protection Introduced

Great Britain's data protection appears to have moved from a more America oriented style to the European one. This is the case, because Great Britain in fact had a lower level of data protection compared to other European
countries before the introduction of the Data Protection Directive. Therefore, the British claim that the European rules were strict compared to their
statutes was not unfounded. In a former research project (Jentzsch 2003a),
I counted the number of data protection rules that existed for credit reporting in a country before and after the implementation of the European Data
Protection Directive. A modified version of this approach is explained in
more detail further below. The number of regulations increased remarkably for Great Britain as visualized in Figure 4.6.

Figure 4.6
Financial Privacy Regulations in Selected Countries

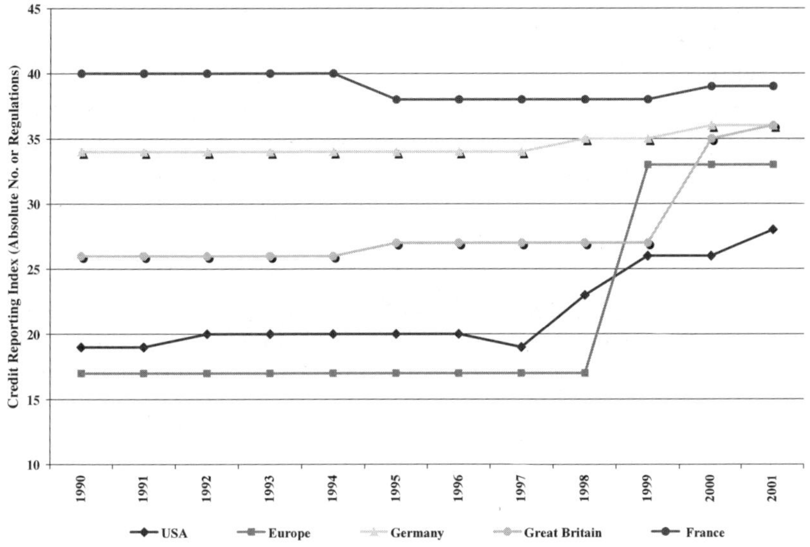

Source: Jentzsch (2003a)

For instance, for Great Britain, the figure shows that over 25 regulations were applicable to credit reporting under the old law. With the implementation of the directive in 1998 this number jumped over 35. The graph also gives an impression of the relatively high data protection level in Germany and in France. The debate about privacy legislation in Great Britain started in the early 1970s with a report by the Younger Committee. This committee proposed 10 guidelines that were intended to provide basic protection of the individual (Carey and Russell 2000: 1). The committee proposals were not implemented, but in 1974 major legislation was enacted to regulate the consumer credit business. The Consumer Credit Act defined consumer credit business broadly and included "ancillary credit businesses," a category that encompasses credit referencing (Goode 1974: 43). The act stated that such business activities required a license, which is normally granted for three years and allows the owner to conduct all activities that are described in it. Any person engaging in any activities for which a license is required without holding one commits an offence.[70] In 1978, the Lindop Committee published a report that dealt specifically with the question of data protection, instead of "general privacy" as in the Younger Committee report. It recommended the establishment of a data protection authority. However, the British authorities did not react until the Council of Europe Convention followed in 1981. Three years later, the Data Protection Act of 1984 was passed, which transposed the minimum requirements set out in the Convention. The Act included eight very broad data protection principles among them access and rectification that were not enforceable in courts, but by the Data Protection Registrar and the Data Protection Tribunal (Carey and Russell 2000: 4). In Great Britain, there are primarily three laws that govern financial privacy: the Consumer Credit Act (1974), the Data Protection Acts of 1984 and the amended one of 1998. The latter transposed the EU Data Protection Directive and brought significant changes to the already very complex legislation in Great Britain.[71] The Data Protection Act of 1998 transposes the Directive 95/46/EC by providing new regulations of the processing of information relating to individuals, including a notice for the purpose of the data collection as well as the types of data that are collected. This Act is the core of privacy legislation in Great Britain (European Commission 1999: 8). The law also provides "principles of good practice", in which data has to be processed fairly and lawfully and only for limited purposes. In the case of inaccuracies, the controller of

---

[70] This is explained in the sections 39.1 and 147.1 of the Consumer Credit Act.
[71] There are data protection laws that are far easier to read than the British one. For instance, compare the German Federal Data Protection Act to the British law.

this data can be mandated to rectify, erase or destroy those data. Prior to the Directive, the situation in Great Britain resembled that of the U.S., because no prior consent to data processing was required. The implementation of EU standards introduced new regulations in the field of individual rights, the legitimacy of data processing, regulations concerning sensitive data and international data flows. Great Britain has a complex system of enforcement and supervision.

Table 4.3
Credit Reporting Regulation in Great Britain

Year	Law and Regulation
1974	Consumer Credit Act
1977	Consumer Credit (Conduct of Business) (Credit References) Regulations 1977 No. 330
1984	Data Protection Act
1988	Data Protection Act
1998	Revised Data Protection Act
2000	Consumer Credit (Credit Reference Agency) Regulations 2000, No. 290
2000	Consumer Credit (Conduct of Business) (Credit References) (Amendment) Regulations 2000, No. 291

For the 1974 Consumer Credit Act, the Department of Trade and Industry issues regulations, while the Office of Fair Trading supervises the enforcement. For the Data Protection Act of 1998, however, the Home Office issues regulations, while the Information Commissioner is the enforcement authority. Concerning the latter act, the Home Office, for example, released roughly 20 regulations, which add precision and clarify regulatory details (Carey and Russell 2000: 7). An overview is given in Table 4.3. The Consumer Credit Act established the obligation to hold a license and some basic property rights to information. So far it has not been revised to any major extent, but there is a reform currently under way. In the period from 1970–2003 there were three laws applicable of which the data protection law changed two times with the amendment of the 1984 Data Protection Act in 1988 and finally in 1998. Great Britain is an example, of a country that went from a more lax approach to increased regulations in credit reporting.

For a long time, the country did have a regime of protection below that of other European countries. This has changed dramatically with the implementation of the EU directive. At the same time, Great Britain has a competitive consumer credit market and high growth rates of credit to households. It also has a highly competitive credit reporting industry, where much merger and acquisition is going on. This is in stark contrast to France.

4.3.3 France: Delayed Implementation

France has one of the strictest privacy regimes in Europe based upon the Act on Data Processing, Data Files and Individual Liberties of 1978. This act created the National Commission for Data Processing and Liberties (*Commission Nationale de l'Information et Libertés*, CNIL), a powerful, independent agency that performs advisory and monitoring functions. Companies that process personal information are expected to register with CNIL. The agency also has the power to deny the license for data processing. This essentially means that a firm cannot enter the market. Regulatory power concerning bankruptcy information is vested in the Banking and Financial Regulatory Committee (*Comité de la Réglementation Bancaire et Financière*, CRBF) chaired by the Minister of Economic Affairs and Finance, including the Governor of the Banque de France. This committee releases regulations governing the establishment of databases for credit and repayment data. By 2004, France had not implemented the EU Data Protection Directive. In February 1998, the administration issued a report that described the changes in the law, but by October of the same year, the Directive should have already been implemented. In 1999, proposed modified legislation was sent to the National Parliament, but no results emerged during the next year. Now the European Commission initiated a case before the European Court against France and four other countries that had failed to transpose the Directive. The CNIL published its opinion concerning the draft bill in September 2000. The National Assembly reviewed the bill, which is intended to strengthen the CNIL and to preserve the level of protection granted by the 1978 law, and it voted in support of it. After the first reading of the bill, however, the process came to a standstill, because of elections in France. The relevant regulations for credit reporting can be found in the Act on Data Processing, Data Files and Individual Liberties of 1978 and the Neiertz Act of 1989. There is also a number of regulations that exist and establish the rules for the FICP (*Fichier national des incidents de remboursement des crédits aux particuliers*, FICP) the database administered by the Banque de France as explained in the section on credit reporting history.

Table 4.4

Regulations of the French FICP

Year	Title of Regulation	File
1986	Règlement No. 86-08 du 27 février 1986 relatif à la centralisation des incidents de paiment	CPII
1989	Neiertz Act (Loi du 31 décembre 1989 relative à la prévention et au règlement des difficultés des particuliers et des famillies), integrated in the Code de la Consommation, Article L333.4, L333.6	FICP
1990	Règlement No. 90-05 du 11 avril 1990 relatif au fichier national des incidents de remboursement des crédit aux particuliers	FICP
1993	Règlement No. 93-04 du 19 mars 1993 modified the No. 90-05 regulation	FICP
1995	Règlement No. 95-03 du 21 juillet 1995 modified the No. 86-08 regulation	CPII
1996	Règlement No. 96-04 du 24 mai 1996 amends the No. 90-05 regulation	FICP
1998	Loi No. 98-657 du 29 juillet 1998 d'orientation relative à la lutte contre les exclusions modified the Code de la Consommation Article 333.4 (Neiertz Act)	FICP
2000	Règlement No. 2000-04 du 6 septembre 2000 modifiant le règlement du 11 avril 1990 relatif au fichier national des incidents de remboursement des crédit aux particuliers modified the No. 90-05 regulation	FICP

The French system is a centralized public credit registry but this was not always the case: the predecessor of FICP was the Centrale Professionelle d'Information sur les Impayés (CPII), administrated by the Association des Sociétés Financières. It was the subject of a declaration before the CNIL in 1989. In 1989 the Neiertz Act established the FICP. Although the private information exchange over the CPII continued until the mid-1990s if was eventually terminated. Obviously it made no sense to continue the database in competition with a public sector register. This resembles the situation in Belgium, where public credit reporting terminated private credit reporting in 2003/2004. France is one of the countries, where the update of its legislation took very long. Only in 2000, two years after the implementation deadline of the EU Directive had expired; draft legislation to update the French law was sent to CNIL for review and consultation. In 2002, the text passed the National Assembly in its first reading, after the Council of Ministers had examined the draft. The Senate on its first reading in April 2003 further modified the bill. At the time of the evaluation of data protection laws for this study (in 2003/2004), France had not yet implemented the Directive, and Ireland and Luxembourg did so only in 2002. In 2004, France finally amended its law to bring it in line with the European Data Protection Directive.[72] In France, only two acts apply to credit reporting: the Neiertz Act of 1989 and the Act on Data Processing, Data Files and Individual Liberties of 1978. The first act has been modified in 1995 and 1998.[73] Therefore, there were two changes of relevance: in 1978 and 1989. [74] Altogether, France is characterized by the central solution of a public monopoly in credit reporting, strict regulation and enforcement of data protection and a relatively high stability of legislation and regulations. I have already stated above that this is paired with a relatively slowly growing consumer credit market.

4.3.4 U.S. and European Approaches to Privacy

In the following, the most important differences between the U.S. and Europe in terms of financial privacy regulation are summarized. First, a short summary of the general historical differences is given, before moving on to international initiatives and the differences in credit reporting. The differences between American and European approaches to privacy must be traced back to their historical roots. The origin of the American understanding of privacy is rooted in the colonial times and the "writs of assistance," unspecified warrants which gave royal officers of the British Crown broad discretion to search homes of citizens for prosecution of violations of British custom laws. This quickly sparked a public debate where opponents of the writs questioned their legality. It was one of the elements that enforced American suspicion against British rule in the colonies. Moreover, it coined the thinking of the Constitution's Fathers. The 4th Amendment was a direct protection against "unreasonable searches and seizures." A further landmark in the evolution of privacy in America was certainly the article "The Right to Privacy" by the Supreme Court Justices Warren and Brandeis in 1890, in this article, the judges state that there is a "right to be left alone." In the 20th Century, this approach is reflected in

---

[72] *Loi no. 2004-801 du 6 août 2004 relative à la protection des personnes physiques à l'égard des traitements de données à caractère personnel et modifiant la loi n° 78-17 du 6 janvier 1978 relative à l'informatique, aux fichiers et aux libertés.*

[73] These amendments were in areas that are not relevant for the subject matter.

[74] Title of the law is: *Loi n° 89-1010 du 31 décembre 1989 relative à la prévention et au règlement des difficultés liées au surendettement des particuliers et des familles.*

the privacy legislation, such as the Privacy Act of 1974, the Right to Financial Privacy Act of 1978, the Electronic Communications Privacy Act of 1986 and the Communications Assistance for Law Enforcement Act of 1994. The review of the history of privacy in America shows that the focus was for a long time on government and unlawful interference with the private sphere of citizens. Federal privacy acts for the private sector were introduced in the 1970s under mounting public pressure (typically after scandals) or because of the threat that individual states began to enact legislation. Several laws in the 1980s and 1990s targeted the private sector. I have summarized some of the most important points in Box 4.5.

Box 4.5 U.S. Approach to Privacy Protection

The most important general differences to the European approach are:

- No comprehensive data protection law (covering private/public sector)
- Laws for the private sector are applied only to a specific industry
- Privacy is regulated at federal and states' level
- Fragmented instead of general data protection oversight
- Private data is primarily the property the data collector
- Emphasis on self-regulation

In Europe, the primary emphasis is on human rights, as stated above. The European constitutions protect the right to privacy and this is based on historical experience with oppressive bureaucracies. After the World War II, centralized databases were regarded with great suspicion, especially if they are in the hands of governments. As computerization started in the 1960s and 1970s there were questions about how fundamental rights to privacy could be preserved in an environment of pervasive computing.

In the 1970s, Germany proved to be the leader in data protection regulation. The state of Hesse introduced the first comprehensive data protection law worldwide in 1970. After that, several other countries followed, among them Sweden and France. Europeans laid down guidelines in the Council of Europe Convention in 1981 and later in the European Data Protection Directive. With this directive they established an area of free information flows and with minimum standards that hold across borders. Box 4.6 summarizes the most important aspects.

Box 4.6 EU Approach to Privacy Protection

The most important general differences to the U.S. approach are:

- Comprehensive data protection laws
- Regulations for private entities hold for all private entities
- Multilayered regulation in some countries
- General data protection authority
- Prior consent for data collection is required (person is owner of data)
- Less emphasis on self-regulation

There is a strong emphasis is on human rights and less trust in industry self-regulation. Moreover, it is claimed that an individual will not be able to lead successful litigation if there is no organizational backup in terms of a data protection authority. More property rights are located at the individual with some countries explicitly following the approach that the data subject is the rightful owner of data (see section on Germany). Today, as Europe is increasingly harmonizing its laws, there is a trend of convergence of data protection regulations across countries. Although regulations itself might be more burdensome in one country compared to another, particularly burdensome are frequent changes in national legislations.

Table 4.5
Regulation of Credit Reporting: A Comparison of Changes

Land	No. of authorities	No. of laws	No. of changes of laws	∅ change of laws p.a.	No. of regulations	∅ change regulations p.a.
1970–2003						
US	5	3	20	0.60	18	0.55
GB	2	3	2	0.06	22	0.66
FR	2	2	2	0.06	14	0.42
GER	1	1	5	0.15	0	0
1990–2000						
US	5	3	14	1.4	10	1
GB	2	3	1	0.1	15	1.5
FR	2	2	2	0.2	7	0.7
GER	1	1	3	0.3	0	0

Table 4.5 maps the regulatory activity in credit reporting regulation and data protection. U.S. and Germany are countries that have changed their

laws more often on average than Great Britain and France. This is interesting as one would have expected a high stability of the legal situation in Germany. The U.S. and Great Britain, on the other hand, have a relatively high average of changes of their regulations. The more such "rules of the market place" are changed the more costly and cumbersome is their implementation for the firms but also their administration and monitoring by regulatory authorities. Because no regulations exist in Germany that could be changed, the country has no changes. In Germany a cooperative approach prevailed where companies would directly discuss with data protection officials and both would find a consent what business practices should be changed (or not). The discussion of globalization usually focuses on goods, services, capital or workforce, less on flows of information. Such flows, however, are necessary for globalization. Free information flow is usually taken for granted and it is not regarded as obstacle. However, there is an on-going discussion of differing data protection regimes around the world. Some countries might in future block information flows to others or use data protection as trade barrier.[75] In the following, the international initiatives are reviewed.

4.3.5 International Initiatives for Privacy

Over the past 30 years, there was an emergence of international agreements recognizable that affects global information flows in terms of setting minimum standards for privacy protection. These agreements sometimes served as example for national legislation. The guidelines prescribed vary in content and nature: some are voluntary guidelines, while others are binding international contracts, where deviation can be sanctioned. Several organizations have been occupied in the past with the subject matter such as the OECD, WTO, EEC, EU and the UN. It depends on the status of the organization as to whether binding guidelines can be established–as is the case on the EU level or within the WTO–or if recommendations only can be given. The latter is the case for the OECD. Deviations are not sanctioned if guidelines are not implemented in national legislation. The international contracts regulate trans-border data flows that are constitute of all movements of personal data across international borders, that is all data imports and data exports.

---

[75] This is a complaint many American scholars have put forth to European policymakers.

OECD Initiatives

20 countries founded the OECD in December 1960 as legal follower of the Organization for European Economic Co-operation (OEEC), an organization founded briefly after the war for the stabilization of Europe and its reconstruction. It was formed to administer American aid under the Marshall Plan. The members of the OECD, which counts 30 members today, are devoted to democracy and market economy. It is mainly the forum of the industrialized countries and has often been a forerunner to policy formulation and analysis. The organization is also devoted to identifying emerging issues that are of trans-border nature and global relevance and for coordination of national policies. This is done by means of consensus; the OECD has mainly the character of a governing and guiding policy forum. One of the main subjects of the OECD encompasses a deepening of economic integration as well as the cooperation in questions of economic and exchange rate policies. The OECD has promulgated a number of guidelines and policy reports aimed at implications of electronic commerce for governments, businesses, and the general public and at providing recommendations for further actions. For instance, the group of countries agreed on the *OECD Guidelines on the Protection of Privacy and Transborder Flows of Personal Data* (1980). These guidelines had the intention to find a balance of ensuring privacy and the free flow of information.

In 2004, approximately 50% of OECD member countries among them Denmark, France and Germany have passed privacy legislation. Others were on the verge of enacting laws. There are different principles concerning data collection: Five years later after agreement on these basic guidelines, the governments of OECD member countries adopted the Declaration on Transborder Data Flows (in April 1985). This is actually not more than a declaration of intention to promote the free flow of information as well as the access to data. Other OECD guidelines for information policy include those on the security of information systems (1992) that addresses the safety of cross-border electronic commerce, including electronic money transactions and Internet payments. Another guideline is on the global information infrastructure. Finally the 1998 Ministerial Declaration on the Protection of Privacy on Global Networks (Organization for Economic Cooperation and Development 1998), which was intended to bridge different national approaches to privacy protection and to provide continued trans-border flow of personal data in global networks. The member states obviously wanted to ensure that OECD Privacy Guidelines are effectively implemented in relation to global networks. Moreover, they claimed that from now on, there should be a periodical review of the main developments and issues in the field of privacy protection. As stated above, the principles have been powerful in terms of serving as examples for national legislation.

Box 4.7 OECD Privacy Principles

(1) Purpose Specification Principle: The purpose of the data collection has to be specified;

(2) Use Limitation Principle: Uses of the personal data should be limited

(3) Security Safeguards Principle: Collection and storage of data should be safeguarded;

(4) Openness Principle: There should be in general a policy of openness with regard to the collection and processing of personal data;

(5) Individual Participation Principle: The individual has the right to participate in the collection, to access and rectify information;

(6) Accountability Principle: The data collector is responsible for measures that are in line with the herein stated principles;

(7) Collection Limitation Principle: The collection of data should be limited for the purposes claimed at their collection; and

(8) Data Quality Principle: The data should be accurate and up to date.

Source: OECD Guidelines on the Protection of Privacy and Trans-border Flows of Personal Data of 1980

United Nations Initiatives

The UN was founded after World War II by agreement of 51 governments. Its main purpose is the advancement of human rights and preservation of peace. This aim was to be achieved through methods of cooperation. The UN is virtually an all-encompassing institution with 191 member countries as of January 2004. The UN is a system of institutions. For instance, the World Bank and the International Monetary Fund are specialized agencies that are linked with the UN through cooperative agreements. Altogether there are 12 such agencies, including the World Health Organization, World Intellectual Property Organization (WIPO), International Telecommunications Union, and Universal Postal Union. The UN characterizes itself as a problem-solving institution, where nations discuss their problems and develop cooperative solutions. It works in a number of fields to promote its economic and social purposes. One of its fields is human rights which includes privacy. The Universal Declaration of Human Rights was the first international statement of such rights when it was adopted by the General Assembly in December 1948. In Article 12 it states that: "No one shall be subjected to arbitrary interference with his privacy, family, home or correspondence, nor to attacks upon his honor and reputation. Everyone has the right to the protection of the law against such interference or attacks." The Economic and Social Council of the UN is in charge of privacy matters. One of its tasks is to prepare reports on the subject matter that are presented to the General Assembly. In December 1990, the organization adopted the *UN Guidelines Concerning Computerized Personal Data Files,* these guidelines establish certain principles for the protection of privacy. For overview purposes, they are given in Box 4.8.

Box 4.8 United Nations Fair Information Practices

(1) Principle of lawfulness and fairness: Information about persons should not be collected or processed in unfair or unlawful ways, nor should it be used for ends contrary to the purposes and principles of the Charter of the United Nations;

(2) Principle of accuracy: Right to accuracy, completeness and relevance of the data recorded;

(3) Principle of purpose specification: Publication or announcement of the purpose which a file is to serve, none of the data should be disclosed for purposes incompatible with those specified except with consent of the person concerned;

(4) Principle of interested person access: Everyone who offers proof of identity has the right to know whether information concerning him is being processed and to obtain it in an intelligible form;

(5) Principle of non-discrimination: Data that could give rise to unlawful or arbitrary discrimination should not be compiled this is especially with regard to data on racial or ethnic origin, color, sex life, political opinions, religious, philosophical or other beliefs and membership of an association or trade union membership;

(6) Principle of security: Necessary security measures for protecting files should be implemented;

(7) Supervision and sanctions: Countries should designate an authority to be responsible for the observance of the principles above; and

(8) Trans-border data flows: Where the legislation of two or more countries concerned by a trans-border data flow offers comparable safeguards for the protection of privacy, data should circulate as freely as inside each of the territories concerned

Source: UN Guidelines Concerning Computerized Personal Data Files of 1990

The Office of the High Commissioner for Human Rights has issued these guidelines as a recommendation for the implementation into national laws. They are sometimes called Fair Information Practices. Privacy is in the UN context clearly seen as fundamental human right. Another body of the UN, the Commission on International Trade Law is also in charge for related issues. It is the legal body of the UN in the field of international trade law. In the past, it has developed a model electronic commerce law that has several intentions, such as to increase the commercial use of international contracts in electronic commerce, to establish rules and norms that validate and recognize electronic contracts and to set default rules for contract formation and governance of electronic contract commerce. The model law is being implemented in many countries and is generally regarded as a useful reference by legislators throughout the world.

World Trade Organization Initiatives

Finally, there is the World Trade Organization (WTO). Although the WTO so far has not contributed to the international regulation of data protection, it soon may play a more important role. Shortly after the World War II, nationals agreed to liberalize world trade and to reduce protective measures that were still in place from the 1930s. Tariff negotiations started in 1946 among the 23 founding parties of the General Agreement on Tariffs and Trade (GATT), a provisory contract with no major organizational back up. Through different rounds of negotiation, the GATT expanded and contributed to reducing tariffs and non-tariff trade barriers. In the Uruguay Round (1986-1994), the countries agreed upon establishing the WTO as organization. This marked the biggest reform of international trade after World War II. The purpose of the WTO is the implementation of a rule-based international trade system instead of a power-based one. Countries are asked to refrain from unilateral actions. The WTO has a list of more than 800 non-tariff trade barriers (or measures) including special fees, subsidies, standards for health and hygiene, control measures, dumping, among others. Such "barriers"–if applied in a protectionist way– increase the transaction costs in international trade and blur competitive cost differences. Some of these so-called "protectionist measures" are deeply rooted in a cultural understanding of how to deal with specific questions such as genetically modified foods, health standards or privacy rules. In the past, the latter has been attacked as "non-tariff trade barrier" erected by Europeans against American companies (Kitchenman and

Teixeira 1998).[76] Compared with other international institutions, the WTO reacted relatively late to developments in international e-commerce. From the beginning, there were a number of problems in coming to terms with the issue. For instance, in e-commerce there was the question if it should be treated as goods or services. The GATT is applied to goods, whereas there is another agreement for services (General Agreement of Trade in Services, GATS). The first step was the declaration on global electronic commerce in May 1998 at Second Ministerial Conference in Geneva, Switzerland. The Declaration asked the WTO General Council to analyze trade-related issues in e-commerce, and to present a progress report to the WTO Third Ministerial Conference in Seattle. In September 1998, a formal working program was established for addressing e-commerce topics. Under the auspices of several committees, the organization analyzes matters such as e-commerce, intellectual property, government procurement, import duties on information technology products and services. The declaration also included a moratorium that stated that each member would continue to refrain from imposing customs duties on electronic transmissions. The initial reports were delivered at Seattle and after the breakdown of negotiations in 1999. There are four bodies in charge for reviewing the trade-related implications of e-commerce: (1) Council of Trade in Services (examines e-commerce issues related to the most-favored-nation treatment, transparency, privacy, national treatment); (2) Council for Trade in Goods (analyzes market access for products related to e-commerce); (3) Council for Trade-Related Intellectual Property (is in charge for protection and enforcement of copyrights and trademarks); (4) Committee for Trade and Development (has to look into the effects of e-commerce and the developing countries).

As known, the 2001 Doha conference placed special emphasis on the needs of developing countries. At the Fourth Ministerial Conference, ministers simply agreed to continue the work program and to extend the moratorium on customs duties. As of 2005 not much had happened. The General Council has identified some topics that are said to touch upon several issues of the multilateral trading system such as the classification of the content of certain electronic transmissions, fiscal implications of e-commerce and the relationship between e-commerce and traditional commerce. Currently it is not clear how the different international organiza-

---

[76] One could argue that potentially every standard that differs from American standards could be labelled "protectionist." The term is often used in a defamatory way without a second consideration if something *really is* protectionist and discriminatory against foreigners or not.

tions will work together. For now the WTO cannot impose international (minimum) standards in data protection and the U.S., as well as Europe, have very different approaches to privacy, as discussed in the relevant sections on the subject matter. In the agreements of the WTO there is just one explicit reference to privacy (see Box 4.9). National laws implemented for the protection of data fall under GATS exceptions that overrule all the other Articles in the agreement. Nothing in the Annex, therefore, limits the members' ability to protect personal data, personal privacy and the confidentiality of individual records as long as these measures are not used to circumvent the other provisions of the Agreement.

Box 4.9 GATS Reference to Privacy

Article XIV (General Exceptions) states that under certain requirements nothing in the GATS should be construed to prevent members from the adoption or enforcement of measures that are necessary to secure compliance with laws or regulations that are not consistent with provisions of the GATS. This includes laws relating to fraud prevention and the "(…) protection of the privacy of individuals in relation to the processing and dissemination of personal data and the protection of confidentiality of individual records and accounts; (…)"

Source: GATS, Article XIV (c) ii

Currently, there is a "safeguard for individual privacy" built into the GATS. I will not discuss which international institution would be the most adequate to safeguard privacy as this leads us to far away from credit reporting. The interested reader is referred to Perez (2003) and Reidenberg (2000) for this discussion.

European Union Extraterritoriality Clauses

At the moment there is not a single international organization in charge for data protection. And there is no international treaty on privacy that includes all the important trading partners and enforceable mechanisms to address privacy breaches. This "vacuum" on the international level increasingly creates problems, because there is a trend to extraterritoriality clauses in the national laws. These clauses require bilateral negotiations among nations regarding their status as either adequate data protection regime or inadequate one. Due to the peculiar situation in the U.S. that I have discussed at length above, the country does not take the international leadership in pushing privacy topics. In Europe, policymakers are still busy with the assessment of other countries' statuses for adequate data protection. As of June 2004, roughly 30 of the 100 countries surveyed had extraterritorial clauses in their national laws. These principles are part of international contracts, such as the OECD Guidelines, UN Privacy Principles, Council of Europe Convention and EU Data Protection Directive (see Box 4.10).

Box 4.10 European Union Extraterritorial Principles

In short, the Chapter IV, Article 25 upholds the following principles:

1. The Member States shall provide that the transfer of personal data to a third country may take place only if the third country ensures an adequate level of protection;
2. The adequacy of the level of protection afforded by a third country shall be assessed in the light of all the circumstances surrounding a data transfer, the rules of law, both general and sectoral, in force in the third country;
3. The Member States and the Commission shall inform each other of cases where they consider that a third country does not ensure an adequate level of protection;
4. Where the Commission finds that a third country does not ensure an adequate level of protection, Member States shall take the measures necessary to prevent any transfer of data of the same type to the third country;
5. At the appropriate time, the Commission shall enter into negotiations with a view to remedying the situation resulting from the finding made pursuant to paragraph 4;
6. The Commission may find that a third country ensures an adequate level of protection by reason of its domestic law. Member States shall take the measures necessary to comply with the Commission's decision.

Source: European Data Protection Directive

In 18 countries, the law explicitly states that the individual data subject has to give his/her consent for the transfer to third countries. In 23 countries, the authority has to be informed about the export of personal data. It is clear that today's technology allows for transfers of large amounts of data across borders. Simply transferring the data somewhere else can easily circumvent high data protection standards. In fact this already happens. The U.S. does not have an extraterritoriality clause. In the past, Equifax has outsourced data operations to Jamaica, Experian and TransUnion planned to outsource operations to the Philippines and India (Hendricks 2003). This provoked an outcry by privacy advocates in the U.S. The blockade of data exports happened as early as 1974, when the Swedish Data Inspection Board stopped the export of personal data to Great Britain, because there was no data protection law in the country (Burkert 1999: 51). This incident as well as others led to the enactment of legislation in Great Britain and to the harmonization through the EU Data Protection Directive. This was a necessity, as data embargoes could soon have threatened the harmonization of the internal market. Article 25 and 26 of the EU Data Protection Directive, therefore, states that personal information can only be exported to third countries if there is adequate protection or under certain exemptions. These exemptions are, for instance, where the data subject has given consent or where the transfer is legally required on important public interest grounds. Two documents of the European Commission are the primary tools for the determination of adequacy (European Commission 1998b, 1998c). According to the EU Article 29 Working Party, adequate protection "is typically achieved through a combination of rights for the data subject and obligations on those who process data (...)" (European Commission 1998b: 5). The Commission finds that such rules only protect the individual's right if they are followed in practice, something that emphasizes that enforcement is as important as legislation. Against this background, the Commission not only analyzes foreign rules incorporated in the law, but also the system of enforcement in the other country. The adoption of a Commission decision involves:

> A proposal from the Commission;
> Article 29 Working Party opinion;
> Article 31 Management Committee opinion (delivered by a qualified majority of Member States);
> Scrutiny by the European Parliament if the Commission has used its executing powers legitimately; and
> Adoption of the decision by the College of Commissioners.

The consequence of a positive opinion is that personal data can flow from the 27-EU member states and three EEA member countries (Norway, Liechtenstein and Iceland) to that third country. The process of evaluation, however, is slow, cumbersome and ineffective. By February 2007, the Commission had recognized only 6 countries (!): Switzerland, Canada, Argentina, Guernsey, Isle of Man, and U.S. Department of Commerce's Safe harbor Privacy Principles, and the transfer of Air Passenger Name Record to the United States' Bureau of Customs and Border Protection as providing adequate protection.

4.3.6 Lessons for Credit Reporting Regulation

The review of the theoretical sides of credit reporting, the current empirical and historical knowledge helps to draw some conclusions about "best practices" in credit reporting regulations. Credit reporting bureaus are established around the world and the industry of risk assessment is booming. Credit reporting could potentially play a huge role in globalization as the international exchange of credit profiles could allow that we trade with someone elsewhere in the world albeit this person is completely unknown to us. Some reputation systems do already exist (such as in online auctioning), but the information comes from decentralized sources such as the users themselves and it is unfiltered. Information technologies allow the collection, storage and processing of financial information on millions of borrowers. But with this comes pressure to regulate the activity as consumers may suffer welfare losses from unimpeded trade in highly personal information. In the following, some lessons for the regulation of this activity are presented.

International standards: No country has to re-invent the wheel in terms of financial privacy regulation. There are already international best practices, codes and guidelines that help to assess which regulation should be at least implemented. For instance, there are OECD guidelines, UN guidelines and the Council of Europe Convention as well as the European Data Protection Directive. For more detail the reader is referred to the national laws in the industrialized countries or to the World Bank's general principles for credit reporting systems which have been drawn up by an American lawyer. It is important to not implement them one to one in a developing country, as national peculiarities should always be taken into account. However, reference to the laws in industrialized countries may help to reduce severe gaps and errors that can be made in the creation of credit reporting rules.

Credit reporting is *no* industry but a network: Although for brevity the word "industry" was used many times, credit reporting is essentially a *network activity*. There are furnishers of credit information, consumers, credit report users (that must not be furnishers at the same time) and credit bureaus. If regulations are applied to this activity, they must cover *all* participants not just credit bureaus as "information circuits." At the minimum consumers should be obliged to report truthful information, information furnishers must be obliged to report accurate, up-to-date and complete information and credit bureaus must have reasonable standards in place to validate (*not verify!*) the information. There must be purpose limitations for the users of credit reports and at a minimum they should be asked to certify contractually for which purposes they use credit reports. Again, each credit reporting system should come with standards of protection for the consumer.

Inform the consumer: Consumers almost always only deal with the *creditor* (i.e. the information furnisher) and not the credit bureau. At this stage, the creditor should inform the consumer about credit reporting. This notice should provide the possibility of some form of consent and include what information is transferred to which parties and what these parties do with the information. In addition, it should contain an explanation which consumer rights exist (such as access or rectification) and how he/she can contact the credit reporting agency. If the consumer does not have the chance to consent, how is he/she informed about the information sharing practices? Many of the consumer's rights are interrelated, one is the precondition of another such as the right to know about information sharing to be able to access information and to update or correct it.

Align incentives and responsibilities: A clear sign of little knowledge about credit reporting is a total placement of the burden of responsibility on the credit bureau. Again, it can only be stressed that credit reporting is a *network*. The credit bureau is only the information circuit. It has only a small incentive to "police" creditors. Common sense helps here: creditors are the clients of credit bureaus. How should the former force the latter to report complete information with zero inaccuracies if they risk loosing the client? Policymakers must place responsibilities and liabilities on the parties on which they must be logically placed: the consumer, the creditor and the credit bureaus as they are all network participants.

Reporting inaccuracies and adequate sanctions: Some regulators try to implement liabilities that would reduce errors in the credit reporting system below a 1% error rate. They intended to establish criminal offences for the reporting of inaccurate information. With such liabilities in place who would risk to go to jail for credit reporting? I am convinced that not even regulators would dare to operate under their own standards! The reporting of inaccuracies should not be a criminal offence and it is not in the modern data protection laws of the industrialized countries. However, there should be administrative fines for the intentional and repeated reporting of inaccurate information for the party reporting this information. These fines should be high enough to make a difference. However, there is also imprisonment for severe breaches.

Dealing with purpose creep: I have at length discussed the forces that are at work in markets for information. It is very likely that concentration can be observed. Companies in competition will try to get information from as many sources as possible to increase borrower coverage. They will version the information, bundle it and they have the incentive to sell it to as many customers as possible. I leave it to the reader to think about the consequences for personal privacy. The purposes for which the information is used should be related to the purposes to which the consumer *originally consented*. Credit information should *not* be used for *employment assessment* or any other purpose which is unrelated to credit and of which the consumer has not been informed. Unrelated purposes are usually those for which the consumer has not provided consent in the first place. It might very well lead to a "lock-out" of the labor market, an experience made by regimes that allowed this activity in the past (U.S., South Korea and China). For consumers this might lead to a vicious circle where they cannot find a job and cannot pay back their loan. It should be sufficient to verify some data categories and to apply psychometric test to applicants.

Monitoring and supervision: Credit reporting has long been an activity that somehow operated in the "background:" consumers did not know about credit bureaus and the only direct contact was between credit bureaus and creditors. Although this changed remarkably in the 1990s, credit bureaus only get into the spot light if there are scandals. The activity of information sharing is vital to credit markets and may have negative effects for consumers. Therefore, regulators should ensure that they monitor and supervise credit bureaus. This can be done proactively or reactively. Proactive are all measures that do not demand consumer complains or other evidence of privacy breaches, reactive demands exactly this. Proactive measures are annual reports, audits, discussion among other activities. Reactive measures are all activities that are directed at the company which supposedly is breaching law. Many European authorities employ the reactive approach for the simple reason of being understaffed. Credit bureaus should furnish authorities with aggregate information on the credit market and on their activities such as dispute settlement.

Dispute settlement: Establish an efficient dispute settlement system. Such a system is only efficient, if responsibilities are aligned meaning that each party dealing with the information can be approached for dispute settlement. Only if there is the threat of a dispute the company has to deal with it will take reasonable steps to ensure that it collects, processes and reports accurate information. Again, there is no use of placing the sole responsibility on the credit bureau. All parties should be demanded to disclose the information they have stored on the individual. This is the case in Europe and as could be outlined in the regulatory sections, it is also increasingly the case in the U.S. Regulators should constantly monitor the use and recalibration of credit scoring models, something that must already be done by banking supervision within the Basel II framework.[77]

Cooperation with stakeholders: For policy makers that are newcomers in this field, it is of no use to draw up regulations in isolation without basic knowledge and without talking to the stakeholders. Credit reporting is a complex activity that involves different parties with different incentives and interests. For the outsider it is often difficult to understand. Cooperation with stakeholders is therefore of utmost importance, because it will help to determine what works in practice and what does not work. There are no "quick fixes" in credit reporting, because numerous parties must alter their reporting standards, transmission protocols and practices.

Using credit bureaus for supervision: Banking supervision authorities will have an interest in using the credit information stored in the credit bureau's databases for their own analytical purposes. However, this is not possible if the property rights to information are completely located at the credit bureau. In this case, regulators would have to rely on the good will of the company to get the information. Therefore, it is suggested to find a compromise and to fix it in the law. Such a compromise could be that regulators are allowed to use the bureau information for purposes that are in the public interest. It was stated that information from public registers is used in a variety of ways. These methods of analysis can potentially also be applied to data of credit bureaus for determination of total indebtedness of consumers, identification of banks that systematically make risky loans or identification of trends in lending and risk distribution and evolution in the market.

---

[77] Basel II is excluded from this book, for a discussion see Artigas (2004).

Dictatorships and autocratic societies: Nowhere in any of the publications about credit reporting by international institutions one may find any roadmap how to deal with countries that have no democratic tradition or that are authoritarian/totalitarian. But advisors that work in the field of credit reporting must take such a situation into account. Should one suggest a credit reporting system with vast data collections about individuals to a country like Zimbabwe, ruled by the authoritarian regime of President Robert Mugabe? The experience in European countries during World War II showed that data can be used for other purposes, for instance for prosecuting people politically. It is therefore of utmost importance not to store certain types of information such as nationality, ethnic origin, political and religious belief among other characteristics described in this book. In the long-run credit reporting systems certainly increase access to finance and with it economic empowerment of people. However, it is questionable if one should implement such a system in an authoritarian regime. In fact it would be useful if an international organization such as the UN would monitor activities of data collection on individuals in such countries.

Dual Regimes (public registers and private credit bureaus): The creation of dual regimes is beneficial for a country. However, regulators should bear in mind that if they wish to have a competitive credit reporting industry, they *must* establish a division of labor among the public and the private credit reporting entities. I have discussed cases where the public registry "crowded out" private credit reporting (cases are France and Belgium). Although a public monopoly certainly has advantages in terms of centralization, there are also disadvantages such as not being under pressure to innovate. It is up to the regulators in the individual country to weight advantages and disadvantages of having both in the market and then to decide which institutional road they would like to take. China seems to be an example, where authorities have decided to establish one immense public register–against the advise from international organizations. Sometimes, centralized approaches are probably not the worst solutions from an economic point of view. How efficient the system will work remains an open question. Policymakers have to keep in mind that once they have embarked on an institutional path, there are considerable costs of changes.

Locating property rights: One of the most difficult fields in the regulation is the location of the property rights to information. This may either be at the individual or at the bank or credit reporting agency. In the past, more and more property rights have been located at the individual in most developed countries, even the U.S. I have suggested that a separation of property rights is a solution that dominates other solutions from an economic point of view. There should be no consent for negative information. For positive information it is a matter of consideration. Positive information increases precision of scoring models. And it enables credit bureaus and banks to conduct other types of scoring for marketing purposes. Again, the exact choice of the location of property rights is a political process and will depend on the privacy preference in a country.

Centralized notification systems: If a country has decided to allow competition in consumer credit reporting, regulators must be aware that several entities collect the consumer's information. The consumer has to go to each individual agency to correct the information if errors occur or disputes or identity theft. This is a major burden, especially considering poor people in developing countries that rarely have the time nor the funds to approach all companies conducting the activity in the market (for instance, South Africa has several credit reporting agencies and a very poor population). Policymakers should consider if the set-up of a notification system is possible in their country or if they can establish an ombudsman how deals with consumer requests. Such systems could act as "centralized circuit" that can be approached by consumers. Over such a system, credit bureaus could notify each other of corrected errors or of identity theft indications. This would reduce the costs for consumers and credit bureaus at the same time.

There are a lot more suggestions that could potentially be given to regulators. As always, the devil is in the detail and credit reporting regulation is no exemption. However, it can be stressed that the historical review in this book made clear that even in the U.S.–the country with generally lower data protection standards–more and more regulations were introduced in credit reporting to increase the protection of the consumer. At the end it is a question of finding the right equilibrium of consumer rights and commercial necessity of disclosing credit information. Eventually it is up to the legislators, regulators and policymakers to strike the right balance.

5 Economic Effects of Credit Reporting

Empirical evidence on credit bureaus and privacy regulation is still limited. There are only few works on the economic effects of credit reporting and even less on privacy regulation. The existing works can primarily be divided into micro and macro approaches. Since 1999, the World Bank has collected data on credit reporting systems by putting questionnaires forth to private and public credit registries. Although there is now more data available than six years ago when I started with this research the knowledge of credit reporting remains incomplete. The following sections will present some insights on the interaction of regulations, credit reporting and credit market development. Three areas are differentiated: micro evidence on credit reporting, data protection and macro evidence of both. The micro approaches analyze the effect of individual data protection measures, while the macro approaches evaluate the overall impact of credit reporting on the credit market. The first sections, however, are devoted to credit scoring, because without it any discussion of credit reporting is incomplete.

5.1 Credit Scoring

Over the past years, credit scoring, automated underwriting and securitization have had a major impact on lending business. A credit scoring model is a statistical decision support system that is based upon a function that takes a set of predictors as inputs and provides a number (score) as output. Credit scoring models help creditors to decide who should get credit or who should be declined and if the person gets credit at which conditions (so-called *risk-based pricing*). The basic structure is the following: The dependent variable Y is a variable for credit risk or the likelihood of repayment (for instance, default or delinquency). The independent variables are predictors that explain Y. The independent variables are derived from the credit report or the consumer's application. Such information encompasses payment history, number and type of accounts, late payments or collections among other things. The performance of the consumer in repaying his/her debt is then derived from the performance of similar types of consumers. The credit scoring system awards points for each factor to predict the likelihood of repayment. The total number of these points is added up for the credit score. The higher the score, the lower is the credit risk and the number typically lies between 300-850. There is an increasing trend to develop different models for predicting delinquency (credit risk), write-offs or bankruptcy. These models differ in terms of variables taken into account. The interaction between the variables might change over time and new variables that are good predictors of credit risk might emerge. Therefore models must be re-estimated and re-calibrated from time to time as it might change its prediction power over the business cycle. Altogether, there are commercially available models with around 30 predictors that do reasonably well in predicting the likelihood of repayment. Usually, these models are proprietary, which means that companies such as Fair Isaac or the credit reporting agencies do not disclose them to the public. Banks sometimes develop these models by using their own information and that of the credit bureau, in other cases they are developed by a third party (such as Fair Isaac) or a credit bureau.

Figure 5.1
Credit Scoring Model Structure

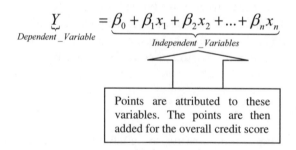

Scoring models are developed as follows: first, a random sample is drawn from a pool of consumers (development sample)–consumers that have been accepted but ideally also those that have been declined. The latter is often not available and there are techniques such as reject inference with which is it possible to statistically infer the behavior of declined appli-cants. Next, the model is estimated and there is the assignment of weights to the characteristics of a borrower. This means the higher the importance of a variable in terms of the relation to credit risk, the higher will be the weight assigned to this variable. Next the model is tested on a different sample (the so-called hold-out sample). The model must work on many different kinds of samples, not only the one it has been developed for. The results from both tests, therefore, must be similar otherwise the model is weak. It is important to note that the scoring model itself is only a decision support system–it does not make a decision itself. It is up to the institution using the scoring system to set the so-called *cut-off score*, which separates good from bad risks. This will be different from institution to institution as the risk preferences and policies are varying from bank to bank. The list below shows the percentage of contribution of different factors to the well-known Fico score from Fair Isaac. For some time, the industry has claimed that it was not possible to explain the score to consumers, because of the complicated statistical models used for its calculation. This is wrong. In the U.S. and other countries there is an increasing number of companies that explain the main influence factors, without revealing the model itself. The contribution to the score is the following:

1. Amounts owed: 30%
2. Length of credit history: 15%
3. New credit: 10%
4. Types of credit used: 10%
5. Payment history: 35%

Depending on what is scored, the result of the estimation informs either about credit risk, bankruptcy risk, probability of repayment or the profitability of the customer. It will be elaborated on those different models further below. Thomas (2000: 151) traces the origin of scoring back to the discrimination of groups studied by Irving Fisher. He was interested in developing discrimination procedures for general classification problems. For this matter, Fisher worked on so-called linear discriminant factors, factors according to which groups can be separated. Although, the model assumptions were restrictive, the models produced results that were relatively robust (Crook, Edelman and Thomas 2002: 41). Fisher's techniques have been used later in a research project for the U.S. National Bureau of Economic Research to discriminate between good and bad loans. During World War II many men were drafted into the military service, among them bank employees, with these men creditors lost valuable expertise. Before being drafted, the experts wrote down "rules of thumb" for their colleagues for the decisions on whom to grant credit. These early versions of "expert systems," together with the increasing power in mathematical modeling and computing developed into the modern scoring model. One of the first firms to enter the field was Fair Isaac as described in the historical chapter of this book. Today, scoring techniques are applied to all kinds of problems. There are different types of scoring models such as application scoring, behavioral scoring, profit scoring or collections scoring. Credit scoring models equate consumer credit risk with defaults, delinquencies or charge-offs. These models are available for specific markets (or portfolios) such as mortgages, auto finance or retail finance. Banks usually work with a number of models. In application scoring, only the information in a borrowers' application is used for the decision as to whether credit should be granted, however, nowadays it is more common to also use credit bureau data. It is also possible for an institution to use different scores as different thresholds for the consumer to qualify.

The bankruptcy score, for instance, is often used secondarily to the credit score. Banks can use both, the credit score and the bankruptcy score in a step-wise qualification procedure for the credit applicant. With a bankruptcy model one can predict either how likely a person is to file for bankruptcy or estimate the bankruptcy loss ratio (bankruptcy losses divided by revenues). The propensity of the consumer to file for bankruptcy is typically assessed by taking into account factors such as high credit utilization and credit limits, the number of late payments, and the number of credit inquiries. Such techniques also enable banks to assess their portfolio in terms of risk, something they need for the capital-to-risk ratio under Basel II. The bankruptcy losses determine how much banks must set aside for loan losses. This score (that is currently not revealed to consumers) works differently compared to the credit score, where a higher number means a better type. A low bankruptcy score is an indicator of low risk of filing for bankruptcy.

Profit scoring focuses on the consumer's profitability. "At present, the emphasis is on changing the objectives from trying to minimize the chance a customer will default on one particular product to looking at how the firm can maximize the profit it can make from that customer." (Crook, Edelman and Thomas 2002: 4). Banks are interested in the profitability of their clients or of potential clients. This could affect the marketing efforts of a bank or the service level the consumer is about to get. For instance, marketing could primarily be focused on the most profitable consumers. For this kind of scoring other information requirements exist, for instance one must have information on the transactions of a consumer and the profit made from them. The problem is that profit is not only a function of the consumer's individual characteristics, but also of the prevailing economic conditions.[78] For instance, revenue scores rank-order revolving credit accounts by the likely amount of revenue they will generate in the next 12 months. There is also collection scoring (i.e. the probability that the consumer will repay the loan after default). For this type of scoring, experts go through the repayment behavior of a person, but sometimes also through demographic information and the correspondence with the borrower. The intention is to find aspects that could be targeted so that the borrower pays

---

[78] A more detailed discussion is provided in Thomas (2000).

back the loan in the collection process as quickly as possible. In the past, insurance scoring drew a lot of attention. Insurance companies use credit reports for their underwriting policies and to set premiums. Underwriting is the process of risk identification and the setting of contractual conditions and prices for personal lines of insurance. Originally, insurers have focused on the physical aspects of risk as in the case where a car is insured. Increasingly, non-physical risk is taken into account. Insurance companies use their own risk-prediction models and they derived the risk of somebody filing a claim also from credit data (so-called insurance claim risk). This score is based upon the credit score, because there is a correlation. The rule of thumb is the lower the credit score, the higher the risk for filing a claim. Somebody who has a low insurance score has a higher propensity to file a claim with the insurance. If the insurance score is high, this is positive, the premiums charged will be lower. There are six categories that might be used by an insurance scoring model: public records, past payment history, length of credit history, inquiries for credit, type of credit in use and outstanding debt.

Personal credit profiles on individuals also increasingly play an important role in small business lending. In this market segment, informational asymmetries are severe. Information gathering is especially difficult as small businesses are opaque. Therefore, small business scoring is partially based upon the personal profile of the business principal (see Asch 1995, Mester 1997). Tests of small business scoring models in the U.S. found that one of the most important indicators of loan performance were the characteristics of the business owner rather than the ones of the business itself (Mester 1997: 5). This is the reason, why data protection also plays a role in commercial reporting–there is an area of overlap, where personal reports are used for business lending. Business information is combined with information on the owner of the business to indicate the likelihood of repayment. The reporting agencies are aware that small firms cannot be rated the same way as large ones. For this type of scoring, there is usually a threshold of what is considered to be a small business (such as less then US-$ 5 million in sales) and credit of less then US-$ 250.000. Small business lending is in general more related to consumer lending than to commercial lending and the main similarity is that the business owner's profile is closely linked to creditworthiness of the company (Bishop 2002). The author also states that his company has compared profiles of small business owners and consumers: that comparison showed that small business owners have in general more delinquencies, more inquiries and older and thicker files. Altogether, there is an increasing trend to diversify scoring techniques and to apply them to many areas in economic life. There is behavioral scoring, attrition scoring, revenue scoring and many other techniques not discussed here. Such techniques are increasingly refined and the models can be customized to individual needs. For instance, the credit card industry uses models for setting prices and conditions of credit cards that differ from the scoring models used for mortgage underwriting. As discussed in the theory chapter of this book, the forces in information markets and the characteristics of information goods inevitably lead to this diversification. It ensures that information is used over and over again–as many times as possible. There are different techniques of credit risk estimation. Discriminant analysis differs from the regression model, because it divides borrowers into high and low default-risk classes instead of estimating the probability of default. Discriminant functions are used to separate groups, as already mentioned, whereby one searches for the combination of variables that separates the two groups best (see Banasiak and Tantum 1999).

Figure 5.2
Credit Scores: Performance Distribution

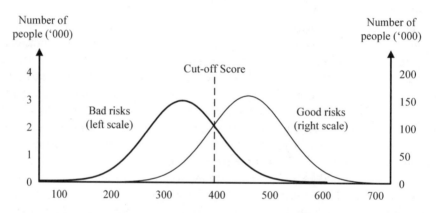

Figure 5.2 shows the distribution of credit scores and the separation of good risks and bad risks in terms of numbers of people. The graph also shows the cut-off point set by the creditor that is between a score of 400. Around this area, cases need further scrutiny. However, below a score of 300, no further scrutiny is required, since the model clearly shows that these are bad risk cases. One of the great advantages of credit scoring is that instead of evaluating each application individually, the credit manager can focus on the shady area, when it is not clear which risk exists. This increases productivity in lending and contributes to a more efficient use of human capital. There are a number of methods applicable for the estimation of credit risk, as stated above. Other methods are recursive partitioning algorithms (classification trees), where a set of borrowers is split into different sub-groups depending on their characteristics. These sub-groups

are then judged as good or bad. With the classification in sub-groups and further sub-subgroups, ever more homogenous groups are created. This classification only stops when some pre-set characteristics of the terminal nodes of the classification trees are met. Among the newer approaches are neural networks (popularly called artificial intelligence). These algorithms detect relationships between variables and default probability, for instance. They allow for learning and flexible pattern recognition. Initial assumptions about the distribution (i.e. the functional form) of default are not necessary. A good overview of the different techniques is provided in Fair Isaac (2003). Despite having models that perform well, they have to be re-evaluated and recalibrated from time to time, because the relationships between the variables might change. There is a range of techniques that can be applied to measure the performance of the model such as Kolmogorov-Smirnov statistics.

Figure 5.3
Receiver Operating Characteristics Curve

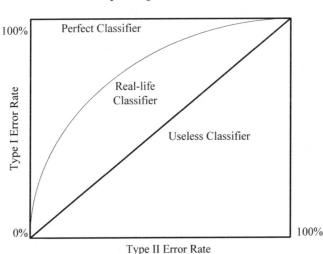

Type II Error Rate
Source: Yang (2002)

Another method is to create the Receiver Operating Characteristics curve (ROC) with which it is possible to compare the classification properties of different scorecards. Yang (2002: 18) explains that in case of a perfect prediction, the curve would follow the axes and classify 100% of bad risks into the "bad risk category" and 0% into the "good risk category." The ROC-curve is a plot of the proportion of correctly classified good accounts against the proportion of incorrectly classified bad accounts for all possible cut-off levels. "The higher the curve, the better is prediction, and consequently the larger is the area under the curve, the better is the model performance." (Andreeva, Ansell and Crook 2003: 5). This is an important tool to evaluate the efficiency and performance of a model. Figure 5.3 shows the perfect classifier sorts all cases that are bad loans into the "bad loan" category. However, this is only an ideal case. The real-life classifier would be a curve in between the perfect classifier and the useless one. Other methods include cross-validation for small samples, bootstrapping and jack-knifing which are not further explain herein (the reader is referred to Crook, Edelman and Thomas 2002 or Fair Isaac 2003). Altogether it is important to note that models must be re-evaluated from time to time as some relationships in the model change. In addition, it is important to evaluate the quality in terms of the purposes they are supposed to serve. This approach also has implications for regulators that will have to evaluate the models of banks under the Basel II regime.

5.2 Empirical Evidence on Data Protection

What is the economic impact of financial privacy restrictions? Do such restrictions negatively impact on credit scoring models? What are the sources that reduce the efficiency of predictive models? In the following sections, these questions are discussed in-depth by evaluating recent literature. This discussion is not only concentrated on privacy restrictions, but also touches upon other problems that directly have to do with statistical data protection (erroneous data, under-representation or selection bias).

5.2.1 Data Protection and Credit Scoring

In the following, the interaction of financial privacy restrictions and credit scoring is reviewed. There are several topics that should be taken into consideration. First, there might be general problems of information availability unrelated to data protection. This would be the case if the introduction of certain variables into the scoring model would raise public concern and protest. Second, data protection acts might restrict the availability of certain variables that might be predictive. Thirdly, some variables might not be available simply for the reason of being difficult to collect. In the subsequent sections I will discuss evidence on all of these problems. In an early survey, Chandler and Parker (1989) compare data from credit bureau files with that from credit applications. Their main question is as to whether the predictive power of a model increases if–in addition to application data–also credit bureau information is used. This is indicative for the question if an increasing information amount really adds to prediction power. Their samples consist of 1.500 bankcard applicants, 5.000 retail revolving card applicants and over 10.000 applicants for non-revolving cards. The authors test as to whether the larger data set (which combines credit bureau information and application information) outperforms the application data in predicting risk. The application data includes variables such as age, former and current residence, job, housing status, income, banking relationship and debt ratio. For testing the prediction precision of credit bureau information, the authors experiment with three information sets that show increasing detail. For the first set they only used the number of inquiries by lenders resulting from the application at different institutions and the worst credit rating. The second set included the aforementioned variables as well as, for example, new trade lines opened. The last and most detailed set included all the previous variables and information on the number of accounts by the lender (bank revolving and bank non-revolving). The authors built several models to score applicants. The predictive power of the credit scoring formula is tested with the Kolmogorov-Smirnov statistic to measure its ability to separate creditworthy and non-creditworthy accounts. In the models built to score bankcard applicants, results indicate that predictive power increases with the number of variables in the information sets. For bankcards, application-data yielded the lowest predictive power, whereas the detailed credit bureau model yielded the best predictions. It even improved in prediction power by excluding applications data for credit cards and revolving retail debt. In the category of models built to score retail card applications, the combination of application plus detailed credit bureau information outperformed the two other models. For the other product, the non-revolving charge card account, similar results were found. The authors concluded that predictive power rises for every card product *as the level of credit bureau detail increases.* The more data is available on the borrower, the greater the ability of the scoring model to separate good and bad risk. These results do not directly refer to privacy restrictions, but rather general information availability. Credit bureau data apparently serves the purpose of separating good and bad risks better than application data only.

Boyes, Hoffman and Low (1986) go one step further in the analysis of data protection restrictions and information availability. The authors analyze the impact of the Equal Credit Opportunity Act (ECOA). This act prohibits specific variables such as race can be used in lending decisions. The authors state that restricting important creditworthiness variables results in portfolio adjustments. On the macroeconomic level, the level of credit granted to all applications could decline. The authors use for their discriminant analysis a non-random sample of roughly 2.600 borrowers who applied for credit cards over the period of 1977-1980. In a probit analysis, their credit-granting equation simulates the behavior of the bank. The authors test for differences between the credit-granting equation and the default equation concerning variables like marital status, number of dependents and age. While marital status is not significant in either equation, number of dependents is associated with more defaults (but not reflected in the credit-granting behavior of the lending institution) and a higher age is a sign for less risk of default. By using a proxy for race (racial make-up of the neighborhood), the authors also test for racial discrimination. Race can also serve as proxy for the stability of income. The authors find a significant role of the variable in the default equation. However, the surveyed institution does not take this into account when making lending decisions. Instead, the opposite is the case: more credit is allocated to minorities, *in order to avoid charges* of ECOA violation. There are some methodological problems as the authors themselves note (Boyes, Hoffman and Low 1986: 219). First, a non-random sample is used which produces results that cannot be generalized and that hold only for the specific sample used. Second, the race variable is only a proxy, the authors actually test for racial make-up of the neighborhood and third, no evidence is offered on the trade-off of benefits received by the minorities through access to credit versus the portfolio reallocation.

Zandi (1998) makes another interesting observation in this respect. One striking characteristic of the U.S. economic expansion in the 1990s was the apparent deterioration of credit quality of U.S. households. Although there are several reasons involved, the number of nearly 6% of all households filing for bankruptcy was alarming (Zandi 1998: 156). The author discusses the question as to whether macroeconomic data should be integrated into scoring models or not. As one of the main reasons behind the deteriorating credit quality he sees the lowering of loan standards between 1993 and 1995. This standard is approximated by the loan-to-value ratio on mortgage loans. Yet this is not the complete picture. There was a surge of credit card solicitations and originations in the 1990s. For credit cards as well as most of the other types of household lending, the acceptance standards were lowered and sub-prime lending markets burgeoned during the same time (such markets encompass lending to those with below-the-average credit scores).

In the second half of the 1990s, consumer debt growth slowed also due to a tightening of lending standards by senior loan officers (Zandi 1998: 158). One consequence of this is the stabilization of the household debt-service burden. Zandi states that a scoring model's predictive capacity may be reduced by business cycle fluctuations; therefore, it has to be recalibrated with such fluctuations. The author sees a need for incorporating macroeconomic data in the models (for example the Leading Economic Indicators, LEIs), because the models are built upon historical data based on the economic situation that prevailed historically. "Since economic conditions lead credit quality performance by six to twelve months, the LEIs will lead changes in credit quality by as much as twelve to twenty-four months." (Zandi 1998: 166).

Avery, Calem and Canner (2000) discuss if concerns about reliability of scoring models are justified. They raise several issues: (1) Problems with omitted geographical and individual variables; (2) problems due to wrong measurement in credit reports; and (3) problems due to inappropriate populations or products. First the methodological approach is discussed. The authors select a representative sample of ZIP-codes stratifying the U.S., meaning the ZIP codes were randomly selected from each stratum. Next, Equifax provided the authors with proprietary credit bureau data individuals residing in the ZIP code areas. The tests were then made with the Mortgage Score (TMS) of Equifax. The authors use proxies for individual characteristics created from ZIP-code demographics as controls.[79] They explain that the mortgage score is computed from the same variables as the consumer credit score hence it has a similar aggregate distribution. Altogether scores of 3.4 million individuals were selected that were aggregated into 2.5 million households.

The problem of omitted variables is analyzed as follows: the authors explore how scores vary across ZIP codes by using the median score in the individual ZIP codes and the proportion of individuals (households) in the ZIP code with low credit scores. These measurements are regressed on proxies for regional and local market conditions and individual economic circumstances. The results will be summarized further below.

The authors assess the importance of errors in variables and other information problems. The credit report gives an incomplete picture due to a lack of data on rent or utility payments. Another problem is associated with types of errors and omissions in credit records.[80] It appears that omissions are caused by lenders who only report payment incidents or do not report to all three credit bureaus. This might result in models that are biased by assigning distorted decision weights to variables. This in turn implies inaccurate quantification of risk. The completeness of files is also referred to as "depth of credit files."

---

[79] The company did not provide information on income, education, etc.
[80] This topic will be discussed in more detail below.

Problems due to inappropriate populations refer to population coverage that is if the scoring model is developed for a population that does not cover all potential credit applicants. If the model is applied to a non-random subset of the population, it cannot mirror the behavior of the underrepresented population. Another bias arises if models are developed for a wide range of consumer products, but used for only a narrow category such as mortgages. If scores do not reflect the actual risk, banks choose a "wrong" cut-off and credit allocation inefficiencies could arise. The question is if these inefficiencies are really *economically significant*. Some of the applicants might get more credit than their risk profile would suggest and others get less. This might cancel each other out when generalized to a large group of people. The evidence suggests that omitted variables such as local economic conditions should raise some concern. Areas with high unemployment rates have median scores that are lower than areas with low unemployment. In areas where unemployment is persistently high, counties have a higher average credit score. The explanation for this phenomenon is that creditors apply tighter standards in economically weaker areas (Avery, Calem and Canner 2000: 537). The proxies for economic conditions show a significant effect on the differences in the credit scores. The median scores across urban, suburban and rural areas are relatively evenly distributed. However, the median score is lower in areas with high minority populations, high poverty rates and low house values or lack of education. For the creditworthy omitted variables are less of a problem, but: "For the 20% of individuals (15% of households with mortgages) with low TMS scores, however, obtaining credit may be more of a problem." (Avery, Calem and Canner 2000: 538). Under-representation of less educated and very poor people might bias the selection. The results on depth of credit reports are interesting. To approximate completeness, the authors take the age of the population in the ZIP code, which is statistically related to the median score. Younger applicants are on average less likely to have extensive credit histories. Where a larger share of the population is older than 60 years, credit scores have a much higher median. This primarily reflects differences in age-related credit usage behavior and income stability. There is significant variation in bureau scores across economic, location and demographic characteristics. This suggests that omitted variable and depth issues in fact require some attention. With regard to coverage, those with very low income or little education may be under-represented in the data that are used to develop scoring models. The failure to not make adjustments to economic conditions could lead to inefficiencies. Currently there seems to be no method for incorporating macroeconomic and regional information in scorecards. The use of scorecards not including this information can result in inappropriate pricing decisions (Avery, Calem and Canner 2000: 545). There are some interesting implications from a supervisory point of view: "The cumulative effects of these potential biases may raise questions about the adequacy of loss reserves and capital. Examiners may find it difficult to evaluate the safety and soundness of portfolios of scored loans." (Avery, Calem and Canner 2000: 528)[81]

The above discussion shows that inefficiencies do not always originate in data protection regulations: lack of variables and under-representation among other factors do play an important role. Bostic and Calem (2003) go one step further and test the impact of privacy restrictions directly. The authors differentiate three categories of data restrictions: (1) legal limitations on what may be collected (privacy laws); (2) time limitations on storage of adverse information (privacy laws); and (3) public concerns over certain variables (privacy culture). Whereas the first category and the second are clearly legal restrictions, the third category is based on considerations of public reactions. These reactions could be negative if variables are included that are not directly under the control of the borrower, such as regional economic data.

Table 5.1
Prohibited Bases in Selected Countries

Variable	U.S.	Germany	UK	France
Gender	1	0	0	0
Marital Status	1	0	0	0
Ethnic Origin	1	1	1	1
Color of Skin	1	0	0	0
National Origin	1	0	0	0
Age	0	0	0	0
Political Opinion	0	1	1	1
Trade Union Membership	1	1	1	1
Religious Belief	1	1	1	1
Health Data	1	1	1	0

Note: "0" indicates that there are no legal restrictions and the variables can be used in scoring. A "1" this denotes restrictions. For age to be used in the U.S. scoring models must not assign a negative value.

---

[81] The question here is as to whether a regional variation in scores should lead to different risk weights assigned to the loans within a portfolio.

Table 5.1 gives an overview of the prohibition of sensitive information in different countries. 0 indicates that there are no legal restrictions and the variables can be used in scoring, 1 this denotes restrictions. Although incorporated in the OECD and UN privacy principles as discussed above, it differs from country to country what variables are forbidden. For instance, age is generally allowed in European countries, however, in the U.S. there is the special rule that it might be used in scoring, but only if it is assigned a positive value. In addition, the gender variable is not allowed in scoring models, however, it is allowed in European countries. But there are also other restrictions such as retention periods for specific categories of information (see Table 5.2). Together with the prohibited bases, these are data privacy restrictions that do have a direct impact on scoring models, although this must not always be economically significant. Characteristics can be approximated in a less intrusive way than referring to race or health. Bostic and Calem (2003: 314) explain that the ECOA may have different effects such as: (1) overt discrimination: decisions are made upon prohibited bases; (2) disparate treatment: A lender treats the same credit qualities differently based upon prohibited bases; and (3) disparate impact: members of a protected group are negatively impacted.

Table 5.2
Retention Periods for Specific Data Categories (in Years)

Country	U.S.	GER	UK	FR
Information Sharing	+/ -	+/ -	+/ -	-
Delinquency (30-90 days late)	7	3	6	5
Payment history	2	3	3	0
Closed/Paid accounts	10	3	6	0
Default (180 days late)	7	3	6	5
Enquiries/searches	1	1	1	n/a
Law Suits/Judgments	7	3	6	8
Bankrupt/Liquidation	10	5	15	8
Administration Orders	7	3	n/a	n/a

Note: "+" denotes positive information and "-" denotes negative information, see Box 2.1 for explanation of these data categories.

Privacy always reflects a societies' judgment of what data should not be shared. This does not mean that such restrictions always have negative impacts on the efficiency of credit allocation. For instance, if recent payment behavior is a better predictor of credit risk than data that are a decade old, information that is 8 years old might not be used by credit reporting agencies. In this case, the retention period of 10 years has no efficiency decreasing impact. Restrictions on time limits of storage of data only matter if the data are highly predictive after becoming legally obsolete.[82] The ECOA banned the gender variable in scoring models for the purpose of limiting gender-based discrimination of women. The authors ask whether models that incorporate prohibited bases are more predictive than policy-compliant models. They used roughly 1.200 mortgage loans and applied logit analysis to analyze the relationship of loan delinquency, credit scores and the gender variable. Again, the TMS of Equifax is used. In their model, loan performance is regressed on a series of variables that are said to influence repayment. The estimations show that repayment behavior of women differs compared to men: "Thus, at each point over the credit score distribution, female borrowers had a delinquency rate that was less than or equal that of the male borrowers." Bostic and Calem (2000: 325). There is a gender-based performance gap, because the ratio of delinquency rates to credit scores is unequal across scores. For instance, in the range of 660-720, the delinquency rate for males is three times higher than for females. The adverse impact of the prohibition of the gender variable differs across score ranges. Privacy restrictions can run counter to economic efficiency and even may have the *opposite impact of their original intention*. Women here are pooled together with men–some of them pay more for credit considered their lower risk. This is evidence for data protection restrictions that lower the efficiency of a credit decision in terms of correctly pricing credit.

Instead of testing the impact of one individual data protection restriction, Barron and Staten (2003) are interested in the overall effect of positive and negative data sharing on the efficiency of credit allocation. The bottom line is whether prohibited variables cause fuzzy risk predictions, because they reduce a scoring model's decision efficiency by deteriorating screening and separation effectiveness. For this matter, two risk scoring processes are simulated, one under the Australian regime (negative information only) and one under the U.S. regime (positive-negative information sharing). The authors want to demonstrate that more information leads to

---

[82] Research from Fair Isaac cited by Barron and Staten (2003: 295) shows that more recent late payments are more predictive than older ones. However, some derogatory information remains to be predictive even when it ages.

better performance of the model. For this matter, they build a generic credit-scoring model that uses credit reports and not application data. For the simulations, the authors build a model with the full set of variables. In a next step, those not available in the simulated environments were dropped from the set of potential variables and the model was re-estimated based upon the remaining ones. The sample of roughly 312.000 new accounts was randomly drawn from a database that encompassed ten million credit records of U.S. citizens. To get a picture of the performance of the accounts (opened in 1997), their development over the next two years was followed. For performance the authors took the typical default measure of accounts becoming 90 days or more delinquent within the past two years. "For simulations the full set of bureau variables (500 and more) were available that were being marketed commercially by Experian in 1999." (Barron and Staten 2003: 291). The models were built by using subsets of this range of information. For the U.S., the model was estimated based upon 84 variables, for Australia 37 variables were used. The authors state that commercial scoring models usually contain 15-20 variables as some might capture the same or similar effects. For a common commercial model a small number of highly predictive variables is sufficient.

For each model, the individuals were ranked according to their credit score. By choosing a specific approval rate and comparing default rates for both types of probit models, one can judge effectiveness. The authors show that a change of the reporting environment results in changes of the cost and availability of credit. For a given approval rate, the full model produces lower default rates as the negative-only model. The gap between the full model and the negative only model decreases with increasing approval rates. Prediction power can be measured in type-I and type-II errors. The former, errors of omission, occur when goods risks are denied credit and the latter, errors of commission, when bad risks are accepted as borrowers. The authors demonstrate that both types of error increase under the negative regime. In a series of estimations, the authors analyze what happens if models are developed on sector-specific data. This could be retailer data or bank data, for example. They separate into: (1) positive-negative model; and (2) data on retail loans only. For the latter, the variables had to be re-calculated to reflect retail experience. This time the sample entailed roughly 67.000 retail accounts. Also, in this environment, the default rates are different. For the full model they are lower than for the sector-specific one, for which approval rates were also lower. In exchanging the retail model for a bank credit card model, the results show that the deterioration of the model is smaller: "This is an interesting result that suggests, among other things, that much of the predictive power in the full model derives from how customers acquire and handle their bank credit cards." (Barron and Staten 2003: 302). This result might be unique to the U.S. due to its highly developed credit card market. All in all, the authors draw several conclusions: (1) less credit is available in markets with restricted data sharing; (2) less credit might impair consumer spending; and (3) noisier variables might be used instead of less noisy ones.

A further point is due here. As the authors remark (Barron and Staten 2003: 309, Footnote 9) that being delinquent does not mean that these accounts are not profitable: "The argument that two borrowers who experience serious delinquency could differ on profitability is essentially the same argument that supports the addition of positive information to a score card that formerly contained only negative payment information." Creditors and credit bureaus are increasingly applying profitability scoring. A limited number of variables for predicting default is sufficient, but for marketing uses and profitability scoring more data are needed. There are indications that for different countries, different sets of variables are predictive. The credit behavior of Australians differs from that of Americans or Germans. Credit markets produce different types of information, for instance in the U.S., there is more credit card information available than in many European countries. Avery, Calem and Canner (2004a) find that although there are numerous benefits arising from credit scoring, there are also some drawbacks. These problems are due to imperfect predictions lacking three types of data: (1) local economic conditions; (2) marital status; and (3) adverse personal trigger events. The authors survey a large cross-section sample of credit records on U.S. consumers. The evidence suggests that a failure to consider local economic variables and unexpected individual events diminishes the effectiveness of the scoring models. The authors distinguish households with chronic financial problems from those with an unanticipated income shocks. The default probability is found to be smaller when credit problems were isolated in the past that is when they are clumped together in one month, for example. For individuals that had a repayment problem confined to a single month, the likelihood of default is 8% lower compared to those that have repayment problems stretched over a year. This type of borrower is not "irresponsible" compared to cases where the problems are chronic and stretch over a longer period of time. Temporary trigger events such as bad health or divorce require special attention. Newly divorced or separated persons exhibit a higher probability of default. But the likelihood of individuals to default also depends on local economic circumstances such as a recovery of the regional economy. For instance, in areas that undergo a recovery, the credit score will overstate the likelihood of default. In any case, there might always be one or more unlucky circumstances clumped together that lead to financial problems. The authors conclude that there are potential benefits from expanding the use of situational data, "a question for further research is whether modifications in the structure of the credit reporting system could be made, to permit the increased use of individual situational information that would yield greater accuracy in prediction and lower average credit losses and cost of borrowing." (Avery, Calem and Canner 2004a: 13). It is questionable if society would accept some of the suggestions, the authors probably had in mind. For instance, just recently medical information received special protection in the U.S. as it may now only be disclosed to another party after the consumer's opt-in. Instead, credit reporting agencies should further optimize their models by including the time variable that is as to whether financial problems were clumped together or not. The above surveys are the only ones that are publicly accessible by the conclusion of this literature survey. Other studies might exist, but they are either proprietary or otherwise not accessible.[83] One of the reasons why credit scoring had such a tremendous growth since the 1960s was the demand for credit cards: "The number of people applying for credit cards each day made it impossible in both economic and manpower terms to do anything but automate the lending decision." (Crook, Edelman and Thomas 2002: 3). Whereas the manual review of files and the expert judgment of the earlier credit granting process usually took some days, this is now done in seconds. This is especially the case in the U.S., where current levels of indebtedness are relatively high. In a testimony before the House Financial Services Committee in April 2003, Federal Reserve Board chairman Alan Greenspan said:

> *"There have been a lot of complaints about inaccuracies (...). But there is just no question that unless I have some major sophisticated system of credit evaluation continuously updated, I will have very great difficulty in maintaining the level of consumer credit currently available (...)."*
> (U.S. Federal Reserve Board 2003)

As discussed in the theory chapter, information sharing must reduce credit rationing and expand credit by pricing in more and more formerly underserved or denied households. There is evidence for the U.S. that this is the case. Table 5.3 shows that the percentage of families having any card increased from 51% (1970) to 76% (2001). The Table indicates that at the same time, the number of households with cards that have a credit facility increased over the past 20 years. In addition, an increasing number of

---

[83] I have requested several times surveys from different credit bureaus that were quoted somewhere. Usually, these surveys where not made available to me.

households take on debt (see Table 5.4). In 1983 roughly 69.6% of households had some kind of debt, which stood at 75.1% in 2001. Home-secured debt was 37.4% in 1983 and increased to 44.6% in 2001, over the same time, credit card balances increased from 37% to 44.4%.

Table 5.3
Percentage of U.S. Families Owning a Credit Card

Ownership	1970	1977	1983	1989	1995	1998	2001	2004
Own a card:								
- Any card	51	63	65	70	74	73	76	74
- Retail Card	45	54	58	61	58	50	45	58
- Banktype Card	16	38	43	56	66	68	73	95
Own card with balance:								
- Any Card	22	34	37	40	44	42	55	58
- Retail Card	15	25	29	28	24	19	n/a	n/a
- Banktype Card	6	16	22	29	37	37	n/a	n/a

Note: Data are only available until 2004, Source: Federal Reserve (2002)

The percentage of households with installment credit and other lines of credit, fell during this period. This increase in indebtedness, however, depends on many factors, not just the credit reporting system. One aspect is the cultural acceptance towards the use of credit. This is difficult to measure and could be subject to further research. In highly competitive environments, one would also expect a broader access to credit as well as in low interest rate environments. Another advantage of credit scoring is the opportunity for risk-based pricing. Edelberg (2003) tests the assumptions as to whether the premium per unit of risk increases because of risk-based pricing. Debt levels react accordingly and the spread between the category of borrowers with the highest risk and that with the lowest should increase. High credit risks would get access to credit but at higher prices (premium). For an increase of 0.01 points in the probability of bankruptcy, the corresponding interest rate increase tripled for mortgages, doubled for automobile loans and even rose almost six-fold for second mortgages.

Table 5.4
Percentage of U.S. Households with Debt

Indebtedness	1983	1989	1992	1995	1998	2001	2004
Any debt	69.6	73.0	73.6	74.5	74.1	75.1	76.4
Home secured	37.4	40.0	39.1	41.0	43.1	44.6	47.9
Installment loans	n/a	50.1	46.1	45.9	43.7	45.2	46.0
Credit card balance	37.0	40.4	43.8	47.3	44.1	44.4	46.2
Other lines of credit	11.2	3.2	2.4	1.9	2.3	1.5	1.6

Note: Data are only available until 2004, Source: Federal Reserve

Table 5.4 maps the increase of the number of U.S. households with debt. Borrowing levels and access to finance has changed: especially low-risk households could increase their borrowing and their financing costs fell. For high risks, on the other hand, increases in risk premiums implied that their borrowing as a whole either increased little or sometimes even fell. However, there is evidence that the inequality in credit terms increases. Credit scoring can help to monitor regional developments in credit markets and changes of overall credit quality. One of the most widely used scores in the U.S. is the FICO score by Fair Isaac. It has the range of 300-850 with higher scores denoting better credit risk (see Figure 5.4). Only 11% of U.S. consumers reach a score of 800 and more, the largest percentage of households is in the upper two categories: the range from 700-749 and from 750-799. Fair Isaac states that over 75% of credit applications in the U.S. use scores and the majority of banks get scores from the three bureaus to evaluate borrowers. Credit scoring has important effects on efficiency and productivity. Current levels of consumer indebtedness are only sustainable, because of the improved techniques of borrower evaluation.

Figure 5.4

National Distribution of U.S. FICO Scores

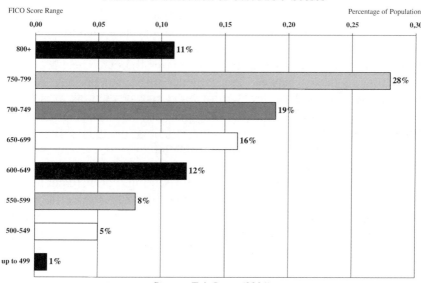

Source: Fair Isaac (2001)

Disadvantages or perceived problems encompass several aspects, social ones as well as technical ones. First, there might be the uncomfortable feeling that a decision with considerable impact on the life of the individuals is "made" by a "computer system" (for critical remarks, for instance, see Capon 1982).[84] Moral and political concerns of having "computerized decisions" resulted in Article 15 of the EU Data Protection Directive which states:

> *"Member States shall grant the right to every person not to be subject to a decision which produces legal effects concerning him or significantly affects him and which is based solely on automated processing of data intended to evaluate certain personal aspects relating to him, such as his performance at work, creditworthiness, reliability, conduct, etc."*

It is the financial institution that sets the cut-off point at an acceptable level of risk. Still many consumer associations criticize that scoring models are a "black box," a non-transparent process that is not explained to the public. One of the reasons for this non-transparency is the proprietary status of the models and the increasing competition among credit bureaus and scoring companies. Since the techniques are a property and "trade secret," the

---

[84] Again, it is the human being who makes the decision to use an automated decision support system. Of course, some humans outsource the decision to computers, but this in itself is a human decision.

techniques and weighting of variables are rarely disclosed except probably for supervision purposes. However, bureaus and scoring companies increasingly explain the driving factors behind the score. One concern is that credit scoring has a disparate impact on certain groups such as females or minorities. Some critics emphasize that information that enters scoring models could be of minor quality which biases the outcomes. Moreover, correlations that exist between the variables might be spurious. Above I have already discussed the problem of fuzzy risk predictions. It is true, a model is only as good as its input. However, this input may vary from region to region and from country to country. One of the main differences is positive and negative information. Information sharing regimes differ as well as the definitions of variables. It is important to acknowledge the characteristics of variables that are used for scoring. For different reasons, these variables can be of minor quality, which can blur the efficiency of the separation decision. The variable filter process identifies a combination of the most predictive variables, but this combination is subject to change. Therefore, scores are time-contingent. Models have to be re-estimated otherwise they may be too optimistic or too pessimistic. A Senior Loan Officer Opinion Survey by the Federal Reserve Board in November 1996 showed that 56% of 33 banks that used scoring models "failed to accurately predict loan-quality problems by being too optimistic. The bankers attributed part of the problem to a new willingness by consumers to declaring bankruptcy." (Mester 1997: 11). The author further states that in response to this development, 54% of the banks have redefined and re-estimated their models and 80% have raised their cut-off scores. The credit score is in many occasions private property just as the model. Increasingly the score is also disclosed and explained to consumers. Firms in the U.S. already provide score simulators. They enable consumers to simulate the impact of taking out more credit. Altogether transparency is on the rise. Some confusion surrounds the fact that credit scores from different bureaus almost inevitably differ. The sources for these differences are different data furnishers, varying updating cycles, different analytical techniques and a variance in data errors. The consumer is not able to tell from which agency the bank should get the record. To cope with the problem of inconsistent scores, products are offered that synthesize scores. For instance, financial service providers that get three credit scores (and possibly have their own) have to decide which one is the primary for them. The combination of more than one score could lead to a higher one.

Table 5.5
Fico Scores and Interest Rates in the U.S.

Credit Score (Lower bound)	Credit Score (Upper bound)	Interest Rate (30-year fixed rate mortgages)
720	850	5.586%
700	719	5.711%
675	699	6.248%
620	674	7.398%
560	619	8.531%
500	559	9.289%

Source: Fair Isaac, updated daily on the website.

Table 5.5 is one of the few examples, where a company champions consumer education and directly discloses the effects arising from differing credit scores. For consumers it might in some occasions be better to wait until the score changes again before taking up credit. There is some controversy over how accurate scoring models are, as discussed above. Automatic underwriting and scoring are increasingly applied to all kinds of business decisions such as lending, retail and telecommunication. Although credit scoring can lead to a denial of credit, the most important impact for the majority of credit-active population is risk-based price discrimination and very fast credit decisions. The overwhelming majority of credit decisions is positive. There are a number of other statistical problems, besides data quality, I have discussed them above. Altogether credit scoring has advantages and disadvantages, but the advantages certainly outweigh disadvantages. However, it has to be kept in mind that often unpredictable life events lead to payment defaults and these cannot be foreseen by a model (Jentzsch and San Jose Riestra 2006).

5.2.2 International Differences in Credit Scoring

Little is known about the international differences in credit data prediction power and scorecards. Countries differ concerning terminology and range of data collected. So far, attempts to model a European scorecard have been rare. The forerunner of this research is the Credit Research Centre at the University of Edinburgh and one of the first works there is that of Howe and Platts (1997). These authors ask the question if data across European countries change their predictive power from country to country or if it is possible to build one single European scorecard. They select five countries to represent the different regions in Europe: UK, Germany,

Greece, Belgium and Italy. Next they choose retail credit as their area of interest and pool the data they got from Experian for all of these countries. Since the variables used for the individual countries differ they had to select the ones that are common to all of them. Around 20 variables fulfilled this requirement. Next, the variables were classified. Apart from the single European scoring model, the authors build five regional models through re-classification and re-weighting of the variables. This excludes specific regional and client information that is used for regional models and that enhances their predictive power. European countries exhibit remarkable differences in credit use.

The variations in credit produce different "information environments." For instance, in the UK, credit card penetration is higher therefore there is more data available on credit card use. Consumer credit penetration and mortgage credit also vary from country to country. Howe and Platts (1997) included the following variables: residential status, home telephone, credit card, number of dependants and negative bureau data. They state that "certain attributes are far more predictive in certain countries than in others." (Howe and Platts 1997: 8). They estimated the European scorecard by using the common variables, regional ones (re-classification and re-weighting of common variables for each country) and five portfolio scorecards. The performance of a scorecard in separating good from bad risks can be measured with the following criteria: the information value, the Gini-Coefficient, the reduction of bad loans at a given acceptance rate or the increase of accepted loans at given default rates. The outcome is interesting. Introducing a European scorecard would have different effects in the countries, but in general the card "scores" worse than the country model and much worse than the retail models. For instance, in the UK, the European model would increase bad debt by 9.09% (Howe and Platts 1997: 15). In Belgium the European and country model come relatively close followed by Greece, Germany and Italy. The predictive capability can be improved and the amount of bad loans reduced by choosing a country model rather than a EU model. The authors conclude that we "must accept our differences and therefore the need to be scored differently." (Howe and Platts 1997: 17). The predictive power of the borrower's characteristics varies from country to country.

Andreeva, Ansell and Crook (2003: 7) ask the question as to whether it is possible to apply a single generic scoring model to populations of several European countries. Their cases are Belgium, Germany and the Netherlands. Generic models are developed for scoring geographically or socio-economically different populations, whereas customized models are only applied to the specific purpose/population they have been developed for. For their survey, the authors chose the retail card segment, 16 variables are common to all of the countries. Next to the three national models, the generic model is build on a data set that unifies data from the three nations. Besides this, the authors also construct three fully customized models. Again, the level of prediction of risk for the same variables differs across the countries. The authors observe some general patterns that hold irrespective of the country.[85] The ranking of attributes in terms of their significance also varies. To test the generic model performance, the authors applied it to the following samples: a) a hold-out sample aggregated from each of the national hold-out samples; and b) each national hold-out sample individually. With this approach, they were able to show that the generic model performs well and shows only a minor loss of prediction quality compared to national models. For developing the customized models, the authors used full data sets (application and credit bureau data) for the individual countries and several further country-specific variables. These models had a higher performance compared to the generic one. This higher power largely stems from the scope of information entering the models.

The authors conclude that generic scoring is a viable option provided that the data is harmonized between the countries. It is especially an option if the countries are geographically and economically close and if, despite the differences in predictors, some common patterns exist. For instance, in all countries married applicants are better risks than singles, homeowners are better risks than tenants and older borrowers are less risky than younger ones. In terms of acceptance rates–important for the consumer– the models differ. So for the consumer *it does make a difference*, which model is employed (the generic or the customized one) because this might increase or decrease the chance of being accepted.

The authors conclude that harmonized scoring would be feasible for some parts of Europe given that there are general patterns in the distribution of good and bad risks and that there is enough harmonized information for building a European model. However, there is the necessity for further harmonization of characteristics collected in different countries. This also holds for credit bureau characteristics, because of the lack of harmonization of data collections in the bureaus.

5.2.3 Macroeconomic Evidence on Credit Reporting

There are few works that test for the economic effects of credit reporting (regulation) on the macro-level. "Macro" denotes the global effects of credit reporting. The beginning of economic research on privacy is rooted

---

[85] For example, marital status is predictive across countries.

in the works of Posner (1978, 1979, 1980), Stigler (1980) and Hirshleifer (1971, 1980). The roots of this research can be traced back to the Chicago school of law and economics. The first works were mainly empirical and tested specific assumptions about privacy. These papers are more political economy oriented. Stigler (1980) analyzed congressional voting behavior on privacy legislation and supporting constituents. For this matter, he takes data on voting records, income, education and urbanization from 1977. He shows that the support for privacy laws is positively correlated with urbanization; however, it is negatively correlated with educational level. He also explains that those that could be considered bad risks (because of impaired credit reports or legal convictions) are politically organized and translate their interests into regulation in their favor. Stigler argues that the higher the percentage of such groups in the state, the more restrictive is privacy legislation. In his eyes, such restrictive statutes redistribute welfare from good risks to bad risks, because they tend to reduce employment, wages and increase interest rates. It is difficult to believe that the benefiting groups such as ex-criminals or African-Americans are better organized than the financial services industry. The latter is well known for contributing largest amounts to campaign finance. Additionally, Stigler's empirical analysis might be incomplete, as he does not control for any other important factors. This will be discussed in greater detail for Posner (1981). Posner conjectures that an economic approach to privacy implies that privacy is a "concealment of information:" "By reducing the amount of information available to the buyer in the labor market (the employer), it reduces the efficiency of that market." (Posner 1981: 405) This "*more information is always better*" doctrine is still held by many economists and policy makers today. All market participants have the incentive of concealing deficiencies either of their products or persona. With the concealment of information some costs may rise: there might be additional search costs or plain mismatches stemming from the reduced transparency. Posner (1980: 406) equates the "fraud of selling oneself" with a seller who is lying about his products. Concealment of information is based upon: (1) concealment as social insurance or buffer for bad health; (2) disclosure of criminal records reducing the prospect of rehabilitation; and (3) information overload reducing the processing of large data amounts. For instance, the concealment of a criminal record of a schoolteacher shifts the wealth consequences from one group to another–the school children, in case of a convicted abuser. Posner regards every reduction in the amount of information–in labor, credit or marriage markets–as a reduction of the efficiency of allocation of resources. The author is especially interested in the economic effects of the privacy laws on the state and federal level in terms of non-disclosure of credit reports or criminal records. Posner supports the political economy argument of Stigler. As source of this legislation, the author suspects pressure from groups with more arrests or convictions and poorer credit records than the average population. Although these groups would not be cohesive enough to form political coalitions, they would strongly overlap with racial and ethnic groups such as African- or Hispano-Americans: "Given laws that forbid discrimination against members of these racial and ethnic groups, it may be in their interest to press for passage of laws that also forbid 'discrimination' against people with poor credit records and lengthy criminal records." (Posner 1981: 407). This would lead to a "redistribution of wealth from whites to members of these racial and ethnic groups." With a regression analysis, Posner intends to underpin his assumptions. His model assumes the following: the dependent variable is a privacy law related to either criminal records or credit reports.[86] His independent variables are proxies for minorities, migration into the state,[87] income per capita in the state,[88] tax burden and the progression of the state income tax. The latter two variables are proxies for measuring the redistributive activity in the state. The results show that most of the variables are insignificant, which remains unexplained. In all cases, the migration variable remains insignificant, but it still constitutes for Posner the "social cost of privacy," because frequent changes of residence inhibits collection of information on these persons. Some further important variables are absent, such as GDP per capita, technology or banking regulation. Despite these drawbacks, Posner makes some important points: information disclosure has distributive wealth effects, which individuals must take into account. The first empirical survey of information sharing in credit markets is that of Pagano and Jappelli (1993). The authors collect information on 14 OECD countries and divide them into two groups: those with widespread information sharing and those with exchange on a smaller scale.[89] The authors compiled information on the absolute number of credit reports (excluding mortgage reports), credit reports per capita and per US-$ 10.000 of consumption. One proxy for the size of the credit record database in a country is how long the credit bureau existed in that country. Further variables are mobility of borrowers (changes of residence per year and frequency of moves between communities with more than 1 million inhabitants).

---

[86] This variable is either 0 if there is no law, 1 if there is one law in either category or it is 2 if there are laws in both categories.

[87] The variable is in all regressions not significant.

[88] The variable is significant only in two cases.

[89] These 14 countries are: U.S., Great Britain, France, Italy, Spain, Japan, Finland, Netherlands, Australia, West Germany, Sweden, Belgium, Norway and Greece.

The regression shows that there is a correlation between the number of credit reports (scaled by consumer spending) and consumer mobility. In a second regression, with the number of credit reports as dependent variable, the coefficient of mobility is positive and significant, whereas the coefficient of consumer credit is insignificant. The authors find that countries with credit bureaus that are active on a larger scale, exhibit high mobility of consumers and deeper consumer credit markets, whereas countries with little information sharing have thinner credit markets and lower mobility (Pagano and Jappelli 1993: 1707). The authors argue that information sharing is positively correlated with advances in information technology. In fact only advances in information technology facilitate large-scale information sharing. The size of the market increases the incentive to share information, which in turn leads to the expansion of the market. Altogether, the benefit of setting up a credit bureau rises with:

1. Increases in loan demand;
2. Household mobility;
3. Decrease of operational costs of the credit reporting system;
4. Uncertainty about borrower quality; and
5. Number of participants in the credit reporting system.

Especially when banks are faced with large numbers of unknown and mobile borrowers, they will have an incentive to exchange information. Regulatory barriers may reduce the competitive pressure among banks that arises from sharing information with competitors. The difficult question here is as to whether higher information sharing leads to more lending or if it is the other way round. Remarkable is that the simple regression with the dependent variable does not show a significant coefficient for consumer credit that means that there is no significant relationship between credit reporting and consumer credit lending in that specification.

Van Cayseele, Bouckaert and Degryse (1995) approach the topic from a different angle. Their model was explained in the theory chapter of this book. The main interest is the interaction of information sharing mechanism and the resulting market structure for banks. The authors compile 48 observations on eight countries for varying points in time (but all within the 1980s).[90] They identify three types of countries: those without a register, a negative-only and with a positive-negative register. Two questions are of interest:

---

[90] The countries are Belgium, Finland, France, Germany, Italy, Netherlands, Spain and Sweden.

1. Does an information environment with a negative or no register lead to more outlets per bank compared to a positive information environment?
2. Do more banks enter the market in a positive information environment as compared to a negative one?

The variables in the regression are the number of banks, the total number of outlets and consumer credit volume. In the first regression equation, the number of banks serves as dependent variable, whereas the independent variables are dummies for the existence of a positive or negative credit bureau, respectively. The same is done with the number of outlets per bank (as a dependent variable). The number of banks and outlets are the interdependent variables. Next, two equations are estimated that are relying on the same dependent variable, but include: (1) the revenue on consumer credit, (2) revenue on total non-bank deposits, and (3) personnel cost in the banking industry. The argument behind this is that higher revenue must attract more banks and more outlets. The second independent variable measures the deposit activity of banks. The equations are estimated by the Ordinary Least Squares method (OLS). The results suggest that in a positive-negative information sharing regime, there are less outlets per bank. The authors conclude that information sharing plays a role in the bank market structure. In the positive-negative information environment more and smaller banks emerge. However, more outlets are opened when a negative information environment exists compared to a positive-negative one. An interesting aspect is that the authors test for outlets and numbers of banks as being substitutes at the market level. But there might be also endogeneity at work here: It could be that smaller banks are more inclined to share data than larger banks. This seems to be one of the more convincing explanations considering the historical evidence in the U.S. and the development of the credit reporting system there. After all consumer banking is mainly a local business, even today.

One of the most comprehensive surveys to date is Jappelli and Pagano (2002). The authors divide their country sample into three groups depending on the existence of a credit bureau before 1994 and if there is a negative or a positive-negative bureau. In the specifications, the dependent variable is bank lending to GDP.[91] For the independent variables, the authors use categorical dummies for information sharing, further explanatory

---

[91] Bank lending to GDP is the ratio of bank claims on the private sector to GDP in 1994/1995. Although this indicator is usually available for a larger sample of countries, it includes lending to private businesses and households.

variables are the growth rate of GDP, rule of law, creditor rights and the legal origin of the commercial code of each country. The legal variables are introduced to control for the fact that countries with high values on those proxies mostly exhibit deeper credit markets. In the regressions they find that negative and positive information sharing is statistically significant. The estimates indicate that with the sharing of information, the ratio of bank lending to GDP is more than 20% higher (24.77% with negative information only and 23.18% with positive information). After excluding influential observations, the quality of the regression increases and so do the coefficients of both information sharing variables (Jappelli and Pagano 2002: 2034). The authors also approximate information sharing with other variables. For instance, they use the per capita number of credit reports and the number of years the agency is in business. Here, the results are somewhat surprising: none of these variables have coefficients that are statistically different from zero. This means that there is no discernible relationship of bank lending and information sharing approximated by metric variables. Moreover, it also does not make a statistical difference if the information is exchanged through a public or private credit bureau. A further regression is relating information sharing and default rates. It is difficult to find good variables for defaults for a large and international country sample. Two proxies would be at hand: non-performing loans or loan loss provisions. The former reflects information on loans that are handed over for collection and the latter reflects the bank's anticipation of future losses. The authors decide to use something else: the ICRG indicator ranging from 0-50 with 50 denoting the maximum risk.[92] The OLS estimates indicate that credit risk is in fact correlated with the information sharing dummies (on a 10% significance level): "According to the point estimates of these regressions, the presence of information sharing reduces credit risk by 3 or 4 points, between one third and one half of the sample average of credit risk (...)." (Jappelli and Pagano 2002: 2035). This sample average is a score of 7.77. Countries with no data exchange display a high credit risk score of 15.20 and countries with positive data exchange only 7.14. Countries that exchange only negative information exhibit only 5.11 in credit risk (Jappelli and Pagano 2002: 2032).

Next, the relationship of non-performing loans, credit risk and information sharing is tested. The regression predicts that a reduction of the credit risk variable of 3 points translates into a 1%-point reduction in the fraction

---

[92] The indicator is somewhat noisy, because it includes different kinds of risks. Respondents of this survey are asked for their perceptions on loan default and restructuring, delayed payment of supplier credits, repudiation of contracts by governments, losses from exchange controls, and expropriation of private investments.

of non-performing loans. The authors conclude that default rates are negatively correlated with the information sharing indicators. A further result is that private and public sharing arrangements have no differential impact on lending activity. In countries where private bureaus already exist, it is less likely that the government sets up a public one and public credit registries tend to be established in countries with poorly protected creditor rights (Jappelli and Pagano 2002: 2037). All in all, the authors state that credit market breadth is associated with information sharing and that total bank lending is higher in countries where information exchange is "more solidly established and intense." (Jappelli and Pagano 2002: 2039). This association exists when one controls for intervening variables such as country size or GDP growth, rule of law and creditor rights. Moreover, they find that credit risk is mitigated. It is not easy to draw conclusions about the direction of information sharing and bank lending, "there is a causality issue that our reduced form approach cannot address." (Jappelli and Pagano 2002: 2031). Theoretical models show that information sharing increases lending and reduces defaults. The same models however, also suggest that where credit is more abundant lenders have a stronger incentive to set up a credit bureau (Jappelli and Pagano 2002: 2031). Another aspect is that highly developed markets such as the U.S. have deep credit markets, but also competition among banks and non-banks. The technical infrastructure might also be important. Altogether it can only be stated that information sharing is higher in countries where there is more demand for credit and hence higher bank lending per capita. In a report by the World Bank (2003: 64), it is stated that there is a strong association between the wealth of a country and the presence of private credit bureaus. It is also observable that in highly concentrated banking markets it is less likely that a private credit bureau exists. World Bank researchers confirm the above results of Jappelli and Pagano (2002) that countries with poor creditor rights tend to establish public credit registries. Also, countries that score lower on the rule of law variable are more likely to have a public credit bureau. This is a substitution to make up for a private one. The reputation effect established through the credit reporting system seems to partially offset problems in enforcing contracts. The general impact in credit markets is that better law enforcement and stronger creditor rights are associated with deeper credit markets across countries. The impact of information sharing rises when it is controlled for creditor rights. The development perspective in the report is interesting. The World Bank poses the question what works best for credit markets considering different stages of development:

> *"For the poorer half of the sample, information sharing has greater impact than creditor rights. But in the richer countries, the effect of credit information sharing is less significant than that of creditor rights. Legal protections–important everywhere–have more impact in rich countries."* World Bank (2003: 65)

There are new insights into the relationship of public and private registries. For instance, if both are separated in the analysis (not one single dummy for an existing registry), then private bureaus have a positive and significant impact on credit depth and public registries are insignificant. If countries are grouped by income, the poorer half of the sample shows that both types of bureaus are associated with more private credit. The effect of public credit bureaus in poor countries rises with higher coverage. In the richer half of the countries the public credit registries have no association with private credit.

5.3 Estimating the Effects of Data Protection

What are the effects of data protection if we do not just look at one restriction, but the overall regime of regulation? Does it make a difference when countries regulate financial privacy stricter? How can data protection be measured? In the following, a proxy for data protection is developed that includes information on data protection in credit reporting as well as on enforcement mechanisms. Privacy protection in credit reporting is more than the restriction of the use of some variables. In theory chapter, the interaction of property rights (assigned by data protection laws) and disclosure was explained. The dominant strategy would be to share the information and to extend larger amounts of credit to better risks. Additionally, it was stated that it is not optimal to assign the whole set of property rights to information to the individual. The individual could then avoid disclosing negative information, but this information is crucial for overall stability of the banking system. It is important to have a credit reporting agency in the market, as bad risks will be exposes as such. Empirical analysis of these questions is difficult due to non-existent data or due to the fact, that some of the proxies first had to be developed.

5.3.1 Sample, Variables and Index

For the following analysis, the evaluation of 100 countries and their legal regime was included (see Table 5.6). This sample is based upon the country sample that the World Bank used for its Doing Business Project in

2004/2005. Countries can request World Bank evaluation, therefore this sample might have been expanded later on. Only a minority of these countries have data protection or credit reporting laws. But for those that do, I compiled information on law and regulations to map the rules applicable to credit reporting. Six questions were posed to compile information for a global overview:

(1) Does the constitution provide a general clause on privacy?
(2) Is there a general data protection law in effect?
(3) Does the country have a bank secrecy act?
(4) Does the country have a specific credit reporting act in effect?
(5) Are there any codes of conduct for the credit reporting industry?
(6) Are there any industry guidelines?

Since 2005, a number of countries have introduced new laws and regulations—they would now achieve higher ratings in this evaluation regime. These later developments are not acknowledged here. In former publications (Jentzsch 2003a), I have already evaluated countries in terms of their data protection regimes. This evaluation takes into account the clauses that exist in laws and regulations. It will be explained in greater detail, further below.

Table 5.6
Sample for the Survey of 100 Countries

Countries 1-25	Countries 26-50	Countries 51-75	Countries 76-100
Albania	Egypt	Lebanon	Singapore
Algeria	Ecuador	Lithuania	Slovak Republic
Argentina	Ethiopia	Latvia	Slovenia
Armenia	Finland	Madagascar	South Africa
Australia	France	Malawi	Spain
Austria	Georgia	Malaysia	Sri Lanka
Arab Rep.	Germany	Mali	Sweden
Bangladesh	Ghana	Moldova	Switzerland
Belarus	Greece	Mongolia	Syrian Arab Rep.
Belgium	Guatemala	Morocco	Taiwan
Benin	Honduras	Mozambique	Tanzania
Bolivia	Hong Kong	Nepal	Thailand
Bosnia Herze.	Hungary	Netherlands	Tunisia
Botswana	India	Nicaragua	Turkey
Bulgaria	Indonesia	Niger	Uganda
Burkina Faso	Iran, Islamic Rep.	Nigeria	Ukraine
Cameroon	Ireland	Norway	UA Emirates
Canada	Italy	Pakistan	United Kingdom
China	Jamaica	Philippines	United States

Table 5.6
Sample for the Survey of 100 Countries (cont.)

Countries 1-25	Countries 26-50	Countries 51-75	Countries 76-100
Colombia	Japan	Poland	Uruguay
Côte d'Ivoire	Jordan	Portugal	Uzbekistan
Croatia	Kazakhstan	Romania	Venezuela
Czech Republic	Korea	Russian Fed.	Vietnam
Denmark	Kenya	Saudi Arabia	Yemen
Dominican Rep.	Kyrgyz Republic	Senegal	Zambia

The legal situation in the countries was analyzed by taking the data protection laws, the credit reporting laws and further regulations (if existent) into account (Table 5.7). This Table shows that of 100 countries, 80 had privacy clauses in their constitutions, 35 countries had data protection laws–meaning laws that either cover the public-private sector or the private sector only. 96 countries had a bank law; many of those contain clauses on bank secrecy. Only seven countries had an industry specific law–although until 2007 this number increased, but the recent development is not taken into account here. Six countries had official codes of conduct (not private ones). The latter are often voluntary industry initiatives, but they are not counted here. Finally 22 countries had industry guidelines. This shows that the majority of countries does not follow the approach of applying an industry-specific law.

Table 5.7
Legal Design of Financial Privacy in 100 Countries

Legal Foundations	Number of Countries
Privacy clause in Constitution	80
General Data Protection Act	35
Banking Act	96
Credit Reporting Act (excl. individual articles)	7
Public Codes of Conduct	6
Industry Guidelines	22

It is often the case that the general legislation only provides some fundamental principles, while detailed regulations of financial privacy can be found in accompanying regulations. Therefore, to understand how a law is implemented one must also read the regulations. The complete evaluation form applied to the rating of the countries is displayed in Table 5.8. The Table shows that there are six components of the rating:

(1) Supervisory authority;
(2) Property rights to information;
(3) Obligations for credit bureaus;
(4) Trans-border data flows;
(5) Tasks of information furnishers; and
(6) Sanctions.

Whenever the relevant clause mentioned in Table 5.8 existed in the law, the country was assigned one point ("1"). For instance, if the law established a supervisory authority, the country was assigned 1, if not 0. The overall legal design was not included in the rating, because of the very general nature. In the following, the components (1)-(6) are called "variables." The individual clauses as mentioned in Table 5.8 are called indicators. For instance, "supervisory authority" is called variable, whereas existence, oversight or investigation powers are called indicators. Likewise, trans-border data flow is called variable, whereas import and export of personal data are called indicator. For the variable "obligations for credit bureaus" the indicators are the obligation to register, the definition of a purpose of the data collection, notification of the data subject, disclosure of the data only for specific purposes, etc. For each of them, the law or regulation has to set a provision to be counted into the index.

Table 5.8

Evaluation Instrument

Evaluation Criteria	
Legal Design (not rated)	**Obligations of Credit Bureaus (OC)**
Constitution	Register or License
Data Protection Act	Purpose of collection
Banking Act	Notification about data collection
Credit Reporting Act	Disclosures only for specific purposes
Codes of Conduct	Minimum fee for disclosure
Industry Guidelines	Accuracy of data required
Supervisory Authority (SA)	Up-to-date data required
General existence of any authority in data protection	Reaction to consumer requests (days/weeks)
Oversight over public sector	Time limit for dispute with consumer
Oversight over private sector	**Trans-border Data Flows (TBDF)**
Competence in oversight over credit reporting industry	Export of personal data only with consent
Competence to investigation	Export of personal data only with notification of authority
Competence to hear complaints	Export of personal data forbidden
Competence to administer lists of data controllers	Import of personal data forbidden
Competence to conduct audits	Extraterritorial clause in the law
Property Rights to Information (PR)	**Tasks of Information Furnishers (IF)**
Data subject has the right to opt in (consent)	Accuracy of reports required
Right to access the data	Notification of consumer about disclosure of data to credit bureau
Right to correct the personal data	Notification of consumer in case of adverse action
Right to have false information deleted	Dispute settlement mechanisms
Right to block information	Requirement to disclose own information
Right to know to whom information is disclosed	Requirement to update data
Right to stop marketing	Requirement to report complete data
Special restrictions on sensitive data exist	**Sanctions (SC)**
Special restrictions on historical data exist	Monetary Fines
	Imprisonment

The indicators are added to produce the variable. The first variable rates the power, the law (or regulation) assigns to the supervisory authority. It is the competence to oversee the private sector or the public sector (in case of a PCR, for instance). The competence to oversee credit reporting is singled out, because some countries assign the competence for private sector data protection to one government body and the competence to regulate credit reporting agencies to another. Of interest are also powers of the supervisory authority (for complaints, investigation of cases, etc.). International contracts were also included for comprehensiveness, although they are for expository purposes only. The reader is referred to the Tables in the Appendix for details. Here, the results are displayed. If a country does not reach any values in any of the aforementioned categories, it is clear that nothing exists in this country–meaning no law and no regulations. One of the most important variables collected is the property rights to information variable. This variable explains how much power a data subject has to determine how the personal information is used. The most important rights are: the right to opt in to the collection of data by another party (consent), the right to access the data, the right to correct them, the right to have false information deleted, the right to block information in case of dispute, the right to know to whom information is disclosed, the right to stop marketing, special protections for sensitive information,[93] and special restrictions for historical data.[94] Although there is no legal distinction between the credit reporting agency and information furnishers in Europe (both are "data controllers"), I separated them to account for the U.S. legislation, where information furnishers are separately defined. There are certain obligations credit bureaus have to take care of when operating in a regulatory environment: duty to register or acquire a license from an authority, specification of the purpose of data collection, notification of consumers about the ongoing data collection and specification of the reasons for data disclosures. Further important aspects are as to whether there is a minimum fee for disclosure, accuracy requirements for the credit bureau, requirements that data has to be up-to-date, time limits on reaction to consumer requests (within days/weeks) or limits for dispute settlement with the consumer. Trans-border data flows are also evaluated, although they play a minor role in credit reporting. For instance, the following restrictions were included: export of personal data only with consent of the individual or export of personal data only with notification of the authority. The law also sometimes provides more restrictive measures such as a complete prohibition of

---

[93] These are political beliefs, trade union membership, religious belief, and medical information, colour of skin or sexual preferences.
[94] These are data retention periods.

the export of personal data. In addition, in European laws the existence of "extraterritorial clauses" is common. The legislator demands that other third countries to which data is exported must provide an adequate standard of protection (so-called "European adequacy standard"). Moreover, rights/obligations of information furnishers also have to be evaluated. This is usually the bank, retailer, telecoms or any other party that sends the information to the bureau. The following legal points are evaluated in the law: accuracy of reports, notification to consumers about disclosures to credit bureau, notification of consumer in case of adverse action, dispute settlement mechanisms, requirements to disclose data stored (including any credit report), requirement to update data and requirement to report complete data. Lastly, sanctions include fines and imprisonment. The latter kicks in especially in cases of severe and repeated privacy intrusion. One might think that the sanction category is superfluous, once there is a law, there should be provisions to put teeth into it. However, there is a difference if just monetary fines are applied or if criminal offences are introduced. The results are given in the Appendix:

1) Table 5.9, 5.10 and 5.11 show the laws, where only data protection and credit reporting laws were included in the analysis inclusive their regulations (for comprehensiveness banking acts are also included); and

2) Overall results from the evaluation are presented in the Table 5.12 in the Appendix, where "1" denotes the existence of a clause and the values are added for the individual fields. Note that this is a snapshot of the legal situation which nowadays changes especially in Asia and Africa at a fairly fast pace.

It shows how many "points" a country achieved in individual categories. Although this is a rather rough approximation method, it maps credit reporting regulation in a country fairly well.

Figure 5.5
International Data Protection Standards Compared

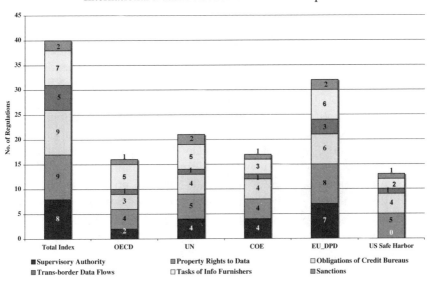

The results could be used in different ways. First, the rating contains general data protection measures, therefore one may calculate an *EU Data Protection Index* that can be compared to other indices. It is also possible to calculate an *OECD index* which contains only the indicators of the OECD guidelines. For comprehensiveness, U.S. Safe Harbor agreement and Council of Europe Convention are also rated. The results are presented in Figure 5.5, the total index used for credit reporting has 40 indicators (all derived from Table 5.8). In terms of the comparison, contracts and guidelines are of different character: some of them are legally binding, such as the EU Data Protection Directive, others are voluntary such as the Safe Harbor Agreement between the European Union and the U.S. As can be immediately noticed, the EU Data Protection Directive provides the highest number of regulations, taken here as proxy for strength of data protection. Safe Harbor as voluntary agreement provides the lowest level of protection. One might derive from this that companies that sign into Safe Harbor are certainly *not* on European data protection level, although they claim it.

Figure 5.6
Credit Reporting Regulation in Selected Countries

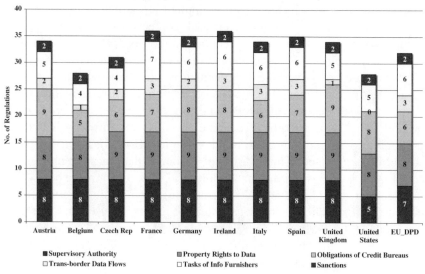

Figure 5.6 presents a detailed overview of countries and their credit reporting regulation rated according to the methodology explained above. None of the surveyed countries reached the level of 40 regulations. But as the figure shows, Germany, France and Ireland have a relatively high number of data protection regulations. And there is a noticeable difference to the level of data protection in the European countries and in the U.S. The latter country in comparison falls short in financial privacy regulation. Again, the number of regulations are taken here as indicator for the strictness of the data protection regime. However, one cannot really state that a country with twice as much regulatory rules has a twice as strong data protection regime. The number of rules is merely an indicator (proxy) for the latent variable "strength of data protection" which is not directly observable. The figure also shows that data protection regimes differ in their "composition" that is in the number of rules that are applied in individual categories. The comparison of regulatory regimes designed in a structurally different way cannot be conducted by a simple aggregation of numbers. There are a number of drawbacks if working with aggregates as they hide structural differences. In this section, it is briefly discussed why an index is applied. For this some general remarks are due. Indices are defined as the output of

either a formula or the aggregation of various indicators.[95] Most of the features of popular indices are known and have been extensively discussed. One of the reasons why they can be applied are structural problems that arise in inter-temporal or inter-regional comparisons. For international comparisons, for instance, one needs a common base.[96] The World Bank has already explored the development of international indices: "More specific measures of government performance, coupled with more specific measures of governmental processes or institutional arrangements, would permit analyses that provide more indication of which reforms are likely to be effective." (Knack 2002: 17). There are many reasons why indices are preferable to simple aggregations of variables. However, not everything should be aggregated. The addition of variables that are measured in different units is useless from a methodological point of view.[97] The "scaling problem" arises if indicators do not have a common dimension (unit of measurement). Indices should use homogeneously scaled variables (von der Lippe 2002: 4). In addition, if variables are differently scaled, they imply different arithmetic operations. For ordinal data only quantiles may be calculated, interval scaled data allows arithmetic operations (but not sums) and ratio scaled data allows the application of all types of arithmetic operations. The scaling problem implies that sums may not be meaningful due to varying scales or varying units of measurement. To aggregate variables that lack a common measurement unit, relatives can be calculated. This has been described as a necessary condition for deriving a sum, but not a sufficient one for a *meaningful result* (see von der Lippe 2002: 12). In addition, one should take into account that there are different influence factors on the index, if economic and political variables are added, some might change slowly (legal variables), others faster (financial variables). The weighting scheme then determines as to whether the index is lagging, leading and/or co-incidential. One of the main concerns is that simple aggregates change their structure, this implies that a weighting scheme has to be found which introduces weights either from the base or the current structure. In the past, researchers have developed a multitude of indices. The question is what index to pick. Among superlative indices that are typically used for price measurement, Fisher or Laspeyres are preferable, be-

---

[95] The terms "rating" and "score" are used interchangeably with the index (for a functional definition see Eichhorn 1978: 3).

[96] Other authors are applying either macro-indices that approximate overall institutions (Acemoglu, Johnson and Robinson 2001; Rodrik, Subramaniam and Trebbi 2002) or micro-indices that measure specific regulatory environments in capital or credit markets (Barth, Caprio and Levine 2002; La Porta, Lopez-de-Silanes and Shleifer 2002).

[97] One such example are international risk indicators aggregating facts such as "military in politics" and "foreign debt/GDP."

cause they fulfill many aspects required for indices. The inputs in the index is the number of regulations. Problematic is the weighting scheme, because there are "prices" and "quantities" and Laspeyres is usually applied for price measurement. However as "base" one may take the maximum number of regulations achievable in a field and divide it by 2 to obtain x_i^t.[98] As weights, the maximum amount or regulations that exist in the individual variable are chosen. To reduce the problem of implicit weighting, explicit weights must be applied. These weights may be constructed in two ways: (1) they can be derived empirically by using correlation or regression coefficients; or (2) they might be assigned by using maximum values that are achievable in the individual variables. Here, the latter method is used and the explicit weights are denoted with z_i^t for Laspeyres I^L in equation 5.1:

$$I^L = \sum_{i=1}^{n} \left(\frac{x_i^{t+1} z_i^t}{x_i^t z_i^t} \right) \tag{5.1}$$

$$I^L = \left(\frac{x_{sa}^{t+1} z_{sa}^t + x_{pr}^{t+1} z_{pr}^t + x_{oc}^{t+1} z_{oc}^t + x_{tb}^{t+1} z_{tb}^t + x_{if}^{t+1} z_{if}^t + x_{sc}^{t+1} z_{sc}^t}{x_{sa}^t z_{sa}^t + x_{pr}^t z_{pr}^t + x_{oc}^t z_{oc}^t + x_{tb}^t z_{tb}^t + x_{if}^t z_{if}^t + x_{sc}^t z_{sc}^t} \right) \tag{5.2}$$

In 5.2, x denotes the regulatory variable, sa denotes supervisory authority, pr property rights, oc obligations for credit bureaus, tb transborder data flows, if are information furnisher tasks and sc are sanctions. t denotes the base period and $t+1$ the observation period. For Laspeyres, the weights are taken from the base period and used for the base and observation period. Laspeyres fulfils tests such as the identity test, homogeneity[99] and commensurability.[100] However, the index fails the time reversal test, where–if two periods are exchanged–the output is the reciprocal value of the original observation, see equation 5.3:

$$I_{01}^L I_{10}^L = 1 \Leftrightarrow I_{01}^L = \frac{1}{I_{10}^L} \tag{5.3}$$

Where in equation 5.4 the latter term is the time-reverse Paasche index

$$\sum \left(\frac{x_i^1 y_i^0}{x_i^0 y_i^0} \right) = \frac{1}{\sum \left(\frac{x_i^0 y_i^0}{x_i^1 y_i^0} \right)} \tag{5.4}$$

---

[98] This ensures that the index is not artificially depressed.
[99] If all inputs change with the same rate □, the index has to reflect □.
[100] Index should not be affected by a change in unit of measurement of prices or quantities

and not the time reversed Laspeyres index.[101] With the time-reversal test one can determine, as to whether the index has a slight bias. If this test–applied forward or backward–does not result in unity, there is a bias. In addition, the factor reversal test is not fulfilled:

$$\sum\left(\frac{x_i^1 y_i^0}{x_i^0 y_i^0}\right) \cdot \left[\sum\left(\frac{x_i^1 y_i^0}{x_i^0 y_i^0}\right)\right] \neq \sum\left(\frac{x_i^1 y_i^1}{x_i^0 y_i^0}\right) \tag{5.5}$$

This index also fails the circularity test, where in equation 5.6 the subscripts denote the periods 0, 1 and 2:

$$I_{01}^L \cdot I_{12}^L \overset{?}{=} I_{02}^L \tag{5.6}$$

Equation 5.6 can be rewritten as in 5.7. That equation shows that for circularity to hold the index for the overall period has to equal the product of the two indices for the two time intervals 0 to 1 and 1 to 2.

$$\sum\left(\frac{x_i^1 y_i^0}{x_i^0 y_i^0}\right) \cdot \left[\sum\left(\frac{x_i^2 y_i^1}{x_i^1 y_i^1}\right)\right] \neq \sum\left(\frac{x_i^2 y_i^0}{x_i^0 y_i^0}\right) \tag{5.7}$$

The Fisher index would solve some of these problems, but it would at the same time complicate the structure even more. Moreover, some of the above tests are not important for the research matter. The most important criteria is that the index does should have an explicit weighting scheme. For robustness, I have used a number of other variables to approximate the economic and regulatory environment and to control for influences that are important. The rationale here was not to simply repeat the estimations of the other authors. Although that probably would have made the estimations more comparable, I was interested in using less noisy variables. Altogether the database included more than 120 variables covering macroeconomic data, credit markets, privacy regulations and information allocation variables. The data definitions are given in Table 5.13 in the Appendix. For the variables in the model, I usually had one, two or more substitutes approximating the same phenomenon. For instance, for technical infrastructure a telecom index, but also a connectivity index could be used (aggregating information on internet, telecom and mobile phones). For the estimations, I typically chose those variables that maximized the number of observations.

---

[101] For the Paasche index the weights are taken from the observation period and they are used for both, observation and base period.

5.3.2 Evidence on Credit Reporting Regulation

What are the main economic effects of credit reporting regulation? In the following some simple estimations are presented to analyze the interaction of several variables of interest. For simplicity, regression analysis is not discussed in detail, for instance I will not discuss normality or diagnostic tests that have been conducted for the statistical analysis. From the beginning, this research project was driven by the interest in the effects of data protection restrictions and their interaction with the credit market. There are only a few works that attempt to estimate the direct effects of data protection restrictions. In the following, we concentrate on three major fields of interaction:

1. Interaction of regulatory regimes with the information proxies;
2. Interaction of information proxies and credit market variables; and
3. Interaction of information sharing and credit risk.

Do data protection regimes have a negative or positive influence on the allocation of information in the market? This is one of the main questions to be answered. With „information allocation," „amount of information" or „credit reporting" the sales of credit reports on consumers are denoted. I have already discussed in the historical and empirical part of this book that credit reporting agencies collect and process millions of items on consumers. The main question is as to whether increased data protection in credit reporting could in fact make business more cumbersome and lead to lower information sales.[102] In addition: What are the effects of different kinds of regulations on information sharing? Do property rights to information have any discernible effects? A higher score on the credit reporting regulatory index might mean that data subjects have more rights to block sale of their personal information. And a high level of data protection might increase the costs of business in information markets and therefore the costs of the credit report. One may think of a situation where reduced information allocation reduces the efficiency of channeling savings into credit. It was argued in the theory chapter that locating the property rights at the individual can produce inefficient solutions. It will depend on the negative externalities as to whether the location of rights at the bank leads to efficient results. If externalities become too large (in the sense that personal data can be sold to almost anyone with „any kind of business interest"), the social planner would have to find compensation rules. But in general credit reporting should lead to higher lending in credit markets. This is based upon

---

[102] To be more precise, this is the number of credit reports sold/scaled by population.

the theoretical insights and the empirical literature. Before the estimations are presented, some words of caution. It was difficult to find estimates for the number of credit reports sold in the market–these had to be compiled from different sources over the period of five years of conducting this research. Although all countries could be evaluated in terms of their data protection regimes, the number of credit reports sold could not be found for all of them. An additional problem was posed by the collection of credit market statistics. There are no internationally standardized data on credit to households, for instance. In addition, all estimations are also hampered by the endogeneity problem. In addition, not all authors control for variables such as monetary policy or technical progress when estimating the economic effects of credit reporting. Models that do not account for these influence factors could potentially be subject to under-fitting. Due to the explorative character of the majority of works in this field, many surveys suffer from a small number of observations (this one here is no exemption), which increases variance and uncertainty about the statistical results. Moreover, usually, there is no time series data available. For my estimations, the dependent variable is metrically scaled: that is the number of credit reports sold in a country divided by total population ("credit reports per capita"). Therefore, the Ordinary Least Squares (OLS) technique can be applied. Below are the summary statistics of the variables used in the model.

Table 5.14
Summary Statistics for Credit Reporting

Variable	No. of Obs.	Mean	Standard Deviation	Minimum	Maximum
$Sqcridx$	76	0.3970203	0.5441424	0	2.335602
$Crri_L$	100	0.3346053	0.3684854	0	0.9309211
$Loans\_hh$	57	5634.903	10958.75	0.18	57129.81
$Banks$	80	226.6375	951.0202	5	8075
Tel	100	228.0863	224.6114	1.9292	745.57

Note: Variables and abbreviations are described in the Appendix, in Table 5.13.

Table 5.14 shows the summary statistics. *Sqcridx* is the squared credit reporting index. This is the number of consumer credit reports sold in the market scaled by population. *Crri$_L$* is the credit reporting regulatory index, the index that maps regulations. The variable *loans_hh* are the loans to households and *banks* is the absolute number of banks, a rough approximation of competition and concentration. *Tel* denotes telephone mainlines per 1.000 inhabitants and is used as proxy for technological development.

Some variables of potential interest were not significant in the model, therefore I excluded them.[103]

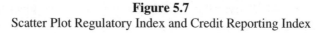

Figure 5.7
Scatter Plot Regulatory Index and Credit Reporting Index

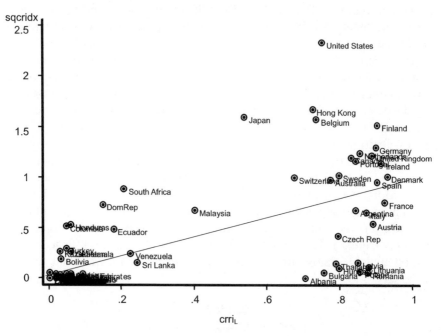

Figure 5.7 shows a positive relationship: the higher the credit reporting regulatory index (the index that measures regulation, $crri_L$), the higher is the credit reporting index (which maps sales of credit reports, sqcridx), see for an explanation Tabl 5.13 in the Appendix. There is potential for influential variables, for instance the U.S. is a Cook's d outlier. This is discussed below. In the origin corner are countries clustered that display low values on both variables, these are mostly developing countries. Although such a separated sample would suggest including a dummy variable for development, it was not significant. The OLS regression model is specified in equation 5.8:

$$Sqcridx = \beta_0 + \beta_1 Crri_L + \beta_2 Loans\_hh + \beta_3 Banks + \beta_4 Tel \qquad (5.8)$$

As the U.S. are an influential observation, a robust regression should be applied. For the record in terms of regression diagnostics, neither multicol-

---

[103] This included a 7-year average of real GDP, interest rates for the monetary policy and an indicator on the informal economy.

linearity nor autocorrelation, heteroskedasticity, outliers or model mis-specification are a problem. Diagnostic tests that were applied a listed in Table 5.15.

Table 5.15
Diagnostic Tests

Problem	Tests Applied
Normality	Kurtosis, Skew, Kolmogorov-Smirnov test
Outliers	Cook's d
Multicollinearity	Pearson Correlations, Variance Inflation Factor
Autocorrelation	Durbin-Watson statistic
Heteroskedasticity	White's test, Cook-Weisberg test
Misspecification	Ramsey RESET test, Link test

Table 5.16 in the data Appendix shows that there is an influence of loans to households on the number of credit reports sold per capita, the number of banks play a role and the telecommunication infrastructure. The primary index of interest, however, was the credit reporting regulatory index, $Crri_L$. Even after accounting for the other influences, it does not seem to have a negative impact on the credit reporting variable. To remind the reader: the index is an approximation of data protection in the field of credit reporting and the credit reporting variable is an estimate of the number of credit reports sold in the market scaled by population and corrected for skew. The regulatory index maps the existence of a supervisory authority, the property rights to information of the individual, the obligations of credit bureaus, the trans-border data flows and the tasks for information furnishers as well as the sanctions in a law (and the regulations). This is index is therefore tailored to the credit reporting activity. Even after experimenting with the index construction or including the absolute numbers of regulations, the insignificance remains.[104] What about the economic significance of the variables? The response variable is raised by .0000157 units for a one unit change (transformed back: 2.4649E-10) of the independent variable *Loans_hh* (loans to households per capita, see Table 5.13 for an exact description). This is hardly a major economic impact. It is small compared to *Tel* that changes the response variable by .0012541 units (transformed back: 1.57277E-06). The impact of the *Tel* variable is also greater than of the *Banks* variable.[105] The variable certainly captures a number of things

---

[104] I have also instrumented for this variable by using a dummy for democracy. This dummy is highly correlated to data protection act existence which in turn is highly correlated with $Crri_L$. This variable, however, was also not significant.

[105] Telecommunication is a proxy for several things, among them wealth of a country.

and might in general be seen as a proxy for the development of the country. Are there any categories of data protection in credit reporting that might have a special importance? Even if the overall regulatory index is not significant–it can be decomposed into individual measures, for instance rules on property rights. This variable, however, was not significant in estimation of a model with the same specification as in equation 5.8, when regulatory index was exchanged for property rights. Also none of the other variables (supervisory authority, obligations of credit bureaus, etc.) was significant. In this specification, therefore, other factors besides credit reporting regulation are important contributors to the amount of loans lent to households. For robustness, variables that measured the same phenomenon were exchanged, but the results remained the same. Further modifications such as inclusion of new variables (a dummy for development, for instance) did also not change the basic result that the credit reporting regulatory index remains insignificant. But even if the regulatory index has no impact on credit information sales, what is the interaction of credit reporting itself and access to credit?

For the interaction of credit reporting and access to finance, there are already some competing explanations. They are only mentioned, because they were extensively discussed elsewhere in this book. Again, simple reestimation of those models would have been possible. However, other authors worked with data sets that were not always accessible. In addition, they worked with different country samples or a smaller number of observations. For comparative purposes, however, I briefly review them here. Jappelli and Pagano (2002) and the World Bank (2004) have provided competing explanations for credit reporting and access to credit in terms of bank lending as percentage of GDP. As noted earlier, Jappelli and Pagano (2002: 2032) find that rule of law and creditor rights are important determinants of bank lending. Moreover, the coefficients of their dummies on type of information sharing (positive/negative) are significant and positive. Even after controlling for influential observations through robust regression, the coefficients on these dummies remain significant. Their result: information sharing increases bank lending. Additionally, the authors experimented with other information indicators such as per capita number of credit reports or the year the registry was established, but the coefficients on these variables were insignificant. The World Bank (2004: 65) finds, that information sharing, creditor rights and better enforcement systems are associated with deeper credit markets. The impact of information sharing is stronger when one controls for creditor rights. Credit reporting, therefore, might compensate for poor creditor protection. The World Bank also found that the relative importance of creditor rights and information sharing depends on country wealth. For poorer countries, credit reporting has a greater impact, but in richer countries the effect of information sharing is less strong. The problem inherent in most analyses is that there is endogeneity present, because credit and information sharing are simultaneously determined. Regarding to the question of causation, textbooks usually suggest that only theory provides a sufficient guidance here (Box 5.1 gives a definition of causality).[106] However, for theoretical modeling the researcher is as well forced to make assumptions about the direction of the effect. These assumptions are usually based on experience. Some refer to economic history as best guidance about causal relationships. History allows a broader perspective and is not focused on a small set of variables.

Box 5.1 Definition of Causality

Causality has been described as being subject to at least four criteria:
(1) Sufficient association between the variables
(2) Temporal antecedent of the cause versus the effect
(3) Lack of alternative causal variables and
(4) A theoretical basis for the relationship
Empirical approaches might be able to answer the first statement, economic history the second one, common sense and empirical insights the third and theory the fourth.

For instance, economic history suggests that lending preceded information sharing and national bank lending preceded national credit reporting. It also suggests that information sharing precedes data protection. If we look at more recent data, privacy protection might be treated as a lagged dependent variable that was determined in some earlier period. Further, common sense suggests that variables such as data protection, bank lending and information sharing are influenced by many other manifest or latent variables, for which a single model can account. There might be not captured influences through bank regulation, informal lending, and borrower mobility or bankruptcy laws. The question is if the models discussed at length in the empirical chapter contain structural equations that must be accounted for. If this is the case, the endogenous variable would violate the OLS assumption, namely that one or more variables are correlated with the error term–in this case a change in error term changes all independent variables. If OLS would be applied, the estimators would be biased and inconsistent. Finding more and more control variables does not solve this problem. To understand the relationship of bank lending and credit reporting one needs "to treat the two variables as jointly endogenous. Thus, [the

---

[106] See, for instance, Hair et al. (1998: 589-590).

equation] considering in isolation is not sufficient to determine the economic meaning of the statistical relationship." (Hausman 1983). Summary statistics are given in Table 5.17. Other influence factors that could qualify as predictors for loans to households are GDP growth, unemployment rates, creditor rights, telephone mainlines per 1.000 inhabitants, absolute number of banks, interest rates and contract enforcement.[107] I explain the variables below. The squared index on credit reporting is again credit reports sold in a country scaled by the population. GDP growth is the growth in 2002, unemployment rates are taken from the same year. Creditor rights measures four powers of secured lenders in liquidation and reorganization processes. A minimum score of 0 represents weak creditor rights and maximum score of 4 represents strong creditor rights. Interest rates are actual annual lending rates. And contract enforcement covers the step-by-step evolution of a debt recovery case before local courts in the country's most populous city.

Table 5.17
Summary Statistics for Credit Reporting and Household Credit

Variable	Obs.	Mean	Standard Deviation	Minimum	Maximum
Loans_hh	57	5634.903	10958.75	0.18	57129.81
Sqcridx	76	0.397020	0.544142	0	2.335602
Gdp	91	2.342383	2.190784	-3.109875	10.2655
Unemployment	64	10.21139	6.759896	0.5	29.9500
Creditor rights	100	1.95	1.018763	0	4
Tel	100	228.0863	224.6114	1.9292	745.5700
Banks	80	226.6375	951.0202	5	8075
Interest Rates	85	15.28906	11.53702	1.86	53.8000
Contract enforce.	99	3.731559	0.973204	0.7303	6.0088

A number of variables are significantly correlated with loans to households ($p<0.05$): *Sqcridx*, *Tel*, *interest* and *contract enforcement*. The other ones are not significant, which does not automatically imply that there exists no relationship. Figure 5.8 shows the expected positive trend: the higher the values on credit reporting, the higher the amount of lending to households per capita. This association would indicate what other authors have also assumed: the higher the information sharing in a country the higher should be lending to households. Information is the necessary structure in credit markets and credit reports enable creditors to assess creditworthiness of a

---

[107] Creditor rights and contract enforcement are variables from the World Bank (2004)

borrower. Therefore, countries with higher values on the information sharing variable should in fact have higher bank lending. Again, there is a cluster of countries near the origin. These are again the developing countries
that have low values on both variables: relatively little household credit
and little information sharing. Other countries seem to be outliers, such as
Japan. The country has a very high value on the loan variable. Also, outlier
identification techniques showed that a robust regression must be applied.

Figure 5.8
Scatter Plot of Credit Reporting and Access to Credit

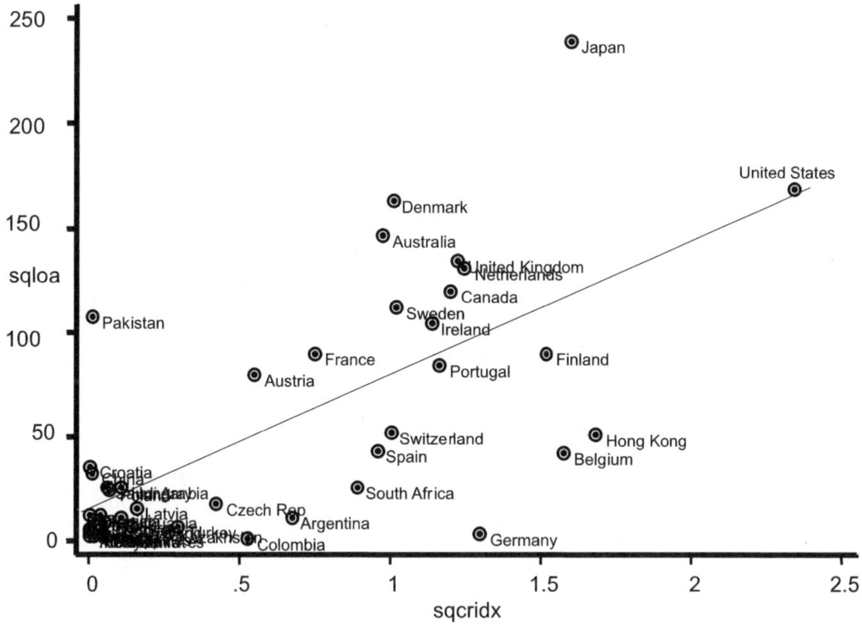

The robust regression is displayed in the Table 5.16 in the Appendix.
For the model, the following variables are introduced: creditor rights, telephone mainlines per 1.000 inhabitants, interest rates as well as contract enforcement. The equation estimated is 5.9:

$$Sqloans = \beta_0 + \beta_1 Sqcridx + \beta_2 Creditor + \beta_3 Tel + \beta_4 Int + \beta_5 Contract \qquad (5.9)$$

The equation shows that some of these variables might have an influence
on the variables of loans to households. The latter also had to be corrected
for skew. There are well-known rules of thumb how to correct for skew.
The strongest transformation, for instance would be to take the inverse of a

variable, a weaker form is the logarithm. With the latter one has to be careful, if the variable has a lot of zero values the result is an error message (the log of zero is undefined). Therefore, some researchers add small numbers for the variables that are zero–but this is only preferable if "zeros" do not have a special meaning. This approach is not applied here as zeros in our context mean that there is simply no law or regulation in the country. Not many variables remain significant in this model (see Table 5.16). For instance, there seems to be no significant relationship between loans to households and creditor rights as well as contract enforcement (*Contract*). Two other variables are significant, the technical infrastructure and interest rates (*Interest*) that approximate the monetary policy. The main indicator of interest was the credit reporting variable (*Sqcridx*). This variable does shows a weak statistical relationship. However, if there in endogeneity, the parameters might be biased and the estimators inconsistent. With the Durbin-Wu-Hausman test (DWH) one can check if it is necessary to use an instrumental variable (Gujarati 2003):

$$Sqloans=\beta_0+\beta_1 Sqcridx+\beta_2 Crights+\beta_3 Tel+\beta_4 Interest +\beta_5 Contract +\varepsilon_1 \qquad (5.10)$$

$$Sqcridx=\beta_0+\beta_1 Crri_L+\beta_2 Loans\_hh+\beta_3 Banks+\beta_4 Tel+\varepsilon_2 \qquad (5.11)$$

The DWH test works as follows. First the residuals ε_1 and ε_2 are obtained from the parallel equations 5.10 and 5.11. Next, the endogenous variable (here: *Sqloans*) is regressed on all "exogenous" variables that is on all variables exogenous to the dependent variable to obtain ε_3 in 5.12):

$$Sqloans=\beta_0+\beta_1 Crights+\beta_2 Tel+\beta_3 Interest+\beta_4 Contr+\beta_5 Crri_L+\beta_6 Banks+\varepsilon_3 \qquad (5.12)$$

Two conditions indicate if endogeneity is present: (1) No correlation between ε_3 and ε_4; (2) the coefficient of ε_3 is significantly different from zero. For obtaining the residual ε_4 the reduced form equation must be estimated as in 5.13:

$$Sqcridx=\beta_0+\beta_1 Crri_L+\beta_2 Banks+\beta_3 Tel+\beta_4 Sq\_loans+\beta_5\varepsilon_3+\varepsilon_4 \qquad (5.13)$$

As stated, if endogeneity is present there is *no correlation* between ε_3 and ε_4–according to my tests this condition is fulfilled, because I do not find a significant correlation between those variables. However, the second condition is that the coefficient of ε_3 is significantly different from zero. This is also the case (for brevity results are not displayed). Therefore, it seems like a 2 stage least squares regression (2SLS) should be applied. This regression is an OLS regression that uses a newly created instrumental variable. I do not display the results, because all coefficients in that regression were insignificant, once applied. If there would have been a higher number of observations, another functional form could have been applied, but this is not really possible with the low number that is present here. The OLS results might not be robust, the credit record variable is significant in simple OLS regressions (not displayed), in robust regressions it becomes insignificant (pointing to influential outliers in the simple OLS) and this remains the case in 2SLS regression. There is more research needed which focuses on the quality and number of variables used. If the number of observations could be increased, there would be probably more evidence on another functional form of the model. For now it must be concluded that the credit reporting indicator is not significant once one accounts for endogeneity. Under these circumstances, the model has to be rejected, as it poses no good explanation of loans to households.[108]

This can have a number of reasons. One reason is, as stated, the quality of the variables which might be noisy. The other is probably the low number of observations. It is not really possible to conclude that there is no statistical relationship, because these results are only indicative and further research has to improve upon the estimation techniques as well as the variables. However, by the time this study was concluded, better variables were not available. Next, the interrelation of the credit reporting and credit risk is analyzed. Figure 5.9 shows the non-performing loans as variable that is to be explained, plotted against the credit reporting index (the information allocation).

The developed countries, on the other hand, show lower values on non-performing loans and higher ones on credit reporting. This is the relationship one would expect: the higher the information allocation, the lower is the credit risk. A note of caution is due. It is problematic to find good indicators for credit risk for large country samples. The only proxies for credit risk available are either the average of impaired loans, loan loss provisions or the ratio of non-performing loans. Many of these variables are distorted by differences in national accounting standards or differing bank regulations.

---

[108] Note that these results are not comparable to the other authors' results and there is not a contradiction at this point.

Figure 5.9
Scatter Plot of Credit Reporting and Credit Risk

Banks also differ in what they consider to be a "non-performing loan." Therefore, they are only a crude proxy unfortunately including loans for households and companies. In the figure it appears that the higher the values on the credit reporting proxy (meaning the sales of credit records on consumers, not the regulation of credit reporting), the lower the values on the non-performing loans indicator.

The response variable is metrically scaled therefore it is possible to apply OLS. Next, the summary statistics are displayed of the potential candidate variables (Table 5.18). There are a number of variables that could influence the ratio of non-performing loans to total assets. They are displayed in the Table. The results show that not all of them seem to have a (linear) association with credit risk.

Table 5.18
Summary Statistics for Credit Risk

Variable	Obs.	Mean	Standard Deviation	Minimum	Maximum
Sqnpl	71	2.374977	1.157172	0.2236068	5.634714
Sqloa	57	49.01078	57.36354	0.4242641	239.0184
Sqcridx	76	0.397020	0.544142	0	2.335602
Pcr_exist	100	0.46	0.500090	0	1
Creditorrights	100	1.95	1.018763	0	4
Contractenf.	99	3.731559	0.973204	0.7303	6.0088
Interest	85	15.28906	11.53702	1.86	53.8

In Table 5.16 (in the Appendix), the only coefficient that stays significant is the credit information proxy (*sqcridx*). It has the expected negative association with the credit risk variable. All the other coefficients are not significant. The model is a "reduced approach" as there are certainly a number of other variables that influence the ratio of non-performing loans. Overall the results are not more than indicative and further research has to work for finding better proxies for the sales of credit reports. For robustness checks, far more models than the ones displayed here were estimated. However, this essentially did not change the results. In terms of the strictness of credit reporting regulation, I could not really find any detectable negative effects of credit reporting regulation and the sale of credit records in credit markets. I tested different specifications (by exchanging proxies) and controlled for developing country status.

The results did not change. This might be due to noisy proxies. However, another explanation would be that credit reporting regulation on the overall level is by far not as important as other variables, such as the demand for credit. Also, there were no discernible negative effects of the individual components of the regulatory index. This must not imply that there are no effects at all, only they were not apparent in this type of model. It has been stated on several occasions that credit reporting has positive effects on credit markets. Credit reporting is one important ingredient for credit markets, but its effects might be sometimes overstated, as other factors are also important such as banking competition, creditor rights or bankruptcy laws. There is reason to assume endogeneity in the relationship. Further research will certainly find better instruments than the ones used herein. While every researcher hopes to find significant results, *not finding them* is sometimes also a valuable outcome. It might help to put some of the emotional discussion about privacy into a perspective: data protection *does not* have hampering effects. It goes hand in hand with economic development, technological progress and democracy. The right regulations in place might help to reduce some of the adverse effects that might stem from the large-scale collection and distribution of highly personal data.

5.4 Evidence on Information Inaccuracies

Credit reporting agencies collect information on million of borrowers. This information is monthly updated with billions of data items. It is clear that such amounts of information cannot be without mistakes. Which problems arise if credit reports really do contain errors? Do such errors have an impact on the pricing of credit? These questions are controversially discussed in the U.S., but they are also increasingly relevant in other countries. It is remarkable that there is almost no independent research on the quality of credit reports even though this is subject to much controversy. Especially in the U.S., lobby groups for consumers and for the industry or industry-sponsored research centers publish competing commentaries and surveys. Independent research conducted by scholars that have no political or financial interests are rare. Another observation is that there were virtually no reliable statistics until very recently. Instead policymakers have stressed the importance of the system, an example is FTC Chairman Muris who stated in 2001:

> *"I call this the 'miracle of instant credit.' (...). This 'miracle' is only possible because of our credit reporting system. The system works because, without anybody's consent, very sensitive information about a person's credit history is given to the credit reporting agencies. If consent were required, and consumers could decide - on a creditor-by-creditor basis - whether they wanted their information reported, the system would collapse. Credit histories are one of our most sensitive pieces of information. Their use is, and should be, restricted and protected."*
> (U.S. Federal Trade Commission 2001)

American policymakers seem to be convinced about the superiority of their system. This is reflected in the strive of delegates to make statements about the "best credit reporting system in the world."[109] So far, neither the FTC nor the Federal Reserve Board has reliable time series on the subject

---

[109] Policymakers put forth this question to several advisory bodies in Washington in 2003 during the debate surrounding the renewal of the Fair Credit Reporting Act. Members of Congress members asked the Congressional Research Service how they could justify that the American system was the "best of the world."

matter. It seems like the only way to come to terms with this sensitive issue is to "force" agencies to cooperate in giving away data to researcher. This can only be done by Congress. It is important to acknowledge that this is the (incomplete) information basis upon which regulatory measures are drawn up. Policymakers have not put any efforts in studying the impact of the Fair Credit Reporting Act (implemented in the 1970s!) and its revisions in 1996 and 1998. Up until now there was no knowledge on how–if at all–these measures have improved data accuracy. Yet, policymakers still vote on acts that are intended to improve the system. Uninformed policymaking is not confined only to the U.S.: In other countries even less knowledge exists about "noise" in credit reports. Considering the importance of the credit reporting system for financial service providers this is surprising. It was not until 2003–a decade after increasing consumer complaints and increasing pressure from public interest groups, that Congress understood that research has to be conducted. It took a pessimistic account of the General Accounting Office in 2003 to push this through:

"Information on the frequency, type, and cause of credit report errors is limited to the point that a comprehensive assessment of overall credit report accuracy using currently available information is not possible. Moreover, available literature and the credit reporting industry strongly disagree about the frequency of errors in consumer credit reports, and lack a common definition for 'inaccuracy.'"
(General Accounting Office 2003)

Additionally, the Office stated that the lack of information undermined any meaningful discussion about what could be done to improve the system. It recommended an independent assessment of the accuracy of credit reports. Section 405 of Fair and Accurate Credit Transaction Act (FACTA) mandates the FTC to conduct an ongoing survey on the accuracy and completeness of information contained in consumer reports, and to submit biennial reports to Congress on its findings and conclusions. This has to go hand in hand with recommendations for legislative and administrative action. This is planned for an eight-year period, beginning six months from the date of enactment of FACTA.

The FTC and the Federal Reserve are required to jointly study the performance of credit reporting agencies and data furnishers in their compliance with the new FCRA in terms of procedures and timeliness for investigation and correction of disputed data. Additionally, they are mandated to study the completeness of information. So far two major avenues have been employed for the improvement in the quality of credit profiles: reasonable procedures on the side of credit reporting agencies and the consumers' rights to access and correct information. In the following, I review the surveys in this field and then discuss measurement and economic effects of errors.

5.4.1 Errors in Credit Reports

A note of caution: most of the following material reviewed here does no live up to academic standards. Some of the publications are just descriptive, others are not publicly accessible or their methodology is not made available. It is not possible to generalize the results. There is some material on the U.S., but virtually no works on other countries. This is not surprising considering that credit reporting agencies and scoring model builders would have a rather low interest in publicly discussing what is wrong with reports. As Hand (2001: 152) writes: "An issue of fundamental importance is that of data quality, for the results of any analysis and the performance of any predictive model can be no better than the quality of the data fed into it." The author states that all too often, the data quality is rather poor or samples might be distorted by taking into account only accepted borrowers. Missing values are incorrectly recorded and overriding (of decisions of the credit scoring model) occurs. One of the first inaccuracy surveys publicly reported is that of Williams (1989). James Williams was at that time president of a mortgage reporting company, Consolidated Information Services, in Flanders, New Jersey. He analyzed statistics on the frequency of mis-merging errors. Mis-merging occurs when the matching process leads to the combination of information of two different persons, for instance. For example, the author identified errors in the rating of an account as either satisfactory or delinquent. As a user of credit reports, the company had access to them. In a random sample of 1.500 reports, the firm found an error rate of 43%.[110] In the early 1990s, the consulting firm Arthur Anderson conducted a survey for the industry association Associated Credit Bureaus (now Consumer Data Industry Association, CDIA). The non-random sample encompassed 15.703 denied applicants, where 1.223 persons requested copies of their profiles constituting 7.78% of the sample. Only a fraction of those requesting their report started to dispute it, altogether 304 cases (24.85% of requesters). And again only a fraction of those resulted in a real revision of the adverse credit decision (36 cases). Arthur Anderson extrapolated this by stating that in only 0.23% of cases, the error would lead to a revision in the credit decision. This survey, the

---

[110] This report was re-printed in the transcripts to the June 1990 hearings in the U.S. House of Representatives (1990: 517-539).

Credit Report Reliability Study of February 4, 1992 conducted by the ACB Consumer Information Foundation, claimed at that time to be "the only scientific study of credit report accuracy and reliability." However, the results cannot be generalized, as the sample was explicitly *non-random*. Therefore, the assumed 0.23% is not informative for the whole credit reporting system. In addition, ACB (later CDIA) was the association of the three credit bureaus. These repositories keep databases on all credit-active U.S. citizens: a random sample therefore would have been possible.[111] The fact that over 30.000 information furnishers contribute data and some millions of consumers certainly not always fill out applications perfectly should suffice for the conclusion that the error rate must be higher than 0.23%. The survey is not publicly accessible and the firm name Arthur Anderson does not contribute to its credibility.[112]

The industry association also presented some aggregate statistics around the same time. It showed that in 1989, approximately 450 million reports were generated of which consumers requested roughly 9 million credit reports (approximately 2%).[113] Of these 9 million reports, 3 million were in fact disputed (that is 33% of the total) and 2 million were altered in the reverification process (66% of the disputed records). Not all of these changes were the result of an error in the report. Some were the result of the routine updating of files with the most current information. The General Accounting Office (2003: 7) reports that it also requested data from the CDIA. For this response, the association delivered data from a reseller who gathered information over a two-week period. It showed that of 189 mortgage consumers, only 2 discovered errors in their reports (roughly 1.06%).

In addition, the office indicates that in its discussion with information furnishers, they indicated that the information they provided and that was maintained by the agencies was accurate in 99.8% of cases. Is this a credible estimate? Furnishers were criticized in the 1990s for their repeated delivery of incorrect information that spoiled the (corrected) information in the repository. In 2003, the CDIA stated that the repositories sold 2 billion credit reports to their clients. Consumers requested an estimated 16 million credit records of which 84% of requests happened after adverse action and only 5% out of a consumer's curiosity.

In a statement before the Committee on Banking, Housing and Urban Affairs of the U.S. Senate in 2003, the president of the CDIA, Stuart K.

---

[111] These samples are needed for scorecard development.

[112] As is well know, the company suffered a severe loss of reputation after being involved in several scandals, the largest one of them being Enron.

[113] The aggregate statistics from ACB are from its response to questions printed in the transcripts of the September 1989 hearings in the U.S. House of Representatives (1989). The same hearings report statistics for TRW that are comparable.

Pratt, disclosed aggregate data for which reasons U.S. consumers request information. Table 5.21 shows a fraction of total disclosures with percentages rounded.

Table 5.19

Results of Dispute Resolutions

Categories of Dispute Solution	Percentage of Cases
Data verified as reported	46.0
Data modified/updated as per furnisher instructions	27.0
Data deleted as per furnisher instructions	10.5
Data deleted due to statutory time limit	16.0

Source: Consumer Data Industry Association, quoted in General Accounting Office (2003)

The first category (data verified as reported) means that the reinvestigation confirmed the disputed data. The second one is modification after reinvestigation.[114] The third is data that has been identified as incorrect after discussion with the furnisher and the fourth category means that data has to be deleted when the reinvestigation processes drags on for too long. Again, also disputes that result in consumer education or simply verify data cannot be taken as proxy for information quality. Disclosures are made for several reasons, some of them completely unrelated to inaccuracies. The General Accounting Office (2003: 7) reports that five main types of disputes make up 90% of consumer disputes:

1. Claims that account has been closed;
2. Dispute of account status, payment history or payment rating;
3. Dispute of current balance; and
4. Statements that the consumer is not the owner of the account.

The latter hints at the fact that there are "mis-merging" errors that are not only the agencies' responsibility but that might also occur, because consumers use different forms of their name (such as with or without initial, for instance). The frequency of disputes, the types of disputes (which are encoded) and the outcome are recorded by the credit reporting agencies. Therefore, providing this data to the public should not be a problem. Currently, the consumer cannot choose to what agency the personal data are transmitted. However, if this would be the case and errors and disputes would be publicly available, consumers would have an incentive to have the data transmitted to the most reliable agency. Agencies, on the other hand, would have an incentive to compete for consumers. However, since

---

[114] This must not imply that the information is incorrect. It also holds for updated data.

data ownership rests with the agency, this cannot be achieved at the moment. There are some other surveys to mention, as they are in stark contrast to the industry surveys. Public interest groups such as U.S. Public Interest Research Group (PIRG) in Washington, the Consumers Union and the Consumer Federation of America conducted these "studies." For instance, the U.S. PIRG conducted 6 surveys in the period 1991 to1998.[115]

It reports that between 1989 and 1992, the complaints against credit bureaus ranked first place with the FTC. In this context, it is only refered to the last survey, despite several repeated requests, PIRG did not furnish the me with the other surveys. This is no major drawback, because the approach is unscientific and does not produce any reliable results. PIRG asked its own staff in 10 U.S. states to request the most recent copy of their reports from either one, two or all three credit reporting agencies. Their 88 staff members obtained altogether 133 reports and filled out a questionnaire after reviewing them. Such a sample is *definitely not* representative as claimed (see PIRG 1998: 17). In the publicly available survey from 1998, the consumer organization found that 29% of the credit reports (39 of 133) contained serious errors that could have resulted in denial of credit. "Serious errors" were defined as accounts incorrectly delinquent, accounts that did not belong to the consumer, and listings of public records or judgments that belonged to someone else. These categories showed the following rates: 19% contained unrecognizable or incorrect accounts, in 13% of the reports, accounts were incorrectly listed as having been delinquent and 1 report listed a judgment belonging to somebody else. There were also a number of other problems that not automatically lead to credit denial. The survey found that 41% of the credit reports included personal information that was outdated, belonged to somebody else or was misspelled. 5% had incorrect names, 5% had incorrect birth dates and 3% incorrect social security numbers. In 20% of the reports important financial data such as a credit card, loan or a mortgage was missing, as it would have demonstrated the consumers' creditworthiness. Altogether mistakes of some kind were found in 70% of the consumer records. Again these results cannot be generalized.

The Consumers Union, another association, also conducted a study in 1991 and in 2000. As in the above reports, the Union defined as "serious errors" such that could have resulted in credit denial. The reports that were analyzed were also requested in a non-random manner. In Consumers Union (1991) the organization asked 57 consumers in different states of the U.S. to get their credit reports from TransUnion, Equifax and Experian.

---

[115] There was no survey in 1997.

Altogether 161 reports were obtained. 48% contained errors of some kind and nearly 20% serious mistakes that could have resulted in a denial of credit (Consumers Union 1991). Additionally, the organization reported that one in three participants said that third parties had access to their credit reports without their consent. In Consumers Union (2000) 25 staffers or their family members requested 63 reports of which over 40% contained errors of some kind.

In the mid-1990s, the National Association of Independent Credit Reporting Agencies (now National Credit Reporting Association) also looked into this issue.[116] The association is the interest group of small agencies and resellers in the U.S. It examined 1.710 files from the three bureaus. The first group of files were three-merged reports, credit reports that were merged from the three bureaus. The second group was the so-called mortgage reports that reconciled the conflicting information from two repositories by merging it with the application information and by conducting a consumer interview. The association was assessing missing, outdated and duplicated information. In the first group of reports, approximately 29% of accounts were duplicates,[117] 15% of inquiries were duplicates, and 26% of the public records. 19% of all reports had outdated trade lines, 44% missing information. In the second category of the reports, the merged mortgage reports, 19% had trades added after the application information was taken into account, 11% had trades added after investigation and 16.5% had derogatory information deleted after an investigation had been conducted. In 3% trades had to be removed because they did not belong to the consumer and in 2% even information from public records had to be deleted.

The Consumer Federation of America (2002), again another association, has also recently conducted a survey. An interesting twist is that it focuses more on credit scores. In the first phase of the survey, 1.704 files were selected of which 1.545 had at least one score from one of the three agencies, the rest was excluded. Some records were chosen for further review based upon three selection criteria: (1) A score variance of 50 points and more between highest and lowest score; (2) proximity to threshold defined as having a middle score in the range of 575-630 and a range of high and low score greater than 30 points; and (3) if the file was directly at the prime and sub-prime lending threshold of 620 points. Altogether 591 records satisfied the criteria and were flagged for further review. Of the initial 1.545 files 29% had a range of 50 points or more, 11% had a middle score be-

---

[116] This is cited in Consumer Federation of America (2002).

[117] Such accounts are also known as trade lines or trades (past and current loans, lines of credit etc.), as the association explains.

tween 575-630 points and a 30-point range and 2.7% had their highest scores either above 620 and their lowest one below 620. Some of these files satisfied multiple criteria. The authors of the survey note: "The review found considerable variability among scores returned by the three credit repositories. Because the repositories all use the scoring model provided by Fair, Isaac, and Company, this considerable variability among scores suggests considerable differences in the information maintained by each repository. Fair, Isaac, and Company attribute variations in credit scores to variations in credit data." (Consumer Federation of America 2002: 22) The variance in the credit scores is attributed to several sources, such as the differences in scoring models, differences in information sources and difference in updating cycles or in the applied statistical model. The organization also states that the authors of the study looked at the differences produced by the models, but they were negligible. For the results, see Table 5.20.[118]

Table 5.20
Score Ranges and Variation

Range of Scores (between highest and lowest score)	Percentage
Range < 20 (extremely consistent)	21%
Range ≥ 50 (middle)	31%
Range ≥ 100 (high variance)	5%

Source: Consumer Federation of America (2002)

The mean range between the lowest and the highest score was 43 points. The median is a better measure, it stood at 36 points. Because the middle score is often used for the loan approval, the authors plotted the middle score of the credit reports against the range between highest and lowest score. There is a slightly negative correlation between the middle score and the variance of the scores: "This means that, on average, files with low middle scores have slightly greater variability among their scores, relative to files with high middle scores." (Consumer Federation of America 2002: 22). Furthermore, the survey stipulated that each report contained four primary reasons contributing to the score. The survey authors observed that for 82% of the explanations the following four reasons were important:[119]

---

[118] The numbers reported do not add up to 100% because some of the reports fulfilled multiple criteria.

[119] There are altogether 40 standard reasons as the reports were reviewed, but the four were the most important for the 591 analyzed reports.

1. A serious delinquency, derogatory public record or collection filed (37% of all explanations);
2. A serious delinquency only (20% of the explanations);
3. Proportion of balances to credit limits is too high on bank revolving or other revolving accounts (15% of the explanations); and
4. Derogatory public record or collection filed (10% of explanations).

The organization tried to find out how many of the credit reports had inaccuracies that could have either resulted in adverse decision or in more unfavorable of credit terms. The criteria for selection were scores between 575-630 points with a range of more than 30 points (258 files met that criteria). Variation may have positive or negative effects as it could lead to better or less-than-favorable credit terms. In 57% of the cases the researchers could not find out if the inconsistencies inflated or depressed the score. In 22% of the cases scores seem to be artificially high and in 22% they were too low. The lower ones might lead to worse credit terms: "However, these figures are based on the assumption that, in the absence of contradictory information, all information that was reported by only one repository was accurate. The figures likely underestimate the actual number of borrowers who are at risk because they do not account for information that is simply incorrect, does not belong to the borrower, or has been contested and removed from one or two repositories, but not from all three." (Consumer Federation of America 2002: 25) In a next step, the results of the first part of the survey were to be validated. For this matter 502.623 merged records were collected. The following kinds of errors where considered:

(1) Errors of omission (information not being reported by all repositories); and
(2) Errors of commission (inclusion of incorrect information or data not being reported by all repositories).

Figure 5.10 shows the frequency of point ranges between high and low scores. It is a unimodal skewed curve with a long tail. This means that the highest frequency is reached in the score range of 21-30. These score ranges might lead to either better or worse credit terms. There is only a small percentage of scores that have high ranges of 150+. However, cumulative there is a non-negligible percentage that shows ranges of 100+ which may result in credit denial. If risk-based pricing is used, it has large effects on the price of credit. Errors must not automatically lead to an increase of the risk premium charged to consumers. However, the impact of errors might be stronger for thinner credit files. This nonlinear relationship also holds for information that is added: The first derogatory entry is likely to have a greater negative impact than additional items.

Figure 5.10
Frequency of Point Ranges between High and Low Scores

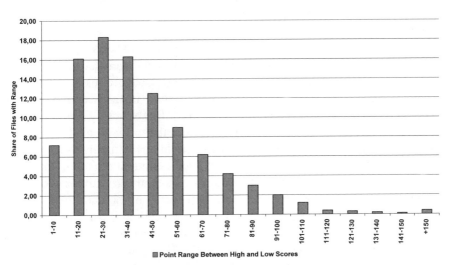

Source: Consumer Federation of America (2002)

In the third phase of the study only 10% of the records were reviewed, altogether 51 files. There were a lot of omitted accounts: 78.4% of files missed a revolving account in good standing, 33.3% missed a mortgage account, 66.7% missed another type of installment account. One in ten records lacked satisfied, paid or dismissed bankruptcies, among other omissions. 43.1% of the reports conflicted with regard to how often the consumer was 30 days late, 29.4% with regard to how many times he/she was 60 days late and 23.5% with regard to how many times he/she was 90 days late. This has an influence on credit scores. In roughly 80% of cases, the balance of revolving accounts or collections was inconsistent and in roughly 96% the inconsistencies were related to an account's credit limit. Of importance for the score is the latest credit activity: for instance, 26.1% of consumer files contained a defaulted account without any date of activity. The authors of the survey state:

"While the findings suggest that there may be some statistical equilibrium between those consumers who have artificially high scores and those who have artificially low scores, such statistical averaging is irrelevant to the in-

dividual consumer who is penalized based on errors in his or her credit report." (Consumer Federation of America 2002)

For an improvement of the system, the Consumer Federation of America suggests that legislators should require creditors to immediately provide the report to the consumer and the score in case of adverse action. Any score that results in a less than best price for consumers should trigger re-evaluation. Regulators should strengthen the requirements for complete and accurate reporting and additionally, government agencies should conduct regular surveys of credit scoring systems. I have already discussed Avery, Calem and Canner (2000) to some extent in the sections on the economic effects of data protection. Therefore, I only briefly repeat the issues they identified. The authors explain that there are significant variations in bureau scores across economic, location and demographic characteristics. Therefore, attention should be given to omitted variables, bias and depth issues (completeness). Concerning coverage, those with very low income or little education, may be underrepresented in the data used to develop scorecards. Avery, Calem and Canner (2003: 71) are more concerned with incomplete information than with inaccuracies. This survey has been conducted by the Federal Reserve Board to find out about the quality of credit reporting information that might be of some value for market monitoring. For this matter they examined a nationally representative sample of 248.000 consumers (as of June 1999). The sample was drawn by one of the credit reporting agencies. Lenders do have a strong incentive to report incomplete information to cushion competitive effects, therefore the completeness of information might be of some concern. Regulators regard the following areas of special importance, because they are sometimes not reported or inconsistent:

1. Credit limits;
2. Current status of accounts with positive balances;
3. Non-derogatory accounts or minor delinquencies; and
4. Collection agency data and public records.

The results of the Federal Reserves' inquiry are the most informative: for instance, 33% of open revolving accounts in the sample had no credit limit reported. A whopping 70% of consumers had a missing credit limit for at least one or more accounts. As the authors note, this might induce substitution effects: "If a credit limit for a credit account is not reported, credit evaluators must either ignore utilization (at least for accounts without limits) or use a substitute measure such as the highest-balance level. The authors' evaluation suggests that substituting the highest-balance level for the credit limit generally results in a higher estimate of credit utilization and probably a higher perceived level of credit risk for affected consumers." (Avery, Calem and Canner 2003: 71) The incentive of data furnishers to not report credit limits to hide the true (low) credit risk of a majority of consumers may result in higher scores depending on the substitution variable that is used by lenders to fill this gap. It is the consumer who eventually pays the price for this incompleteness. On the other hand, if minor delinquencies are not reported credit scores will be inflated. 8% of all accounts were currently not reported, but the last update showed positive balances. The authors suspect that either a transfer or a closing of these accounts occurred. The accounts could be paid or are delinquent, therefore data are inaccurate as reported. This in turn may bias the picture: for instance if accounts have been closed, the creditor mistakenly assumes that the borrower holds more accounts than is actually the case. If accounts are in good standing, but are not reported, this might result in an artificial depression of the score. Additionally, there is also a problem with data from public records, collection agencies and inquiries. The Federal Reserve found that about 40% of consumers with public records have more than one record and 40% with collection records also have more than one of them. The regulators examined those and found that many of the entries pertain to the same occurrence, hence are duplicates, but are reported multiple times. This also could significantly influence the credit standing.[120] Another problem is based upon inquiry data.

Credit bureaus are obliged to report inquiries of creditors. Such an inquiry may result from two situations: either the consumer shops around and compares financing possibilities or he or she tries to apply for different loans at different places. The latter might be an indicator of fraud. The loans for which the consumer applies are usually encoded. This enables differentiation. However, an astonishing 98% of creditors did not report the code for which credit the consumer applied. There are two effects stemming from the data limitations identified by the regulators:

(1) Duplications, omissions and ambiguities affect the scorecard and might incorrectly assign a risk factor to joint group performance; and
(2) Duplications, omissions and ambiguities affect the model's assessment of individual credit risk.

---

[120] Around 50% of records with major derogatory information are exhibiting these problems.

This can have either positive or negative effects for the consumer by inflating or deflating scores: "Even consumers with no such problems in their files can be affected. For example, a consumer with an unpaid major derogatory that is correctly reported will look the same as a consumer with a paid, but not updated, major derogatory." (Avery, Calem and Canner 2003: 72). The former borrower will have a slightly "over-optimistic," the latter an "over-pessimistic" score. In Avery, Calem and Canner (2004b), the authors examine the quantitative effects of data limitations on consumers. For this matter, they estimate the changes in consumers' credit scores that would result from "correcting" data problems in their credit records. The basis of their survey was a nationally representative sample of 301.000 consumers, drawn from the database of one credit reporting agency. For roughly 250.000 consumers they also obtained the score. For testing of the effects of errors in the credit reports, they developed a scoring model. The authors then designed a series of simulations to estimate the effects of the data quality issues. These issues are the ambiguous state of stale accounts, the failure to report credit account information, unreported credit limits and problems with collection agency accounts, public records or creditor inquiries. A further insight is that some data problems do have a stronger effect than others. For instance, problems with collection accounts have a larger impact on the score of consumers. Additionally, the impact of a correction differs across "score groups:" consumers with lower credit scores see a larger impact of the change when a problem in their file is corrected. This also holds for consumers with "thin" files. One of the main results is "(...) that the proportion of individuals affected by any single type of data problem appears to be small, with the exception of missing credit limits, which affected almost one-third of the individuals in the sample used for the simulations." (Avery, Calem and Canner 2004b: 321) The other main result is that the correction of the data problems or omissions has only a minor effect on credit scores. This is easily explained. As many consumers have "thick" credit reports, meaning reports with a lot of accounts, the effect of an individual data error is negligible. Secondly, credit scoring models are usually designed in a way where they do take data problems into account. Thus, correcting the problems is unlikely to materially change the risk evaluation and access to credit for an individual.

There has been the first major public study on credit report accuracy in the U.S. as demanded by the Fair and Accurate Credit Transactions Act (U.S. Federal Trade Commission 2004). The sections in the FACTA demand from the FTC to report on four issues related to credit report accuracy and to conduct an 11-year ongoing survey of accuracy and completeness. The four important topics discussed are the following:

1. Tackling merging errors: What effects a requirement would have that demands from credit bureaus that they must match more key information for merging files;[121]
2. Credit report disclosure: What effect a disclosure of the credit report has after an adverse action by a creditor who used that report;
3. Negative information notice: What effects a notice has that is given to the consumer after negative information has been added to the file; and
4. Completeness: Are there any information items that are not reported, but that could be potentially useful for determining a consumer's credit rating

The report does not really present new numbers, as it was the initial study of the FTC in this field. However, the authority already draws conclusions about the above issues. In terms of the first proposal, the FTC states that if implemented, there should be less "mixed files." However, if there is no perfect match, the system might establish a new credit report for a consumer who already has a report (so-called "fragmented file"). The number of these files could increase. Concerning the second proposal, the FTC states that if there would be a measure to disclose exactly the same report as the creditor has reviewed, identity theft might increase. There are more effective means, for instance, to notify credit report users when an address (indicated to creditors) "substantially differs" from the address on file. Thirdly, there is the negative information notice. The FTC estimates that the costs for this measure could be significant. Additionally, it could contribute to identity theft. Therefore, the authority suggests that an opt-in system, where the consumer chooses to receive notices. Finally, there is the question of completeness. In this area, the FTC states that there are several types of items that could be beneficial to the consumer such as rent and utility payments. But there are also barriers to this type of reporting which should be addressed. Altogether the FTC wants to study the effects of the FACTA measures first, before implementing or suggesting further legislative measures. For this matter, it will conduct the ongoing studies.

During the course of the research, the first steps to a more rigorous analysis of errors in credit reports have been made. The U.S. is the country that takes the lead in this matter, because Congress asked the regulators to analyze the issue in greater detail. This is necessary considering that 2 billion credit reports are sold per year and the industry and consumer associations analyzed negligible small samples. There is virtually no material on other countries regarding inaccuracies in reports. There is, however, an

---

[121] Items to be matched include name, Social Security number or address.

abundance of material on how to enforce one's right as a consumer in case of errors. For Germany, the only discussion on mistakes in credit reports happened in 2000. 17 members of a TV reporter team got their credit records from a bureau. In 15 of the records, the agency delivered incomplete and obsolete information. The data lacking most frequently was that on mortgage loans, bank accounts and credit card contracts. In an unscientific self-test I had my own credit record disclosed by a bank. It lacked a major credit and the regular payments I made on it, therefore, my credit report was incomplete as well.

5.4.2 Origin and Impact of Credit Report Errors

Credit report inaccuracies might either have positive effects or negative effects for the consumer, depending on the kind of error. However, this is the crux: What *exactly is an error*? Is missing information or obsolescence also inaccuracy? Stakeholders and policymakers disagree. Consumer associations define "serious errors" as those that have a high probability of resulting in denial of credit (for instance, PIRG 1998). These are either: (1) accounts incorrectly marked as delinquent, (2) credit reports containing credit accounts that do not belong to the consumer, and (3) reports listing public records or judgments that also do not belong to the consumer. This excludes positive errors that tend to inflate scores and give only an incomplete picture. The Consumer Federation of America (2002) survey discussed above at least includes positive and negative errors. The industry, on the other hand, considers only those errors as real errors that have a discernible impact on a person's creditworthiness (General Accounting Office 2003: 10). The rationale is that this has economic consequences, whereas a misspelling of the name might not. To solve these questions it is not enough to present data on consumer disputes. Such data are primarily related to the errors that were disputed by consumers after adverse action. There is a whole population of errors in credit reports that might have gone undetected in the past, although this might change now in the U.S. with the free credit report. Only a random sample of credit records and direct analysis will help to shed some light on this. While it could very well be the case that information inaccuracies cancel each other out on average over a whole population of consumers–some get higher and others lower scores– this statistical argument does not count for the individual consumer. The individual might get worse terms for mortgages, for instance, which might make a price difference of several thousand dollars over the years.

What is the driving force behind error rates? There are several parties that are part of the credit reporting networks–all of them carry responsibility for the accuracy of the credit information. It is wrong to assign the full responsibility of errors to the credit bureau. This is a lesson, many policymakers around the world have not learnt yet. All of the parties in the network share responsibility. This includes consumers and banks. All of these parties contribute to inaccuracies. Three main parties are involved in producing errors in the credit reporting system. Firstly, consumers not always provide consistent information. Sometimes they might use initials at other times not. Also, some might misspell their identification numbers. Some consumers might even confuse addresses when they moved recently. Creditors and other information furnishers, on the other hand, might input inaccurate information and send this to the credit bureau (see Figure 5.11). This is the case if bank employees are negligent and write down misspelled social security numbers or names.[122] This seems to be a major source of errors that end up in credit reports. Credit bureaus might match the wrong information and put together data that does not belong in one report (merging errors).

Figure 5.11

Common Causes of Errors in the Credit Reporting Process

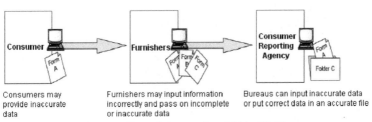

Source: General Accounting Office (2003)

Usually credit reporting agencies take several key factors as identifiers (such as name, date of birth and social security numbers), but still merging of two unrelated consumers might occur. Relatively little is known about the quality measures implemented by the credit reporting agencies. As the General Accounting Office (2003: 12) notes, the agencies have started to develop systems for improving accuracy since the "reasonable procedures" standard took effect in the FCRA of 1970. One of the arguments is that credit scoring models are highly predictive of credit risk on the aggregate

---

[122] The latter happened to the author, when a bank employee noted "Deutsch" (German) from the passport as last name. This would probably have been to chance to take on another identity.

level and that they are recalibrated if necessary. This is true, because there are indications that statistical errors cancel each other out on the macro level. For the overall scoring model it might hold that it is indeed correct, however, when fed with incorrect information or neglecting important items that should be included the resulting individual score might be either too optimistic or too pessimistic about the borrower's probability of repayment. There is a general lack of data on information inaccuracies. Therefore, the overall impact of data protection regimes on inaccuracies cannot be assessed. However, the impact on individual consumers might be large: "Consumer access to credit, housing, insurance, basic utility services, and even employment is increasingly determined by centralized records of credit history and automated interpretations of those records." (Consumer Federation of America 2002) There is the tendency to centralize databases in other countries than the U.S., including Germany and UK.

On the scale of possible impacts, the most extreme is certainly the denial of credit, insurance or employment. When employers ask for the credit report, adverse employment decisions could also be based on incorrect information. This might take time to correct and clarify with the potential employer who might get the impression that the potential candidate is a "problem case"–an unfortunate situation for anybody who applies for a job. An important point neglected for some time is risk-based pricing and less-than-optimal contract terms. Risk-based adjustments might lead to a change in contract terms that consumers regard as unfavorable. FACTA requires a creditor who uses a credit report in connection with an application or extension of credit to inform the borrower in case he provides *"terms that are materially less favorable"* than the most favorable terms available to a substantial proportion of that creditor's other customers.[123] In his notice, the creditor must provide the name of the credit bureau and explain that the data influenced the terms of the offer. In such situations, the impact on the inaccuracy would be directly measurable. Another interesting question relates to scoring for insurance purposes and incorrect information in terms of associating credit reports with underwriting results: "if the underlying data lack reliability, how reliable are the correlations alleged?" (Musick 1995: 1). This means–in the worst case–inaccurate information diffuses into other areas of economic life. In a credit-unrelated field such as insurance, contract terms, prices and conditions might be also based upon inaccurate information. As stated, statisticians have found correlations between credit scores and the performance of insurance. To better predict the behavior of the insured individual insurance scoring models are

---

[123] This is the so-called "risk-based pricing notice."

developed. There is the danger here that mistaken information also leads to less than favorable terms in insurance and everywhere else, where the information is used. Logic dictates that all three parties, consumers, creditors and credit bureaus must take *reasonable steps* to provide accurate information. For now, the question what data protection regime improves the quality of the credit information in the market must be left for further research.[124] Only some general conclusions can be drawn about the following aspects that contribute to increasing inaccurate information in credit records: the design of the credit reporting system, the network architecture and competition pressure as well as credit scoring and centralization. First, the design of the credit reporting system: The set-up of the credit reporting might be voluntary. If the system is voluntary liabilities and heavy fines for reporting of inaccuracies induces financial service providers to exit the system. There is a trade-off of costs and benefits of participating.

Second, network architecture: The more participants contribute to credit reporting, the more comprehensive the reports, the greater the risk of errors. Errors cannot be erased and regulators that try to achieve this will not be successful. However, the risk of errors can be decreased and their re-emergence prevented if the system is designed accordingly. If more participants contribute to the report, the error rate will be higher, but probably also the rate of detecting mistakes. In addition, distribution of credit records to more and more parties increases the risk of *propagation of the errors through the system* possibly leading to *"mispricing"* in other areas such as insurance or telecom.

Third, competition pressure: If the system is voluntary and credit reporting agencies try to keep as many information furnishers as possible, then they have no incentive to enforce complete reporting requirements strictly. In such situations it is difficult for credit reporting agencies to approach furnishers that report incomplete information. Furnishers are at the same time the clients of credit bureaus. Or as one industry official has put it: "Some information is better than no information." Credit bureaus are not the right party for enforcing requirements of "complete reporting" for creditors. Fourth, centralization: the more databases are connected, the higher the possibility of errors that lead to inaccurate decisions. Deflated or inflated scores could be used for all kinds of decisions, such as mobile phone contracts, insurance contracts or employment screening. Again, credit reporting is *no industry*. It is a network of participants, where the credit bureau serves as "information circuit." All parties that are active in this network do have the responsibility to contribute accurate information. However, it is the responsibility of legislators and policymakers to learn

---

[124] This was the original idea for my PhD thesis. I will further pursue this matter.

how these systems function and to create an environment free of incentive misalignments or legal responsibilities placed on the wrong parties. One of the worst mistakes, however, is to cut out the consumer by making it difficult for him/her to access the report or by making it very costly. In the following, theoretical and empirical evidence on information sharing and financial privacy is summarized. Information affects uncertainty by altering the probability of events that are assumed by the market participants. It reduces information asymmetries and opportunistic behavior, because it increases the borrower's discipline to conform to the contract. One important result is that information sharing reduces adverse selection and credit rationing. Information has effects on credit market efficiency, banking competition, productivity and welfare. The models classified as "information sharing games" in the theoretical chapter of this book showed another range of possible effects. It was discussed that information sharing is more advantageous as the number of participants increase or in the case where adverse selection is severe. It expands the volume of credit in the market and markets become at the same time more contestable, something that lowers interest rates. Additional effects are a reduction of defaults and credit risk. Welfare losses should be reduced. The optimal length of the credit record depends on the share of good risks and bad risks in the market. The sharing of complete information would terminate any information asymmetries and theoretically would thereby terminate its own existence. Information has features of a public good, exhibits economies of scale (leading to concentration) and its indivisibility and immateriality may lead to problems in information trade. The specification of property rights influences externalities and welfare distribution among the market participants by allowing first-, second- and third-degree price discrimination. Externalities exist if property rights are not fully specified. The network character of information distribution has the potential of reinforcing positive as well as negative effects of information sharing. The microeconomics of privacy shows that regulations that reduce the amount of information or increase informational asymmetries also reduce allocative efficiency of the market. Different models that formalize various property rights regimes underpins this. The assigned property rights determine bargaining power and market outcomes. Inefficiencies in these scenarios might be bargained away (or not). The affected party might be compensated for any potential payoffs that are otherwise realized by not disclosing information. The competitive pressure in the market could lead to an over-excessive accumulation of data on the side of the companies. Some of the above arguments have been further explored with econometric techniques. Micro approaches hereby analyze the effect of data protection restrictions on credit scoring models and their efficiency in separating good risks from bad risks. Early papers show that information sharing with the credit bureau increases predictive power. However, the prohibition of variables, such as gender, has efficiency-decreasing effect. There are a number of statistical problems with scoring models and not all of them can be attributed to data protection restrictions. These problems have been discussed above: errors in variables, selection bias and omitted variables as well as the general reluctance to use variables that might provoke strong public reactions, because they are not under the direct control of the consumer. There have been indications that the sharing of positive data is preferable to negative data because it increases the volume of lending. On the global level, information sharing is associated with a higher ratio of bank lending to GDP and a reduction in credit risk as well as the share of non-performing loans. It could well be the case that data protection restrictions have some negative effects on the micro-level, but that on the macro-economic level, these effects do not matter much due to other factors.

6 Conclusions

This book is the first comprehensive review of the economics and regulation of financial privacy. It is intended to increase the knowledge about the interaction of privacy regulation, credit market development and information sharing. For comprehensiveness, this book provides a discussion of the theory of information and privacy, the history of the credit reporting industry and its regulation and econometric analyses. Through this three-fold approach it is possible to gain in-depth knowledge about credit reporting and its implications. At the same time this work is based upon a unique collection of information on credit reporting systems in 100 countries around the world. A credit reporting system consists of laws and regulations, institutions and the information sharing architecture. The analysis is a major step for increasing the knowledge about this crucial and interesting activity that affects the daily lives of millions of borrowers. It is important to understand such systems as they might provide the critical information structure in more markets in the future–not just credit markets. In the theoretical chapter of this book, it was argued that information markets cannot simply be equated with traditional markets for goods and services. Information has interesting and at the same time peculiar characteristics. It is certainly one of the most interesting subjects of study for economists. For comprehensiveness, literature on property rights was included as well as up-to-date insights from network economics and competition in information markets. I discussed the peculiar features of demand and supply in markets of personal information. Market forces–when left unimpeded–almost inevitably lead to erosion of privacy. This justifies regulatory measures as they have been introduced in many countries around the world. The theory chapter also provides the reader with an up to date overview of microeconomic models–there has been an increasing number of such models in the past four years. With game theory one can model interactions in credit reporting which allows conclusions about the incentives and strategic behavior of markets players in different regulatory environments. This discussion implies that credit reporting is a valuable reputation system in the market and data protection acts help to secure commitment by market participants. In the descriptive part of this book, the history of credit reporting agencies in the U.S., Germany, Great Britain and France was discussed as well as competition and regulation of credit reporting. Moreover, the book now covers all 27 European members. It is interesting how different these systems developed in Europe: some countries have dual systems (public registers and private credit bureaus), others have only a public register or private bureaus. Also, information sharing differs from country to country. The historical perspective sheds light on the origins of the different approaches to privacy on both sides of the Atlantic. It also shows how different credit reporting systems can evolve. In addition, history answers which credit reporting regulations worked, where they worked and for what reasons. And it helps to disentangle cause and effects by referring to what was observable in the past. This is the background upon which current regulatory regimes around the world may be analyzed. The above discussion allowed to draw some conclusions about the impact of regulations and as to whether they contribute to market efficiency. The latter is not always the case. Credit reporting is a crucial ingredient for today's credit markets. However, in the early stages of development, lending has evolved without credit reporting. But credit reporting is now the crucial information intermediation in credit market–without it high volumes of lending would hardly be sustainable.

This book also provides detailed account of the evolution of privacy laws (data protection laws) in Europe and the U.S. A further point was the international political economy of information and data protection, meaning, initiatives by the OECD, WTO, UN and the European Union. Data protection policy on the global scale is still in its infancy. It is not clear which institution will take the lead, this is something that can be derived from the discussion about international guidelines and principles. It will be a long way to international harmonization of regulatory standards. This is partially attributable to the different approaches to privacy protection in Europe and in the U.S.

The econometric analysis in this book is based on insights gained from the theory and history chapter of this book. For evaluating data protection regimes, I developed a form that rates countries in 40 indicators. With this evaluation instrument, 100 countries were analyzed. For mapping credit markets, I collected data on credit markets from more than 50 central banks around the world. The database for the econometric analysis contains more than 100 variables on credit markets, political systems, credit reporting regulation and economic fundamentals. The analysis brought up some interesting insights, for instance, European countries in fact do converge in their data protection regimes, but the U.S. also converges to a higher standard of data protection. At the moment, the level in the U.S., however, is still lower than in Europe. Financial privacy regulation goes hand in hand with democratic development and adoption of information technologies. The analysis also showed that credit reporting regulation has no negative impact on the credit reporting activity on a macro-level. This result is robust in the specification presented here. However, it was also argued that some variables might be noisy proxies or there is some mis-specification. However, the small number of observations does not allow to apply models that are more advanced than the linear one. However, another explanation would be that regulation on the overall level is not as important for credit reporting as other variables such as the distribution of credit, the technological infrastructure and the demand for credit itself.

In the past, it has been stated on several occasions that credit reporting has positive effects on credit markets. This is the case and as stated high volumes of lending are hardly sustainable without it. In addition, credit reporting certainly leads to higher productivity in financial services and to greater stability in the banking sector. However, one should not overstate the impact of regulations, European credit reporting systems show that even under stiff laws (such as in Germany) very high coverage rates of the economically active population can be reached. Many (other) factors are important for the development of credit markets, among them economic growth, consumer confidence and income expectations. Credit risk was another focus. Overall the analysis suffers somewhat from the noisy credit risk indicator that was the only one available for such a large country sample. The credit reporting index appeared to have a negative association with credit risk as expected. The higher volume of information sharing is associated with lower credit risk in the market. In the econometric part of this study it was also discussed what the common problems are, such as endogeneity, low number of observations and noise proxies. Research should continue to improve this situation.

Data protection is the outcome of democratic regimes and economic development. It increases transparency in information markets. Moreover, it ensures that the consumer's basic human rights as well as economic rights are preserved in the information age. The economic analysis of privacy helps to reveal many new insights. It is remarkable how well theoretical approaches help to explain the regulatory pressures that arise if property rights to personal information are not precisely defined. Credit reporting is an excellent example to study welfare effects of privacy and control of personal information. It is also an excellent example to explain the (im)balance of competing interests in information disclosure. For a very long time, the credit reporting industry was sheltered from public scrutiny. However, this has changed with the introduction of information technologies and with the collection and distribution of millions of files on borrowers. The picture about the individual becomes more and more precise. At the same time, the activity of information sharing penetrates other markets and expands to insurance, telecommunication and employment. If these trends continue, the personal profile will become the entry code to economic life. At the same time, policymakers have increasingly located property rights to personal information at the data subject. It is an open question, if the individual will become an "informationally empowered consumer" who controls release and distribution of his/her personal data and who has full knowledge about information flows in the market. Privacy principles seek to establish the balance of individual rights and economic necessity to collect the data. The quest for finding the right balance, however, has just begun.

References

Acemoglu, D., S. Johnson, and J.A. Robinson (2001). The Colonial Origins of Comparative Development: An Empirical Investigation, *American Economic Review* 91 (5): 1369-401.

Acquisti, A. and J. Grossklags (2004). Privacy Attitudes and Privacy Behavior–Losses, Gains and Hyperbolic Discounting, in: J. Camp and R. Lewis (eds.), The Economics of Information Security (Kluwer Academic Publishers, Boston).

Acquisti, A. and H. Varian (2002). Conditioning Prices on Purchase History, Working Paper, University of California at Berkeley, forthcoming in *Management Science*.

Aigrain, P. (1997). Attention, Media, Value and Economics, First Monday 2 (9), www.firstmonday.dk/issues/issue2_9/aigrain/

Akerlof, G.A. (1973). A Theory of Information and Labor Markets. Paper presented at the NSF/NBER Conference on the Economics of Information, Princeton.

Akerlof, G.A. (1970). The Market For 'Lemons:' Quality Uncertainty and the Market Mechanism, *Quarterly Journal of Economics* 84: 488-500.

Allen, B. (1986). General Equilibrium with Information Sales, *Theory and Decision* 21 (1): 1-33.

Allen, B. (1990). Information as an Economic Commodity, *American Economic Review* 80 (2): 268-73.

Allen, D.W. (1999). Transaction Costs, in: Bouckaert, B. and G. DeGeest (eds.), Encyclopedia of Law and Economics (Edward Elgar, Cheltenham), www.encyclo.findlaw.com/0740book.pdf

American Financial Services Association (2001). Credit Card Mailings and Responses, Spotlight on Financial Services (May 2001) www.spotlightonfinance.org/issues/May01

Anderlini, L. and L. Felli (2000). Transaction Costs and the Robustness of the Coase Theorem, Sticerd-Theoretical Economics Paper Series 409, Suntory and Toyota International Centers for Economics and Related Disciplines, LSE.

Anderson, M. and W. Seltzer (2000). After Pearl Harbor: The Proper Role of Population Data Systems in Time of War, in: Statisticians in History (Internet publication).

Andreeva G., J. Ansell and J. Crook (2003). Credit Scoring in the Context of the European Integration: Assessing the Performance of the Generic Models, Paper University of Edinburgh, presented at the Credit Scoring and Credit Control Conference VIII, 2003.

Arthur, W.B. (1989). Competing Technologies, Increasing Returns, and Lock–in by Historical Events, *The Economic Journal* 99: 116–131.

Arthur, W.B. (1994). Positive Feedbacks in the New Economy, *McKinsey Quarterly* 1: 81-95.

Arthur, W.B. (1996). Increasing Returns and the New World of Business, Harvard Business Review (July-August), 74(4): 100-9.

Artigas, C.T. (2004). A Review of Credit Registers and their Use for Basel II, Financial Stability Institute and Bank for International Settlements, Basel.

Asch, M. (1995). How the RMA/Fair, Isaac Credit Scoring Model was Built, *Journal of Commercial Lending* 77 (10): 1-4.

Asian Pulse (2004). South Korean Credit Records withheld to Boost Delinquent Hiring, Asian Pulse (March 16, 2004).

Associated Credit Bureaus (1981). Our 75th Year (Associated Credit Bureaus, Houston).

Avery, B.R., R.W. Bostic, P.S. Calem and C.B. Canner (2003). An Overview of Consumer Data and Credit Reporting, Federal Reserve Bulletin (February 2003): 47-73.

Avery, B.R., R.W. Bostic, P.S. Calem and C.B. Canner (2000). Credit Scoring: Statistical Issues and Evidence from Credit Bureau Files, *Real Estate Economics* 28 (3): 523-47.

Avery, B.R., R.W. Bostic, P.S. Calem and C.B. Canner (2004a). Consumer Credit Scoring: Do Situational Circumstances Matter? BIS Working Papers, No. 146 (January).

Avery, B.R., R.W. Bostic, P.S. Calem and C.B. Canner (2004b) Credit Report Accuracy and Access to Credit, Federal Reserve Bulletin (Summer 2004): 297-322.

Azzi, C.F. and J.C. Cox (1976). A Theory and Test of Credit Rationing: Comment, *American Economic Review* 66 (5): 911-17.

Babe, R.E. (1994). The Place of Information in Economics, in: R.E. Babe (ed.) Information and Communication in Economics (Kluwer Academic Publishers, Boston).

Bakos, Y. and E. Brynjolfsson (1999). Bundling Information Goods: Pricing, Profits, and Efficiency, *Management Science* 45 (12): 1613-30.

Bakos, Y. and E. Brynjolfsson (2000). Bundling and Competition on the Internet, *Marketing Science* 19 (1): 63-82.

Baltensberger, E. (1979). Credit Rationing–Issues and Questions, *Journal of Money, Credit, and Banking* 10 (2): 170-83.

Banasiak M. and D. Tantum (1999). Accurately and Efficiently Measuring Individual Account Credit Risk On Existing Portfolios, *Credit and Financial Management Review* 5(1): www.crfonline.org

Banca d'Italia (2005). Functions, website: www.bancaditalia.it/la_banca /funzioni/functions.pdf

Banco de España (2005). Central Credit Register, website, www.bde.es /faqs/riesgose.htm

Banco de Portugal (2005). Central Credit Register, Banco de Portugal Broschure 5, www.bportugal.pt/publish/cadernos/responsabilidades_ credito_e.pdf

Bandulet, M. and K. Morasch (2003). Would You Like to be a Prosumer? Information Revelation, Personalization and Price Discrimination in Electronic Markets, Universität Augsburg Discussion Paper Series 242 (July).

Banque de France (1994). Le bilan du fichier national des incidents de remboursement des crédits aux particulièrs (in French). *Bulletin de la Banque de France* 9: 99-104.

Banque de France (1995). Évolution de l'activité des fichiers d'incidents gérés par la Banque des France (in French). *Bulletin de la Banque de France* 15: 123-26.

Banque de France (1996). Annual Report 1996 (Banque de France, Paris).

Banque de France (1998). Annual Report 1998 (Banque de France, Paris).

Banque de France (2000a). Règlement No 2000–04 du 6 septembre 2000 modifiant le règlement No 90–05 du 11 avril 1990 relatif au fichier national des incidents de reboursement des crédits aux particulièrs (FICP) (in French).

Banque de France (2000b). Annual Report 2000 (Banque de France, Paris).

Banque de France (2001a). The French Central Credit Register, Fact Sheet No. 115 (August).

Banque de France (2001b). Overindebtedness of Individuals, Fact Sheet No. 119 (August).

Banque de France (2002a). Le Fichier National des Incidents de Remboursement des Crédits aux Particuliers (in French), Note d'Information, No. 129 (March).

Banque de France (2002b). Letter to the author, dated 18 June 2002.

Barron J.M. and M. Staten (2003). The Value of Comprehensive Credit Reports: Lessons from the U.S. Experience, in: M. Miller (ed.), Credit Reporting Systems and the International Economy (MIT Press, Cambridge): 273-311.

Barta, J. and A. Vogt (1997). The Making of Tests for Index Numbers (Physica-Verlag, Heidelberg).

Barth, J.R., G. Caprio, R. Levine (2002). Bank Regulation and Supervision: What Works Best? NBER Working Paper, No. 9323 (November).

Beales, H., R. Craswell, S. Salop (1981). Information Remedies for Consumer Protection, *AEA Papers and Proceedings* 71 (2), 410-13.

Besley, T. (1995). Non-market Institutions for Credit and Risk Sharing in Low-income Countries, *Journal of Economic Perspectives* 9(3): 115-27.

Bester, H. (1985a). The Level of Investment in Credit Markets with Imperfect Information, *Journal of Institutional and Theoretical Economics* 141: 503-15.

Bester, H. (1985b). Screening versus Rationing in Credit Markets with Imperfect Information, *American Economic Review* 75 (4): 850-55.

Bhargava, H.K. and V. Choudary (2001). Information Goods and Vertical Differentiation, *Journal of Management Information Systems* 18 (2): 89-106.

Bhattacharya, D. and A.V. Thakor (1993). Contemporary Banking Theory. *Journal of Financial Intermediation* 3: 2-50.

Bishop, M. (2002). The Next Chapter in Small Business Scoring, RMA Magazine (February 2002): 48-52.

Black, S.E. and D.P. Morgan (1998). Risk and the Democratization of Credit Cards, Federal Research Bank of New York Research Papers, No. 9815 (June).

Bostic, R. and P. Calem (2003). Privacy Restrictions and the Use of Data at Credit Registries, in: M. Miller (ed.), Credit Reporting Systems and the International Economy (MIT Press, Cambridge): 311-35.

Bouckaert, J. and H. Degryse (2004). Softening Competition by Inducing Switching in Credit Markets, *The Journal of Industrial Economics* 52 (1): 27-52.

Brandeis, L.D. and S.D. Warren (1890). The Right to Privacy, *Harvard Law Review* 4(1): 193-220.

Brown, W. (2000). Market Failure in the New Economy (Review of Winners, Losers, and Microsoft by S. Liebowitz and S. Margolis) *Journal of Economic Issues* 34 (1): 219-21.

Bundesverfassungsgericht (2004). Volkszählung: Bearbeitung (in German), www.oefre.unibe.ch/law/dfr/bv065001.html

Burkert, H. (1999). Privacy, Data Protection, German/European Perspective, mimeo, Max Planck Institute.

Calzolari, G. and A. Pavan (2003). On the Optimality of Privacy in Sequential Contracting, mimeo, Northwestern University.

Capon, N. (1982). Credit Scoring Systems: A Critical Analysis. *Journal of Marketing* 46: 82-91.

Carey, P. and C. Russell (2000). Data Protection in the UK (Oxford University Press, Oxford).

Carlton, D.W. and J.M. Perloff (1994). Modern Industrial Organization (Addison-Wesley-Longman, Boston).

Cato Institute (1997). Handbook for the 105th Congress (Cato Institute, Washington).

Chandler, G.G. and L.E. Parker (1989). Predictive Value of Credit Bureau Reports, *Journal of Retail Banking* XI (4): 47-54.

Chandler, G.G. and R.W. Johnson (1992). The Benefit to Consumers from Generic Scoring Models based on Credit Reports, *IMA Journal of Mathematics Applied in Business and Industry* 4: 61-72.

Charlesworth, A. (2000). Clash of Data Titans? U.S. and EU Data Privacy Regulation, *European Public Law* 6(2): 253-74.

Chuang, J. and M. Sirbu (1999). Optimal Bundling Strategy for Digital Information Goods: Network Delivery of Articles and Subscriptions, *Information Economics and Policy* 11(2): 147-76.

Chuang, J. and M. Sirbu (2000). Network Delivery of Articles and Subscriptions, mimeo, Harvard University.

Clements, B., I. Maghiros, L. Besley, C. Centeno, Y. Punie, C. Rodriguez and M. Masera (2003). Security and Privacy for the Citizen in the Post–September 11 Digital Age: A Prospective Overview, Institute for Prospective Technological Studies, European Commission Joint Research Centre.

Coase, R.H. (1937). The Nature of the Firm, *Economica* 4: 386-405.

Coase, R.H. (1960). The Problem of Social Cost, *The Journal of Law and Economics* 3 (1): 1-44.

Commission National de l'Informatique et des Libertés (1978). Décret no 78-774 du 17 juillet 1978 (in French), Official Journal (July).

Commission National de l'Informatique et des Libertés (1998a). 18ème Rapport 1997 (in French), (CNIL, Paris).

Commission National de l'Informatique et des Libertés (1999a). 19ème Rapport 1998 (in French), (CNIL, Paris).

Commission National de l'Informatique et des Libertés (1999b). Electronic Mailing and Data Protection, (CNIL, Paris).

Commission National de l'Informatique et des Libertés (2000). 20ème Rapport 1999 (in French), (CNIL, Paris).

Commission National de l'Informatique et des Libertés (2001). 21e Rapport d'activité 2000 (in French), (CNIL, Paris).

Commission National de l'Informatique et des Libertés (2002). Mail to the author (30 May 2002).

Connelly, B. (2001). Requirements for the Successful Use of Credit Information. In: International Finance Corporation (ed.), Making Small Business Lending Successful (Conference Proceedings).

Consumer Federation of America (2002). Credit Score Accuracy and Implications for Consumers (CFA, Washington, DC).

Consumers Union (1991). Credit Reports: Getting it Half-right, Consumer Reports 56 (7): 453.

Consumers Union (2000). Credit Reports–How do Potential Lenders see You? Consumer Reports 65 (7): 52-3.

CoolSavings, Inc. (2001). CoolSavings, Inc. appoints David Arney Chief Financial Officer (Press Release, October 10, 2001), PR Newswire Association, Chicago.

Cooter, R. and T. Ulen (1995). Law and Economics (Addison-Wesley-Longman, Boston).

Corporate Library (2003). From the 2003 Acxiom Corporation Proxy. public.thecorporatelibrary.net/Transactions/rel_ACXM_2003.html

Council of Europe (2004). Background, website, www.coe.int/T/E/Legal_affairs/Legal_co-operation/Data_protection/Background/

CRIF (2005). History and Profile of CRIF, website, www.crif.com /eng/rtf/press_folder.rtf

Crook, J.N., D.B. Edelman and L.C. Thomas (2002). Credit Scoring and Its Applications (Cambridge University Press, Cambridge).

Davis, G.B. and M. Olson (1985). Management of Information Systems: Conceptual Foundations, Structure and Development (McGraw Hill, New York).

Dell'Ariccia, G. (2001). Asymmetric Information and the Structure of the Banking Industry, European Economic Review 45 (10): 1957-80.

Dell'Ariccia, G., E. Friedman and R. Marquez (1998). Adverse Selection as a Barrier to Entry in the Banking Industry, Rand Journal of Economics 30 (3): 515-34.

DeLong, B. (1997). Old Rules for the New Economy, Rewired (December 9, 1997) www.rewired.com/97/1209.html

Demsetz, H. (1966). Some Aspects of Property Rights, Journal of Law and Economics 9 (October): 61-70.

Department of Trade and Industry (2001). Report by the Task Force on Tackling Overindebtedness (Consumer Affaires Directorate, London).

Deutsche Bundesbank (1998). Die Evidenzzentrale für Millionenkredite bei der Deutschen Bundesbank - Änderungen im Meldeverfahren, Deutsche Bundesbank, Monatsbericht 50 (8), 83-91.

Deutsche Bundesbank (2001). Deutschen Bundesbank Geschäftsbericht 2001 (Deutsche Bundesbank, Frankfurt am Main): 176-81.

Deutsche Bundesbank (2002). Letter to the author (7 June 2002).

Diewert, W.E. (1993). Index Numbers, in: W.E. Diewert and A.O. Nakamura (eds.), Essays in Index Number Theory 1 (North-Holland, Amsterdam): 71-104.

Diewert, W.E. (1996). Axiomatic and Economic Approaches to International Comparisons, University of British Columbia Discussion Paper, No 96-11.

Dixit, A. and M. Olson (2000). Does Voluntary Participation Undermine the Coase Theorem? *Journal of Public Economics* 76: 309-35.

Djankov, S., R. La Porta, F. Lopez-de-Silanes and A. Shleifer (2002). The Regulation of Entry, *Quarterly Journal of Economics* CXVII (1): 1-37.

Economides, N. (1988). Variable Compatibility without Network Externalities, Studies in Industry Economics, Stanford University, Discussion Paper No. 145.

Economides, N. (1993). Network Economics with Application to Finance, *Financial Markets, Institutions & Instruments* 2 (5): 89-97.

Economides, N. (1996). The Economics of Networks, *International Journal of Industrial Organization* 14: 673-99.

Economides, N. (2001). The Impact of the Internet on Financial Markets. *Journal of Financial Transformation* 1 (1): 8-13.

Economides, N. (2003) Competition Policy in Network Industries: An Introduction (June 2003),
www.ftc.gov/be/seminardocs/economides.pdf

Economides, N. and C. Himmelberg (1995). Critical Mass and Network Size with Application to the U.S. Fax Market, mimeo (EC–95–11), Stern School of Business.

Economides, N. and S.C. Salop (1992). Competition and Integration among Complements and Network Market Structure, *Journal of Industrial Economics* 40 (1): 105-23.

Edelberg, W. (2003). Risk-based Pricing of Interest Rates in Consumer Loan Markets, Mimeo, University of Chicago.

Egidi, M. and S. Rizzello (eds.) (2002). Cognitive Economics Critical Writings in Economics (Edward Elgar, Cheltenham).

Eichhorn, W. (1978). What is an Economic Index? An Attempt of an Answer, in: W. Eichhorn, R. Henn, O. Opitz, R.W. Shepard (eds.) Theory and Applications of Economic Indices (Physica-Verlag, Heidelberg).

Eichhorn, W. and J. Voeller (1976). Theory of the Price Index Fisher's Test Approach and Generalizations, Lecture Notes in Economics and Mathematical Systems 140 (Springer-Verlag, Heidelberg).

Estrella, A. (2000). Credit Ratings and Complementary Sources of Credit Quality Information, Basel Committee on Banking Supervision Working Papers No. 3 (August).

European Commission (1998a). Data Protection–Background Information, www.europa.eu.int/comm/internal_market/privacy

European Commission (1998b). Transfer of Personal Data to Third Countries: Applying Article 25 and 26 of the EU Data Protection Directive, Working Document (European Commission, Brussels).

European Commission (1998c). Preparation of a Methodology for Evaluating the Adequacy of the Level of Protection of Individuals with regard to Processing Personal Data: Test of a Method on several Categories of Transfer, Final Report (European Commission, Brussels).

European Commission (2001). Unsolicited Commercial Communication and Data Protection, Report (European Commission, Brussels).

European Commission (2007). Report on the retail banking sector inquiry, Commission Staff Working Document accompanying the Communication from the Commission–Sector Inquiry under Art 17 of Regulation 1/2003 on retail banking (Final Report).

Experian (1996). Form S-1 Registration Statement under the Securities Act of 1933 (Securities and Exchange Commission, Washington, DC).

Experian (2001). Dossier de Presse (in French) www.experian.fr /presse/dossierpresse_0102.pdf

Experian (2002a). Historique Complet (in French) www.sg2.fr/france/ about.htm

Experian (2002b). Experian: Spécialiste mondial des services d'information (in French), www.experian.fr/offres/offres.htm

Experian (2002c). Experian Announces Acquisition of AQM Information Solutions and other Affiliate Credit Bureaus, Release (Sept. 12, 2002)www.gusplc.com/template_press.asp?filename=266&divisionna me=Experian

Experian (2003). Ficheros Badex y Badexcug (in Spanish), website, www.experian.es

Farrell, J. and P. Klemperer (2001). Coordination and Lock-in: Competition with Switching Costs and Network Effects, in: Handbook of Industrial Organization, draft (December 2001).

Farrell, J. and G. Saloner (1985). Standardization Compatibility and Innovation, *Rand Journal of Economics* 16 (1): 70-83.

Fay, S. and J.K. MacKie-Mason (2001). Competition between Firms that bundle Information Goods, paper presented at the 27. Annual Telecom Policy Research Conference (September 25-27, 1999).

Feldman, M.S. and J.G. March (1981). Information in Organizations as Signal and Symbol, *Administrative Science Quarterly* 26 (2): 171-186.

Feldman, R. (1997). Small Business Loans Small Banks and a Big Change in Technology Called Credit Scoring, *The Region* 11 (3): 18-25.

Fickenscher, L. (1999). Experian not just a Credit Bureau Emerges as Data Base Powerhouse, The American Banker 164 (64): 1-4.

Fischer, R.L. and M.F. McEneney (1997). Fair Credit Reforms: Relief and Responsibility for Banks, Banker's Magazine 180 (2): 513.

Flaherty, D. (1989). Protecting Privacy in Surveillance Societies: The Federal Republic of Germany, Sweden, France, Canada and the United States (University of North Carolina Press, Chapel Hill).

Foer, A.A. and J. Rubin (2003). Competitive Conditions in the Mortgage Credit Reporting Industry: Report (American Antitrust Institute, Washington, DC).

Freixas, X., R. Guesnerie, J. Tirole (1985). Panning under Incomplete Information and the Ratchet Effect, *Review of Economic Studies* 52 (April): 173-91.

Freimer, M. and M. Gordon (1965). Why Bankers Ration Credit, *Quarterly Journal of Economics* 79 (3): 397-416.

Furash, E.E. (1995). The Small Business Bandwagon, *Journal of Commercial Lending* 77 (6): 1-4.

Furletti, M. (2002). An Overview and History of Credit Reporting, mimeo, Federal Reserve Bank of Philadelphia (June 2002).

Gehrig, T. (1998). Screening, Cross-border Banking and the Allocation of Credit, *Research in Economics* 52: 387-407.

Gehrig, T. and R. Stenbacka (2001). Information Sharing in Banking: A Collusive Device? CEPR Discussion Papers No. 2911 (June).

Gehrig, T. and R. Stenbacka (2005). Information Sharing and Lending Market Competition with Switching Costs and Poaching, *European Economic Review (forthcoming)*.

Gelpi, R.M. and F. Julien-Labruyère (1994). Histoire du crédit à la consommation (in French) (Éditions la Découverte, Paris).

General Accounting Office (2003). Limited Information Exists on the Extent of Credit Report Errors and their Implications for Consumers, Statement for the Record Before the Committee on Banking Housing and Urban Affaires Washington.

Goldhaber, M.H. (1997). The Attention Economy and the Net, Telepolis (November 1997) www.heise.de/tp/r4/artikel/6/6097/1.html

Goode, R.M. (1974). Consumer Credit Act 1974 (Butterworths, London).

Gosselin, K.R. (2003a). A Market Controlled by the Big 3, article, www.ctnow.com

Gosselin, K.R. (2003b). Big-3 Bureaus Control Billion-dollar Business, The Hartford Courant (06. January 2003), http://www.reporterherald.com

Gottinger, H.W. (2003). Economies of Network Industries (Routledge, London).

Green, H. (2001). Databases and Security vs. Privacy, Business Week Online (October 8, 2001).

Grossman, S.J. and J.E. Stiglitz (1976). Information and Competitive Price Systems, *American Economic Review* 66 (2): 246-253.

Grossman, S.J. and J.E. Stiglitz (1980) On the Impossibility of Informationally Efficient Markets, *American Economic Review* 70 (3): 393-408.

Hadlow, J. (2003). How a Credit Bureau Enhances the Credit Approval and Risk Management Process: Integration of Information and Decision–Making, Presentation at the First Central Asian Credit Bureau Conference, www.cbconference.kazecon.kz/en/mat/default.asp

Hancock, S. (2000). Developing a More Accurate and Efficient Scorecard, *Credit Control* 21 (1/2): 10-5.

Hand, D.J. (2001). Modelling Consumer Credit Risk, *IMA Journal of Management Mathematics* 12: 139-55.

Handzic, M. (2001). Does More Information Lead to Better Informing? in: A. Haringer (ed.) Proceedings of the 2001 Informing Science Conference 19-22 June 2001 (Krakow Poland): 251-256.

Hausman, J.A. (1983). Specification and Estimation of Simultaneous Equation Models, in: Z. Griliches and M.D. Intrilligator (eds.) Handbook of Econometrics I (North Holland, Amsterdam).

Hausman, J.A. and J.K. MacKie-Mason (1988). Price Discrimination and Patent Policy, *Rand Journal of Economics* 19 (2): 253-65.

Hayashi, K. (2002). The Usage-sensitive Price, Two–tier Price and the Self–selective Tariff under Network Capacity Limitation, mimeo, International Institute for Advanced Studies Kyoto.

Hendricks, E. (2003). Testimony of before the Senate Committee on the Judiciary Subcommittee on Terrorism Technology & Homeland Security, Hearing: "Database Security: Finding Out When Your Information Has Been Compromised" (November 4, 2003).

Hickman, W.B. (1958). Corporate Bond Quality and Investor Experience (Princeton University Press, Princeton).

Hirshleifer, J. (1971). The Private and Social Value of Information and the Reward to Incentive Activity, *American Economic Review* 61: 561-574

Hirshleifer, J. (1973). Where Are We in the Theory of Information? *American Economic Review* 63 (2): 31-9.

Hirshleifer, J. (1980). Privacy: It's Origin, Function and Future, *Journal of Legal Studies* IX: 649-66.

Hodgman, D.R. (1960). Credit Risk and Credit Rationing, *Quarterly Journal of Economics* 74: 258-78.

Howe, I. and G. Platts (1997). A Single European Scorecard? Does Data Predict Differently Across Europe? Paper presented at Credit Scoring and Credit Control V Conference (17-19 September 1997).

Hunt, R. (2005). A Century of Consumer Credit Reporting in America, Federal Reserve Bank of Philadelphia Working Paper, 05-13 (June).

Ishiguro, S. (2002). Comparing Allocations under Asymmetric Information: Coase Theorem, *Economics Letters* 80: 67-71.

Jaffee, D.M. and F. Modigliani (1969). A Theory and Test of Credit Rationing, *American Economic Review* 59: 850-72.

Jaffee, D.M. and T. Russell (1976). Imperfect Information, Uncertainty and Credit Rationing. *The Quarterly Journal of Economics* 90 (4): 651-66.

Jappelli, T. and M. Pagano (2002). Information Sharing Lending and Defaults: Cross-country Evidence, *Journal of Banking and Finance* 26: 2017-45.

Jappelli, T. and M. Pagano (2003). Public Credit Information: A European Perspective, in: M. Miller (ed.) Credit Reporting Systems and the International Economy (MIT Press, Cambridge): 81-115.

Jentzsch, N. (2001). The Economics and Regulation of Financial Privacy– A Comparative Analysis of the United States and Europe, John F. Kennedy Institute Working Paper No. 128/2001.

Jentzsch, N. (2003a). The Regulation of Financial Privacy: United States versus Europe, ECRI Research Report, No. 5 (June), Brussels.

Jentzsch, N. (2003b). The Regulatory Environment for Business Information Sharing. Paper prepared for the Vice Presidency World Bank Washington DC.

Jentzsch, N. (2003c). Constructing Regulatory Proxies: Elementary and Superlative Indices as Signals, mimeo, Freie Universität Berlin.

Jentzsch, N. (2005). Public versus Private Credit Registries: Substitutes or Complementary? Presentation at the African Microfinance Conference Cape Town South Africa.

Jentzsch, N. and A. San Jose Riestra (2006). Consumer Credit Markets in the United States and Europe, in: G. Bertola, R. Disney and C. Grant (eds.) The Economics of Consumer Credit (MIT Press, Cambridge): 27-63.

Jones, R. and H. Mendelson (1998). Product and Price Competition for Information Goods, Discussion Paper Stanford University.

Kahn, C.M., J. McAndrews and W. Roberds (2000). A Theory of Transactions Privacy, Federal Reserve Bank of Atlanta Working Paper Series No. 2000-22 (November).

Kang, J. (1998). Information Privacy in Cyberspace Transactions, *Stanford Law Review* 50: 1193-94.

Kahneman, D. and A. Tversky (1979). Prospect Theory: An Analysis of Decision under Risk, *Econometrica* 47 (2): 263-92.

Kallberg, J.G. and G.F. Udell (2003). Private Business Information Exchange in the United States, in: M. Miller (ed.) Credit Reporting Systems and the International Economy (MIT Press, Cambridge): 203-29.

Karstadt Quelle Information Services (2005). KQIS website, www.kqis.de

Kitchenman, W.F. and D. Teixeira (1998). Bureaus do a Credible Job. The Banker 198 (867): 104-6.

Kleinberg, J., C. Papadimitriou, P. Raghavan (2001). On the Value of Private Information, 8. Conference on Theoretical Aspects of Rationality and Knowledge (2001), mimeo.

Knack, S. (2002). Governance and Growth: Measurement and Evidence. Working Paper, World Bank.

Krugman, P. (2000). Networks and Increasing Returns: A Cautionary Tale, web.mit.edu/krugman/www/metcalfe.htm

La Porta, R., F. Lopez-de-Silanes, A. Shleifer and R.W. Vishny (1997). Legal Determinants of External Finance, *Journal of Finance* 52: 1131-50.

La Porta, R., F. Lopez-de-Silanes, A. Shleifer and R.W. Vishny (1998) Law and Finance, *Journal of Political Economy* 106: 1113-55.

La Porta, R., F. Lopez-de-Silanes, A. Shleifer (2002) What Works in Security Laws? www.law.uchicago.edu/Lawecon/workshop-papers/shleifer.pdf

Laband, D.N. and M.T. Maloney (1994). A Theory of Credit Bureaus, *Public Choice* 80: 275-91.

Lamberton, D.M. (1994). The Information Economy Revisited, in: R.E. Babe (ed.) Information and Communication in Economics (Kluwer Academic Publishers, Boston): 1-33.

Lanham, R.A. (1994) The Economics of Attention. Proceedings of the 24th Annual Meeting of the Association of Research Libraries, sunsite.berkeley.edu/ARL/Proceedings/124/ps2econ.html

Laudon, K.C. (1996a). Markets and Privacy, *Communications of the ACM* 39 (9): 92-104.

Laudon, K.C. (1996b). Extensions to the Theory of Markets and Privacy: Mechanics of Pricing Information, in: U.S. Department of Commerce National Telecommunication and Information Administration (ed.) Privacy and Self-Regulation in the Information Age (Washington, DC): 41-8.

Layson, S.K. (1994). Third-degree Price Discrimination under Economies of Scale, *Southern Economic Journal* 61(2): 323-27.

Leclercq, P. (2000). Crédit a la consommation - prévention de la fraude et des impayés (in French), (Commission National de l'Informatique et des Libertés Report, Paris).

Liebowitz, S.J. and S.E. Margolis (1995). Path dependence, Lock-in and History, *Journal of Law Economics and Organization* 11 (1): 205-26.

Liebowitz, S.J. and S.E. Margolis (1996). Are Network Externalities a New Source of Market Failure? Mimeo, University of Dallas, wwwpub.utdallas.edu/~liebowit/netwextr.html

Lopes, A.B. and D. Galletta (2002). Information Value in Electronic Networks: The Case of Subscription-based Online Information Goods. Proceedings of the AOM Meeting 2002, Denver.

Lopucki, L.M. (2003). Did Privacy Cause Identity Theft? *Hastings Law Journal* 54 (4): 1277-97.

Lutterbeck, B. (1998). 20 Jahre Dauerkonflikt: Die Novellierung des Bundesdatenschutzgesetzes (in German), in: B. Sokol (ed.) 20 Jahre Datenschutz - Individualismus oder Gemeinschaftssinn? Bericht über die Fachtagung in Münster.

Luo, Y. (2004). Consumption Dynamics, Asset Pricing, and Welfare Effects under Information Processing Constraints, mimeo, Princeton University.

Lyman, P. and H.R. Varian (2000). How Much Information? Research Project, www.sims.berkeley.edu/how-much-info

Macho-Stadler, I. and J.D. Pérez-Castrillo (2001). An Introduction to the Economics of Information (Oxford University Press, Oxford).

Madison, J. (1974). The Evolution of Commercial Credit Reporting Agencies in Nineteenth-Century America, *Business History Review* 48: 164-86.

Majnoni, G., M. Miller, N. Mylenko and A. Powell (2004) Improving Credit Information, Bank Regulation and Supervision: On the Role and Design of Public Credit Registries, mimeo, Washington.

Maki, D.M. (2000). The Growth of Consumer Credit and the Household Debt Service Burden. Finance and Economics Discussion Paper Series (Federal Reserve Board, Washington DC).

Marquez, R. (2002) Competition Adverse Selection and Information Dispersion in the Banking Industry, *Review of Financial Studies* 15 (3): 901-26.

Maurer, V.G. and E.T. Robert (1997). Getting Credit Where Credit is Due: Proposed Changes in the Fair Credit Reporting Act, *American Business Law Journal* 34 (4): 607-61.

Mester, L. (1994). Why are Credit Card Rates Sticky? *Economic Theory* 4 (4): 505-30.

Mester, L. (1997). What's the Point of Credit Scoring? *Business Review Federal Reserve Bank of Philadelphia* (Sept./Oct.) 3-16.

Metcalfe, R. (1995). Metcalfe's Law: A Network Becomes More Valuable as it Reaches more Users, InfoWorld 17 (40): 53.

Miller, M. (2003) Credit Reporting Systems around the Globe: The State of the Art in Public and Private Credit Registries, in: M. Miller (ed.) Credit Reporting Systems and the International Economy (MIT Press, Cambridge): 25-81

Millon, M.H. and A.V. Thakor (1985). Moral Hazard and Information Sharing: Model of Financial Information gathering Agencies, *Journal of Finance* XL (5): 1403-22.

Murphy, S. (1995). The Advertising of Installment Plans, *Essays in History* 37, etext.lib.virginia.edu/journals/EH/EH37/Murphy.htmlty

Musick, P. (1995). Credit History as an Underwriting Factor: Are the Data Reliable? *NAIC Research Quarterly* I (4): 1-4.

Norris J.D. (1978). RG Dun&Co 1841-1900: The Development of Credit-Reporting in the 19th Century (The Greenwood Press, Westport).

Office of the Press Secretary (2000) The Clinton-Gore Plan to Enhance Consumers' Financial Privacy: Protecting Core Values in the Information Age (Press Release, Washington, DC).

Oi, W. (1971). A Disneyland Dilemma: Two-part Tariffs for a Mickey Mouse Monopoly, *Quarterly Journal of Economics* 85 (1): 77-96.

Olegario, R. (2003). Credit Reporting Agencies: A Historical Perspective, in: M. Miller (ed.) Credit Reporting Systems and the International Economy (MIT Press, Cambridge): 115-61.

Organization for Economic Cooperation and Development, OECD (1985). Declaration of Trans-border Data Flows, www.oecd.org

Organization for Economic Cooperation and Development, OECD (1998). Ministerial Declaration on the Protection of Privacy in Global Networks, www.oecd.org/dataoecd/39/13/1840065.pdf

Padilla, J.A. and M. Pagano (1997). Endogenous Communication among Lenders and Entrepreneurial Incentives, *Review of Financial Studies* 10 (1): 205-36.

Padilla, J.A. and M. Pagano (2000). Sharing Default Information as a Borrower Discipline Device, *European Economic Review* 44 (10): 1951-80.

Pagano, M. and T. Jappelli (1991). Information Sharing in Credit Markets CEPR Discussion Paper 579 (October).

Pagano, M. and T. Jappelli (1993). Information Sharing in Credit Markets, *Journal of Finance* XLVIII (5): 1693-718.

Paquet, G. (1998). Evolutionary Cognitive Economics, *Information Economics and Policy* 10 (3): 343-57.

Paredes, T.A. (2003). Blinded by the Light: Information Overload and Its Consequences for Security Regulation, Washington University School of Law Faculty Working Paper Series, No. 03-02-02, forthcoming in *Washington University Law Quarterly*.

Perez, A. (2003). The WTO and the Protection of Personal Data do EU Measures Fall within GATS Exception? Paper for the 8th BILETA Conference: Controlling Information in the Online Environment.

Pesendorfer, W. (2006). Behavioral Economics Comes of Age: A Review Essay on *Advances in Behavioral Economics*, *Journal of Economic Literature* XLIV (September 2006): 712-21.

Posner, R. (1977). Economic Analysis of Law (Little Brown and Company, Boston).

Posner, R. (1978). An Economic Theory of Privacy, *Regulation* (May/June): 19-26.

Posner, R. (1979). Privacy, Secrecy and Reputation, *Buffalo Law Review* 28 (December): 1-55.

Posner, R. (1981). The Economics of Privacy, *American Economic Review* 71 (2): 405-9.

Pratt, S. (2003). Statement of Stuart K Pratt Consumer Data Industry Association before the Committee on Banking Housing and Urban Affairs United States Senate on "The Accuracy of Credit Report Information and the Fair Credit Reporting Act" (July 10, 2003).

Privacy International (2004). Data Protection Laws around the World, www.privacyinternational.org

Privacy Rights Clearinghouse (1997). Highlights of the 1996 Legislation amending the Fair Credit Reporting Act, www.privacyrights.org

Public Interest Research Group (1998). Mistakes Do Happen: Credit Report Errors Mean Consumers Lose (Public Interest Research Group) www.uspirg.org/reports/mistakesdohappen 3_98.pdf

Raban, D.R. and S. Rafaeli (2003). Subjective Value of Information: The Endowment Effect, mimeo, University of Haifa.

Ramakrishnan, R. and A. Thakor (1984). Information Reliability and a Theory of Financial Intermediation, *Review of Economic Studies* 52 (3): 415-32.

Registry Trust (2004). History and the Scope of the Registry, website www.registry-trust.org.uk

Reidenberg, J.R. (2000). Resolving Conflicting International Data Privacy Rules in Cyberspace, *Stanford Law Review* 52: 1315-76.

Reidenberg, J.R. and P.M. Schwartz (1996). Data Privacy Law: A Study of United States Data Protection (Michie, Charlottesville).

Rodrik, D., A. Subramanian and F. Trebbi (2002). Institutions Rule: The Primacy of Institutions over Geography and Integration in Economic Development, Mimeo, Harvard University.

Rohlfs, J. (1974). A Theory of Interdependent Demand for a Communications Service, *Bell Journal of Economics* 5(1): 16-37.

Rothschild, M. and J.E. Stiglitz (2001). Competition and Insurance Theory Twenty Years Later, *Geneva Papers on Risk and Insurance Theory* 22 (2): 73-79.

Rousseau P.L. and R. Sylla (2001). Financial Systems, Economic Growth and Globalization, NBER Working Papers 8323 (June).

Ryman-Tubb, N. (2000). An Overview of Credit Scoring Techniques, *Credit Control* 21 (1/2): 39-45.

Samuelson, P. (2000). Privacy as Intellectual Property? *Stanford Law Review* 52 (5): 1125-74.

Schmalensee, R. (1981) Output and Welfare Implications of Monopolistic Third-Degree Price Discrimination, *American Economic Review* 71 (1): 242-47.

Schufa Holding AG (2002). 75 Jahre Schufa–75 Jahre Verbraucherkredit, Jubiläumsbroschüre (Schufa Holding AG, Wiesbaden).

Schufa Holding AG (2004). Annual Report 2004 (Schufa Holding AG, Wiesbaden).

Shapiro, C. and H. Varian (2001). Information Rules (Harvard Business School Press, Boston).

Sims, C. (1998). Stickiness, Carnegie-Rochester Conference Series on Public Policy 49 (1): 317-56.

Sims, C. (2003). Implications of Rational Inattention, *Journal of Monetary Economics* 50 (3): 665-90.

Simon, H.A. (1997) Designing Organizations for an Information-rich World, in: D.M. Lamberton (ed.) The Economics of Communication and Information (Edward Elgar, Cheltenham).

Simon, H.A. (1992). Economics Bounded Rationality and the Cognitive Revolution (Edward Elgar, Cheltenham).

Smith, R.E. (2000). Ben Franklin's Web Site: Privacy and Curiosity from Plymouth Rock to the Internet (Privacy Journal, Providence).

Solove, D.J. (2003). Identity Theft, Privacy, and the Architecture of Vulnerability, *Hastings Law Journal* 54 (2003): 1227-76.

Sosna, J. (2002). Der Vorschlag der Kommission für einer Neufassung der Verbraucherkreditrichtlinie, Institut für Deutsches und Internationales Bank- und Kapitalmarktrecht, Report University of Leipzig (in German).

Stigler, G.J. (1961). The Economics of Information, *The Journal of Political Economy* LXIX (3): 213-25.

Stigler, G.J. (1967). Imperfections in the Capital Market, *Journal of Political Economy* 75 (June): 287-92.

Stigler, G.J. (1980). An Introduction to Privacy in Economics and Politics, *Journal of Legal Studies* 9 (4): 623-44.

Stiglitz, J.E. (1975). The Theory of 'Screening' Education and Distribution of Income, *American Economic Review* 65 (3): 283-300.

Stiglitz, J.E. (1987) Economic Organization, Information and Development, in: H. Chenery and T.N. Srinivasan (eds.) Handbook of Development Economics 1 (North-Holland, Amsterdam): 93-160.

Stiglitz, J.E. (2000) The Contributions of the Economics of Information to Twentieth Century Economics, *Journal of Quarterly Economics* 115 (4): 1441-78.

Stiglitz, J.E. and A. Weiss (1981). Credit Rationing in Markets with Imperfect Information, *American Economic Review* 72 (3): 393-410.

Stiglitz, J.E. and A. Weiss (1983). Incentive Effects of Terminations: Applications to the Credit and Labor Markets, *American Economic Review* 73 (5): 912-27.

Stiglitz, J.E. and A. Weiss (1992). Asymmetric Information in Credit Markets and Its Implications for Macroeconomics, *Oxford Economic Papers* 44 (4): 694-724.

Such, C.L. (1985). Interactions between Signaling and Repeated Play with Borrower Default, Stanford Institute for Mathematical Studies in the Social Sciences (Economics Series), 480 (October).

Sundararajan, A. (2003). Nonlinear Pricing of Information Goods, *Management Science* 50 (12): 1660-73.

Swire, P. (1999). Financial Privacy and the Theory of High-tech Government Surveillance, in: R.E. Litan and A.M. Santomero (eds.) Brookings-Wharton Papers on Financial Services 1999: 391-442.

Swire, P. and R.E. Litan (1998). None of your Business: World Data Flows Electronic Commerce and the European Privacy Directive (Brookings Institution Press, Washington, DC).

Sylla, R. (2002). A Historical Premier on the Business of Credit Rating, in: R.M. Levich, G. Majnoni and C. Reinhart, Rating Agencies and the Global Financial System (Kluwer Academic Publishers, Boston): 19-41.

Sylla, R., J.W. Wilson and C.P. Jones (1994). U.S. Financial Markets and long-term Economic Growth 1790-1989, in: T. Weiss, D. Schaefer (eds.) American Economic Development in Historical Perspective (Stanford University Press, Stanford): 28-52.

Taylor, C.R. (2002). Private Demands and the Demand for Privacy: Dynamic Pricing and the Market for Customer Information, Duke University, mimeo (September).

Taylor, C.R. (2003) Privacy and Information Acquisition in Competitive Markets, Duke University, mimeo (June).

The Register (2004). The Growing Problem of Identity Theft (February 10, 2004) www.theregister.co.uk/content/55/34336.html

Thomas, L.C. (2000). A Survey of Credit and Behavioral Scoring: Forecasting Financial Risk of Lending to Consumers, *International Journal of Forecasting* 16 (2000): 149-72.

Tritsch, S. (2003). Family Circus, Boston Magazine Online (February 2003) www.bostonmagazine.com

U.S. Federal Reserve Board (1987). 1986 Survey of Consumer Finances. Federal Reserve Bulletin 73: 761-778.

U.S. Federal Reserve Board et al. (2000). Agencies Approve Final Regulations for Privacy of Consumer Financial Information. Joint Press Release (May 10, 2000).

U.S. Federal Reserve Board (2001a). Federal Reserve Statistical Release – Household Debt-Service Burden, www.federalreserve.gov/releases

U.S. Federal Reserve Board (2001b) Federal Reserve Statistical Release– Charge-off and Delinquency Rates on Loans and Leases at Commercial Banks, www.federalreserve.gov

U.S. Federal Reserve Board (2001c). Title 12 (Banks and Banking) Regulation P (Federal Reserve Board, Washington DC).

U.S. Federal Reserve Board (2003). Testimony of Chairman Alan Greenspan in the Hearing of the House Financial Services Committee on the U.S. Monetary and Economic Policy (April 30, 2003).

U.S. Federal Trade Commission (1997a). Proposed Notices of Rights and Duties Under the Fair Credit Reporting Act 16 CFR Part 601 (U.S. Federal Trade Commission, Washington, DC).

U.S. Federal Trade Commission (1997b). Credit Reports: What Information Providers need to know (U.S. Federal Trade Commission, Washington, DC).

U.S. Federal Trade Commission (1999). The Fair Credit Reporting Act. www.ftc.gov/os/statutes/fcra.pdf

U.S. Federal Trade Commission (2000a). Privacy of Consumer Financial Information Final Rule, *Federal Register* 65 (101): 33646-89.

U.S. Federal Trade Commission (2000b). FTC Issues Final Rule on Privacy of Consumer Financial Information, press release (May 15, 2000).

U.S. Federal Trade Commission (2001a). The Gramm-Leach-Bliley-Act – Privacy of Consumer Financial Information, Presentation, Washington DC.

U.S. Federal Trade Commission (2001b). Protecting Consumers' Privacy: 2002 and beyond, remarks of FTC Chairman T.J. Muris at the Privacy 2001 Conference Cleveland Ohio (October 4, 2001).

U.S. Federal Trade Commission (2003). Identity Theft Survey, Synovate Report, www.ftc.gov/os/2003/09/synovatereport.pdf

U.S. Federal Trade Commission (2004). Report to Congress under the Sections 318 and 319 of the Fair and Accurate Credit Transactions Act of 2003, Report (U.S. Federal Trade Commission, Washington, DC).

U.S. House of Representatives (1989). Fair Credit Reporting Act Hearings before the Subcommittee on Consumer Affairs and Coinage of the Committee on Banking Finance and Urban Affairs, 101. Congress, 1. Session (September 13, 1989).

U.S. House of Representatives (2003). Fair and Accurate Credit Transactions Act of 2003–Report together with additional and supplemental Views, Conference Report, No, 108-263.

Ulph, D. and N. Vulkan (2000). Electronic Commerce and Competitive First-degree Price Discrimination, Mimeo, University of Bristol.

Ulph, D. and N. Vulkan (2001) E-Commerce Mass Customization and Price Discrimination, Technical Report, University College of London.

Unabhängiges Landeszentrum für Datenschutz Schleswig-Holstein (2003). Gemeinsame Pressenerklärung des Bundesbeauftragten für den Datenschutz sowie der Datenschutz-Aufsichtsbehörden der Länder Bremen Nordrhein-Westfalen und Schleswig-Holstein (in German), press release (May 15, 2003).

Van Cayseele, P., J. Bouckaert and H. Degryse (1995). Credit Market Structure and Information-Sharing Mechanisms, in: A. van Witteloostuijn, Market Evolution–Competition and Cooperation (Kluwer Academic Publishers, Boston): 129-145.

Van Cayseele, P., J. Bouckaert and H. Degryse (2006). Entry and Strategic Information Display in Credit Markets, *The Economic Journal* 116 (513): 702-20.

Varian, H.R. (1985). Price Discrimination and Social Welfare, *American Economic Review* 75(4): 870-75.

Varian, H.R. (1996). Economic Aspects of Personal Privacy, Mimeo, University of California at Berkeley.

Varian, H.R. (1997). Versioning Information Goods, mimeo, University of California at Berkeley (March).

Varian, H.R. (1998). Markets for Information Goods, Mimeo, University of California at Berkeley.

Varian, H.R. (1999). Markets for Information Goods, IMES Discussion Paper Series Discussion, No.99–E–9, www.imes.boj.or.jp/edps9 9/99-E-09.pdf

Vercammen, J.A. (1995) Credit Bureau Policy and Sustainable Reputation Effects in Credit Markets, *Economica* 62 (248): 461-78.

Von der Lippe, P.M. (2002). General Introduction and Elementary Price Index Theory, TES Script, www.vwl.uni-essen.de/dt/stat

Westin, A. (1967). Privacy and Freedom (Atheneum, New York).

Williams, J.R. (1989). Credit File Errors: A Report, Consolidated Information Services (August 7, 1989).

Williamson, O.E. (1975). Markets and Hierarchies: Analysis and Antitrust Implications (The Free Press, New York).

Williamson, O.E. (1985). The Economic Institutions of Capitalism–Firms, Markets, Relational Contracting (The Free Press, New York).

World Bank (2003a). Access to Credit Project: Results on the Global Survey of 47 Private Credit Bureaus in 33 Countries, worldbank.org

World Bank (2003b). Access to Credit Project: Results on the Global Survey of 47 Public Credit Registries in 64 Countries, worldbank.org

World Bank (2004). Doing Business in 2004–Understanding Regulation (Oxford University Press, Oxford).

Yang, L. (2002). The Evaluation of Classification Models for Credit Scoring, in: M. Schumann, Arbeitsbericht, No. 02/2002 (Institut für Wirtschaftsinformatik, Göttingen).

Zandi, M. (1998). Incorporating Economic Information into Credit Risk Underwriting, in: E. Mays (ed.) Credit Risk Modelling: Design and Application (Dearborn Publishers, Chicago).

Zuccharini, D. (2001). How Do Businesses Use Customer Information: Is the Customer's Privacy Protected? Prepared Witness Testimony before the Subcommittee on Commerce Trade and Consumer Protection (July 26, 2001).

Glossary of Credit Terms

Arrears: When a bankruptcy case is filed, the borrower owes a certain amount–this amount is called arrears. For instance, if a mortgage loan is owed the arrear would be the mortgage payments, including interest and potential penalties.

Bankruptcy: This term denotes the legal state of insolvency of a consumer, in a more narrow sense it denotes the situation where the borrower has officially declared bankrupt by filing a bankruptcy petition. In the legal procedure, assets are either liquidated or debts are restructured. Different classes of creditors are then paid according to their ranking.

Charge-off: This is an accounting procedure, whereby the amount of a non-collectible balance is removed from the active receivable accounts after the borrower has been delinquent. Debts are usually written off after 180 days. Creditors often hand unpaid debts over to debt collectors. The term is common in the credit card industry. Only if a debt is re-classified as non-collectable, it is actually written-off (see definition of "write off" below).

Closed-end credit: The closed-end credit is a type of credit that has to be repaid within a specific time frame. This is usually the case for non-revolving credit that follows repayment plans that are fixed and have also a fixed end date.

Consumer credit: Consumer credit covers short- and intermediate-term credit extended to individuals for consumption purposes. I define it as excluding loans that are secured by real estate, as is the case for mortgage loans or home equity loans. The category includes revolving credit such as credit card credit and lines of credit as well as secured credit for automobiles, durable consumer goods or other consumption purposes that is non-revolving and paid in installments.

Credit risk: The (estimated) probability that the borrower will not repay the amount owed on time. Although there are different definitions, credit risk in general usually is defined as delinquency or as default; this is being either 30, 60, 90 or 180 days late. The term is also used for a consumer's creditworthiness (credit rating). In information economics, this term is used as a short form for "credit risk of the consumer," where there is a separation in good credit risks and bad ones.

Debt-to-income ratio: The debt-to-income ratio is the total amount owed as ratio to the income of a household. It is either calculated as monthly or yearly average. This ratio is sometimes used for affordability assessments. The total ratio, however, says little about the monthly ongoing payments that reduce the borrower's income.

Default: This term denotes the situation, where the borrower fails to meet his or her financial obligations. Default is often used to refer to accounts that are more than 180 days delinquent.

Delinquency: Delinquency is the situation where the borrower fails to pay when payments are due. Usually, there are late fees applied after a delinquency occurred. The credit business usually distinguishes 30-day, 60-day and 90-day delinquencies with the latter being the most serious. Delinquencies that are over 30 days are usually reported to credit bureaus.

Financial obligations ratio: It is the ongoing monthly burden of the borrower devoted to financial obligations. This obligation adds automobile lease payments, rental payments on tenant-occupied property, homeowners' insurance, and property tax payments to the debt service ratio (see also household debt service ratio).

Home equity: The current market value of a home minus the outstanding mortgage balance. Essentially it is the amount of ownership that has been built up by the holder of the mortgage through payments and appreciation. A home equity loan is secured to the extent of the excess of the fair market value over the debt incurred by the purchase.

Homeowner financial obligations ratio: The homeowner total financial obligations ratio (see definition of Financial Obligations Ratio) adds payments on mortgage, property taxes, property insurance and payments on consumer debt and automobile leases to the debt service ratio.

Household debt: The aggregated sum of short-term and long-term obligations of a household. This includes different kinds of credit categories such as consumer credit and mortgage debt. The term is used to describe the overall indebtedness of a household and is used interchangeably with household credit.

Household debt service ratio: This ratio is the debt service of a household to its after-tax income (also known as household debt service burden or financial obligations ratio). The debt service is calculated as sum of monthly interest and minimum payments. This sum reduces current income and the current consumption, because it increases budget constraints. The payments include payments on outstanding mortgage and consumer debt.

Indebtedness: The term describes the situation of being in debt by owing either a monetary or physical value to another person. Usually the term is used to describe the total amount owed.

Mortgage: A mortgage is a loan secured by real estate. The buyer uses the home as collateral for the loan. For fixed-rate mortgages interest rates remain the same after the loans was taken out. For the variable-rate mortgage the interest varies over time, perhaps moving together with prime rate movements.

Non-performing loans: This term describes a loan that does not earn an income ("perform"). The borrower is either delinquent and does not pay installments or interest. This situation usually precedes loan restructuring. Sometimes the term "non-performing accounts" is used for describing non-performing loans that are at least six months past due.

Non-revolving debt: Non-revolving debt describes all other types of credit that are not captured by the term "revolving credit" (see definition "revolving credit"). This comprises installment plans for financing automobile purchases or other durable goods. Installments are regular payments that have to be made by the borrower to reduce the debt and to pay back the credit. Non-revolving debt might be secured by collateral or real estate.

Open-end credit: Credit that can be used up to a certain limit and that can be paid down at any time. The borrower may use it at any time to any extent up to the amount agreed upon with the bank. Open-end is usually the case for revolving credit.

Personal loan: A personal loan is a small amount of credit that is repaid in installments. It is extended for personal consumption purposes that are the acquisition of durable goods (see also definition "consumer credit". The term is used interchangeably with the term "personal credit."

Private credit: Private credit is a statistical aggregate that describes domestic credit extended by deposit money banks to the non-financial private sector. This sector includes households and commercial entities such as companies or entrepreneurs. The category is typically broader than the category of consumer credit or household debt (see definition "consumer credit").

Renter financial obligations ratio: The renter financial obligations ratio (see definition "financial obligations ratio") adds rental payments on tenant-occupied property to the financial obligations ratio. The rationale behind this is that renters usually have a higher financial burden as homeowners.

Revolving debt: This is a description for a specific type of credit use. Here, the consumer may decide when and to which extent the credit is used (within certain limits) and as to whether the balance is carried over to the next month. Revolving credit can be granted in connection with retail credit, credit lines and credit cards. This type of credit is either secured or unsecured. Unsecured credit is not backed by any collateral instead it is extended based upon the creditworthiness and reputation of a person.

Write-off: When a non-performing loan is determined to be noncollectible it is written off. The "write-off" is the accounting procedure that redefines the loan as loss, meaning that it is moved from the asset side of the balance sheet to the expense side. It is marked not recoverable.

Appendix

Table 5.9 Financial Privacy around the World: Data Protection

Country/ Contract	Data Protection Act or Contract (enacted or suggested as of 2004)	Year	Status
OECD	Guidelines on the Protection of Privacy and Trans-border Flows of Personal Data	1980	in effect
UN	Guidelines Concerning Computerized Personal Data Files	1990	in effect
WTO	Article XIV of the GATS (exceptions)	1994	in effect
COE	European Council Convention 108	1981	in effect
EU DPD	Directive 95/46/EC	1998	in effect
APEC	APEC Privacy Principles	2004	suggested
Safe Harbor	Safe Harbor Agreement	2000	in effect
Albania	Law on the Protection of Personal Data	1999	in effect
Argentina	Personal Data Protection Act	2000	in effect
Australia	Privacy Act	1988	in effect
Austria	Federal Law on the Protection of Personal Data	1978	in effect
Belgium	Law on Privacy Protection	2001	in effect
B. Herzeg.	Law on the Protection of Personal Data	2001	in effect
Bulgaria	Personal Data Protection Act	2001	in effect
B. Faso	Bill	2004	suggested
Canada	Personal Information Protection and Electronic Documents Act	2001	in effect
China	Bill: Personal Data Protection Act		suggested
Czech Rep	Act on the Protection of Personal Data	2000	in effect
Denmark	Act on Processing of Personal Data	2000	
Finland	Personal Data Act	1999	in effect
France	Loi N° 78-17 du 6 Janvier 1978	1978	in effect
Germany	Bundesdatenschutzgesetz	1990	in effect

Table 5.9 Financial Privacy around the World: Data Protection (cont.)

Country	Data Protection Act or Contract (enacted or suggested as of 2004)	Year	Status
Greece	Law on Protection of Individuals with regard to the Processing of Personal Data	1997	in effect
Hong Kong	Personal Data (Privacy) Ordinance	1997	in effect
Hungary	Protection of Personal Data and Disclosure of Data of Public Interest	1992	in effect
India	Bill: Amendments to the Information Technology Act	2004	
Ireland	Data Protection Act	1988	in effect
Italy	Protection of Individuals and other Subjects with regard to the Processing of Personal Data	1996	in effect
Japan	Personal Data Protection	2003	in effect
Latvia	Law on Personal Data Protection	2000	in effect
Lithuania	Law on Legal Protection of Personal Data	1996	in effect
Malaysia	Bill: Personal Data Protection Act	2004	suggested
Mali	Bill	2004	suggested
Netherlands	Personal Data Protection Act	2000	in effect
Norway	Personal Data Act	2000	in effect
Poland	Law on the Protection of Personal Data	1998	in effect
Portugal	Act on the Protection of Personal Data	1998	in effect
Romania	Law No. 677/2001	2001	in effect
Russia	Bill: Law on Information of Personal Character	2004	suggested
Slovakia	Data Protection Act	2002	in effect
Slovenia	Personal Data Protection Act	1999	in effect
S. Africa	Protection of Personal Information Bill	2004	
Spain	Organic Law 15/1999 of on the Protection of Personal Data	1999	in effect
Sweden	Personal Data Act	1998	in effect
Switzerland	Federal Data Protection Act	1992	in effect
Taiwan	Computer-Processed Personal Data Protection Law	1995	in effect
UK	Data Protection Act	1998	in effect

Notes: Countries not listed here do not have a general data protection law, but might have a banking law or a credit reporting law. The Table does not list the regulations accompanying many of the above laws. For abbreviations, see list of abbreviations.

Table 5.10 Financial Privacy around the World: Banking Acts

Country	Banking and Credit Acts (Enactment)	Year
Albania	Banking Law	1991
Algeria	Banking Law 90-10	1990
Argentina	Law of Financial Institutions	1977
Armenia	Law relating to Banks and Banking Activities	1993
Australia	Financial Sector Act	1998
Austria	Bankwesengesetz	1993
Bangladesh	Bangladesh Bank Order	1972
Belarus	Banking Code	2000
Belgium	Loi du 12 Juin 1991 relative au Credit à la Consommation	1991
Benin	Banking Law	1990
Bolivia	Ley de Bancos y Entidades Financieras	1990
Botswana	Banking Act	1995
Bulgaria	Law on Banks	2000
B. Faso	Banking Law	1990
Canada	Bank Act	1999
China	Law of the People's Republic of China on Commercial Banks	1995
Colombia	Organic Statute of the Financial System	1993
Croatia	Banking Law	1989
Czech Rep.	Czech Banking Act	1992
Denmark	Commercial Banks and Savings Banks Consolidated Act	1974
Dom. Rep.	Ley de Monetaria y Financiera	n/a
Ecuador	Ley General de Instituciones del Sistema Financiero	1994
Egypt	Decree Concerning Law No. 205	1990
Finland	Act on Credit Institutions	1994
France	Banking Act 1984	1984
Germany	German Banking Act	1998
Ghana	Banking Law	1989
Greece	Law 2076/92	2002
Guatemala	Ley de Bancos y Grupos Financieros	2002
Honduras	Ley de Instituciones del Sistema Financiero	1995
H. Kong	Banking Ordinance	1997
Hungary	Act on Credit Institutions	1996
India	Banking Regulation Act	1949
Indonesia	Law concerning the Banking System	1992

Notes: See notes at the end of this Table.

Table 5.10 Financial Privacy around the World: Banking Acts (cont.)

Country	Banking and Credit Acts (Enactment)	Year
Iran	Monetary and Banking Law	1972
Ireland	Central Bank and Financial Services Authorities Act	2003
Italy	Banking Law	1993
Jamaica	Financial Institutions Act	1992
Japan	Long-term Credit Bank Law	1999
Jordan	Banking Law	2000
Kazakhstan	Law on Banks in the Republic Kazakhstan	1993
Kenya	Banking Act	1995
Korea	Banking Act of Korea	n/a
Kyrgyz Rep.	Law On Banks and Banking Activity in K.Rep.	1997
Latvia	Law on Credit Institutions	1995
Lebanon	Bank Secrecy Law of September 3, 1956	1956
Lithuania	Law on Commercial Banks	1994
Madagascar	Banking Law	1996
Malawi	Banking Act	1989
Malaysia	Banking and Financial Institutions	1989
Mali	Banking Law	1990
Moldova	Law on Financial Institutions	1995
Mongolia	Banking Law	1991
Morocco	Law N° 1-93-147	1993
Mozambique	Law of Credit Institutions and Financial Corp.	1999
Nepal	Commercial Bank Act 2031	1974
Netherlands	Bank Act	1998
Nicaragua	Ley General de Bancos, Instituciones Financieras no Bancarias y Grupos Financieros	n/a
Niger	Banking Law	1990
Nigeria	Banks and Other Financial Institutions Act	1991
Norway	Act on Commercial Banks in Norway	n/a
Pakistan	Banking Companies Ordinance Act	1962
Philippines	General Banking Act	1999
Poland	Banking Act	1997
Portugal	Banking Act	1992
Romania	Banking Law 58/1998	1998
Russia	Law on Banks and Banking Activities	1996
Saudi Arabia	Banking Control Law	1966
Senegal	Banking Law	1990
Singapore	Banking Act	1999

Notes: See notes at the end of the Table.

Table 5.10 Financial Privacy around the World: Banking Acts (cont.)

Country	Banking and Credit Acts (Enactment)	Year
Slovakia	Banking Act	1992
Slovenia	Law on Banking	1999
S. Africa	Banks Act	1990
Spain	Discipline and Intervention of Credit Institutions	1988
Sri Lanka	Banking Act No. 30	1988
Sweden	Banking Business Act	2000
Switzerland	Federal Law on Banks and Savings Banks	1934
Syria	Money and Central Bank Law	1954
Taiwan	Banking Law of the Republic of China	1992
Tanzania	Banking and Financial Institutions Act	1991
Thailand	Act on the Undertaking of Finance Business, Securities Business and Credit Financing Business	n/a
Tunisia	Law 67-51 Regulating the Banking Profession	1967
Turkey	Bank Act	1993
Uganda	Uganda Commercial Bank Act	1965
Ukraine	Law of Ukraine on Banks and Banking	2001
UA Emirates	Bank Control Act	1966
UK	Banking Act	1987
U.S.	Gramm Leach Bliley Act	1999
Uruguay	Decreto Ley 15322	1982
Uzbekistan	Law of the Republic of Uzbekistan on Banks and Banking	1997
Venezuela	Ley General de Bancos y Otras Instituciones Financieras	2001
Vietnam	Law on Credit Institutions	1997
Yemen	Commercial Banking Law	2001
Zambia	Banking and Financial Services Act	1994
Zimbabwe	Banking Act	2000

Notes: Countries that are not listed here do not have a banking law, but might have a banking law. The Table does not list the regulations accompanying most of the above laws.

Table 5.11 Financial Privacy around the World: Credit Reporting Acts

Country	Industry Laws, Codes of Conduct or Articles (Enactment by 2004)	Year
Belgium	Loi du 10 août 2001 relative à la centrale des crédits aux particuliers	2001
Canada	Consumer Reporting Act	1989
Colombia	Proyeto de Ley Estatutaria No. 71 de 2002 Senado	2002
Czech Rep.	Position No. 1/2001 Publication of the Names of Debtors	2001
Dom. Rep.	Second Resolution of the Monetary Board of the Central Bank (14.2.1997)	1997
Ecuador	Memo for Circulation # INSIS-97-0028 of the Banking Regulatory Agency	2002
Hong Kong	Code of Practice on Consumer Credit Data	n/a
Kazakhstan	Decree No. 443 National Bank	1999
Korea	Use and Protection of Credit Information Act	1995
Malaysia	Central Bank of Malaysia Act 1958	1958
Singapore	Code of Conduct	n/a
Sri Lanka	Credit Information Bureau of Sri Lanka Act	1990
Sweden	Credit Information Act	1973
Switzerland	Konsumkreditgesetz (Articles)	2003
Thailand	Credit Information Business Operating Act	2002
U.S.	Fair Credit Reporting Act	1970

Notes: Some of the above acts have been amended in the years after their enactment. The table above does not list the regulations accompanying most of the laws. The table also contains laws that contain articles about credit reporting.

Table 5.12 Results of the Ratings in Credit Reporting Regulation

Country/Contract	SA	PR	OB	TBD	IF	SC	Total
Total Points	8	9	9	5	7	2	40
OECD	2	4	3	1	5	1	16
UN	4	5	4	1	5	2	21
COE	4	4	4	1	3	1	17
EU DPD	7	8	6	3	6	2	32
US Safe Harbor	0	5	4	1	2	1	13
Albania	7	6	6	3	4	1	27
Algeria	0	0	0	1	0	0	1
Argentina	7	8	8	2	6	2	33
Armenia	0	0	0	0	0	0	0
Australia	8	7	5	2	7	2	31
Austria	8	8	9	2	5	2	34
Bangladesh	0	1	0	0	0	0	1
Belarus	0	0	0	1	1	0	2
Belgium	8	8	5	1	4	2	28
Benin	0	3	2	0	0	0	5
Bolivia	0	0	0	1	0	0	1
B. Herzegovina	7	7	8	2	4	2	30
Botswana	0	0	0	0	0	0	0
Bulgaria	8	7	7	1	4	1	28
Burkina Faso	0	0	1	0	0	0	1
Cameroon	0	1	0	0	0	0	1
Canada	8	7	8	0	7	2	32
China	0	0	0	0	0	0	0
Colombia	0	1	0	0	0	0	1
Cote d'Ivoire	0	0	0	0	0	0	0
Croatia	0	0	0	0	0	0	0
Czech Rep	8	9	6	2	4	2	31
Denmark	8	9	8	3	6	2	36
Dom. Republic	0	5	0	0	0	0	5
Ecuador	0	5	1	0	0	0	6
Egypt	0	1	1	1	0	0	3
Ethiopia	0	0	0	0	0	0	0

Notes: See notes at the end of this Table.

Table 5.12 Results of the Ratings in Credit Reporting Regulation (cont.)

Country	SA	PR	OB	TBD	IF	SC	Total
Finland	8	9	7	3	6	2	35
France	8	9	7	3	7	2	36
Georgia	0	0	1	1	0	0	2
Germany	8	9	8	2	6	2	35
Ghana	0	0	0	0	0	0	0
Greece	8	7	7	4	5	2	33
Guatemala	0	1	1	0	0	0	2
Honduras	0	1	1	0	0	0	2
Hong Kong	8	6	8	0	3	2	27
Hungary	8	6	8	2	6	0	30
India	0	0	1	0	0	0	1
Indonesia	0	0	0	0	0	0	0
Iran	0	1	1	0	0	0	2
Ireland	8	9	8	3	6	2	36
Italy	8	9	6	3	6	2	34
Jamaica	0	0	0	0	0	0	0
Japan	4	5	6	0	4	2	21
Jordan	0	2	1	0	0	0	3
Kazakhstan	0	0	1	0	0	0	1
Kenya	0	1	1	0	0	0	2
Korea	6	7	6	0	4	2	25
Kyrgyz Rep.	0	0	0	0	0	0	0
Latvia	8	7	8	3	6	1	33
Lebanon	0	1	1	0	0	0	2
Lithuania	8	8	8	3	6	1	34
Madagascar	0	1	1	0	0	0	2
Malawi	0	0	0	0	0	0	0
Malaysia	2	6	3	0	3	2	16
Mali	0	3	2	0	0	0	5
Moldova	0	0	1	1	0	0	2
Mongolia	0	0	1	0	0	0	1
Morocco	0	0	1	1	0	0	2
Mozambique	0	0	1	0	0	0	1

Notes: See notes at the end of this Table.

Table 5.12 Results of the Ratings in Credit Reporting Regulation (cont.)

Country	SA	PR	OB	TBD	IF	SC	Total
Nepal	0	0	0	0	0	0	0
Netherlands	8	8	7	3	6	2	34
Nicaragua	0	3	0	0	0	0	3
Niger	0	0	1	1	0	0	2
Nigeria	0	0	0	0	0	0	0
Norway	8	7	9	2	6	2	34
Pakistan	0	1	1	0	0	0	2
Philippines	0	1	1	0	0	0	2
Poland	8	8	7	3	6	2	34
Portugal	8	9	5	3	6	2	33
Romania	7	8	8	3	7	1	34
Russia	0	1	0	0	0	0	1
Saudi Arabia	0	0	0	0	0	0	0
Senegal	0	0	1	0	0	0	1
Singapore	0	0	0	0	0	0	0
Slovakia	8	8	7	3	5	1	32
Slovenia	7	7	8	3	4	1	30
South Africa	0	5	2	0	0	0	7
Spain	8	9	7	3	6	2	35
Sri Lanka	2	4	2	0	0	2	10
Sweden	8	8	5	3	6	2	32
Switzerland	6	7	6	3	3	2	27
Syria	0	1	1	1	0	0	3
Taiwan	8	6	8	2	3	2	29
Tanzania	0	1	1	0	0	0	2
Thailand	7	6	8	1	7	2	31
Tunisia	0	1	0	0	0	0	1
Turkey	0	1	0	0	0	0	1
Uganda	0	0	0	0	0	0	0
Ukraine	0	1	1	0	0	0	2
UA Emirates	0	1	1	1	0	0	3
UK	8	9	9	1	5	2	34
United States	5	8	8	0	5	2	28

Notes: See notes at the end of this Table.

Table 5.12 Results of the Ratings in Credit Reporting Regulation (cont.)

Country	SA	PR	OB	TBD	IF	SC	Total
Uruguay	0	4	2	1	0	0	7
Uzbekistan	0	0	1	0	0	0	1
Venezuela	0	5	2	0	0	0	7
Vietnam	0	1	0	0	0	0	1
Yemen	0	1	1	1	0	0	3
Zambia	0	0	0	1	0	0	1
Zimbabwe	0	0	0	0	0	0	0

Notes: SA denotes supervisory authority, PR property rights, OC obligations of credit bureaus, TBD trans-border data flows, IF are information furnishers and SC are sanctions. Total is the sum of the achieved points.

Table 5.13 Variables

Name (abbreviation)	Description	Year	Source
Banks (Banks)	Absolute number of banks in a country as of the year 2001. Source: World Bank Database on Banking Regulation in 110 Countries	2001	World Bank
Credit reporting regulatory index (Crri$_L$)	Index aggregates and weights 40 indicators of data protection in credit reporting stemming from law and regulations in a country as of 2003/2004. Index is calculated by using the Laspeyres index formula, aggregation and methods are described in Section 5.3.1 in this book.	2003/2004	The author
Creditor rights (Creditor)	The indicator measures four powers of secured lenders in liquidation and reorganization. A minimum score of 0 represents weak creditor rights and the maximum score of 4 represents strong creditor rights. Source: World Bank Doing Business Database 2004	2004	World Bank
GDP growth, (Gdpgw_av)	Average of real Gross Domestic Product growth in a country for the years 1995 – 2002	1995-2002	World Bank
Loans to households (Loans_hh)	This indicator is the loans to households per capita in 2002/2003 (depending on data availability) deflationed by the national CPIs. The statistics have been collected from central banks around the world. Loans include mortgages and consumer credit. Data has been scaled by population and converted to Dollar. The variable is a proxy for credit volume	2002/2003	Central Banks
Interest (Interest)	Interest rates are actual annual lending rates for 2002 from deposit money banks. The data is from the EuroMonitor World Marketing Data and Statistics	2002	Euro-Monitor
Credit Reporting (Information) Index (Sqcridx)	Also termed information allocation proxy. The number of consumer credit reports (collected from different sources) sold in a country in 2001/2002. The number has been scaled by population. To account for skew, data have been transformed to the power of 1/2	2001/2002	The author

Table 5.13 Statistical Variables (continued)

Name (abbreviation)	Description	Year	Source
Loans to households (Sqloa)	This is the variable as described above (see loans to households). It has been accounted for skew by applying the adequate transformation	2002	Central Banks
Non-Performing Loans (Sqnpl)	The squared non-performing loans are a proxy for credit risk. They are an answer to the question (posed by the World Bank to survey subjects) what the ratio of non-performing loans to total assets was at banks as of year-end of 2001. It has been accounted for skew by applying an adequate transformation	2001	World Bank
Contract Enforcement (Contr. Enf.)	Covers the step-by-step evolution of a debt recovery case before local courts in the country's most populous city. Variable is derived from the World Banks' Doing Business database	2003	World Bank
Unemployment (Unempl.)	Unemployment rate in a country as collected by the World Bank in a time series. I took the rate from 2002	2002	World Bank
Public Credit Registry (PCR)	PCR is the abbreviation for public credit registry and is a dichotomous variable that maps the existence of a public credit registry in the market	2002	World Bank
Telephone mainlines (Tel)	This variable maps the telephone mainlines per 1,000 inhabitants in a country in 2001. The source is the International Telecommunications Union	2001	ITU

Table 5.16
Robust and Basic OLS Regressions

Models 5.8-5.10 are estimated by basic OLS technique, if not otherwise noted. See Table 5.13 for variable sources and definitions. P-values are given in parentheses, *** indicates significance on the 1% level, ** on the 5% level and * on the 10% level.

Ind. Variable	Dependent Variable (DV)		
	5.8 (DV: *Sqcridx*) robust regression	5.9 (DV: *Sqloans*)	5.10 (DV: *Sqnpl*)
CRRI$_L$	.2001209		
	(0.281)		
Loans_hh	.0000157		
	(0.011)**		
Banks	.0001278		
	(0.006)***		
Tel	.0012541	.1024324	
	(0.002)***	(0.020)**	
Constant	-.1472649	23.08376	1.208985
	(0.168)	(0.537)	(0.141)
Sqcridx		32.2128	-0.7118757
		(0.040)**	(0.044)**
Creditor		-3.191473	
		(0.569)	
Interest		-.5499558	
		(0.336)	
Contract		-2.709263	0.1938309
		(0.709)	(0.318)
PCR_exist		-18.49391	0.497856
		(0.145)	(0.201)
Unemploy			0.0473075
			(0.073)*
Adj. R^2	-	0.6130	0.3755
No. of obs.	44	44	37

Notes: Sqcridx is the transformed variable "credit reporting index" (number of credit reports sold/population), CRRI$_L$ is the credit reporting regulatory index, loans_hh are loans to households per capita, banks is the absolute number of banks, tel denotes telephone main lines per 1.000 inhabitants, creditor denotes creditor rights, interest denotes interest rates in 2002 and contract is a variable for contract enforcement. PCR_exist denotes that there is a public credit register in a country, unemploy stands for unemployment. Data are described in Table 5.13 in the Appendix.

Printing: Krips bv, Meppel
Binding: Stürtz, Würzburg